South African performance and archives of memory

Manchester University Press

South African performance and archives of memory

YVETTE HUTCHISON

Manchester University Press
Manchester and New York

distributed in the United States exclusively by Palgrave Macmillan

Published by Manchester University Press
Oxford Road, Manchester M13 9NR, UK
and Room 400, 175 Fifth Avenue, New York, NY 10010, USA
www.manchesteruniversitypress.co.uk

Distributed in the United States exclusively by
Palgrave Macmillan, 175 Fifth Avenue, New York,
NY 10010, USA

Distributed in Canada exclusively by
UBC Press, University of British Columbia, 2029 West Mall,
Vancouver, BC, Canada V6T 1Z2

British Library Cataloguing-in-Publication Data
A catalogue record for this book is available from the British Library

Library of Congress Cataloging-in-Publication Data applied for

ISBN 978 0 7190 8373 0 hardback

First published 2013

The publisher has no responsibility for the persistence or accuracy of URLs for any external or third-party internet websites referred to in this book, and does not guarantee that any content on such websites is, or will remain, accurate or appropriate.

Typeset by Servis Filmsetting Ltd, Stockport, Cheshire
Printed in Great Britain
by CPI Antony Rowe Ltd, Chippenham, Wiltshire

CONTENTS

LIST OF ILLUSTRATIONS

ACKNOWLEDGEMENTS

There are many people to be acknowledged for their role in this research project. First, the Leverhulme Trust for funding the project *Performing Memory: Theatricalising Identity in Contemporary South Africa,* which made the research for the monograph possible. Then the staff at all the archives and museums at which I have done research, thank you for help with accessing material. In particular I'd like to thank Esther Esmyol of Iziko for her help with the Timbuktu Manuscript Project, and Estelle Pretorius and Sandra Rhode for their help with accessing primary material on the Voortrekker Monument and history. All the artists who made themselves available for interview and generously shared their work with me. Kim Walker and Peter Lichtenfells at Manchester University Press for their advice and support through the project.

And finally my husband Mike for patiently helping me with the archives, going with me to exhibitions, and quietly keeping me calm and focused when I felt overwhelmed by the task at hand; and my sister Nola for keeping me sane in the hours of writing . . . Thank you!

NOTE ON TERMINOLOGY

Apartheid in South Africa encouraged an essentialising of racial or ethnic difference that resulted in both confusion and offence. Thus, 'Native' was used for people of African origin, and 'European' for people of European origin, no matter how distant. 'Black', as it emerges from the Black Consciousness Movement referred to all people who were oppressed under apartheid, including those classified as 'black', 'Indian' or 'coloured'. Today 'black' may refer specifically to people of African origin, or to the former, broader reference of 'Black'; and 'white' is used to refer to people formerly termed 'European'. The term 'Indian' continues to refer to South Africans of Indian descent, but it is also challenged by some who feel that it does not allow them fully to belong in South Africa. The term 'coloured' was used to refer to people of mixed ethnic origin, including African, Koisan, white, Chinese, and/or Malay. I am aware that this term has particular political connotations in Britain and the United States of America, but where I use 'coloured' it refers specifically to the South African context, where this is the generally accepted form. Today many people call themselves small caps 'coloured' or 'Cape Malay' because they associate themselves with a particular group because of shared cultural and historic associations, beyond ethnic background; while others prefer the term 'Black' (or 'black'). Even the term 'Koisan' (also spelt Koesan) is contested, with many shifts back and forth including 'Khoe', 'San', '/Xam' and even 'Bushman' to refer to indigenous peoples from particular backgrounds and family groups in Southern Africa. I have tried to clarify my usage by context, resisting terms like 'so-called' wherever possible.

Introduction

Memory is a weapon. Only a long rain will clean away these tears.
(Junction Avenue Theatre Company, *Sophiatown*, 2001: 205)

For decades theatre in South Africa had a specific role: to 'protest' injustices, to break silences, to provoke debate on issues in spaces that could facilitate discussion, often actually during performances. This theatre was about lived experiences that were often officially denied. As Fugard suggests, play-makers like himself sought 'to witness as truthfully as [they] could, the nameless and destitute (desperate) of this one little corner of the world' (1983: 172). This witnessing extended beyond telling one's own stories, to the dramatisation of those of wider communities. These plays were not about the past; they explored present realities, while rehearsing possibilities for the future.

Then, in 1990 Nelson Mandela was released from prison and South Africa negotiated its transformation. The first fully democratic election was held in 1994, and in 1995 the Truth and Reconciliation Commission (TRC) began to work towards the hearing of thousands of personal testimonies in open and closed sessions throughout the country from 1996 to 1998, covering the period from 1960 to 1990. The material from the Commission was reviewed and collated into a seven-volume *Final Report*, the last of which entered the public domain in 2003. William Kentridge referred to the TRC as 'exemplary civic theatre, a public hearing of private griefs which are absorbed into the body politic as a part of the deeper understanding of how the society arrived at its present position' (1998: ix). This public event challenged many assumptions in South Africa: the relationship between what is perceived as public and private, between theatre and society, between memory, myth and history. It simultaneously, and perhaps paradoxically, sought to address the past in relation to individual narratives, while creating a single coherent, national narrative of the 'rainbow nation'.[1] David Coplan formulates the significance of the final report on the Commission, saying that 'the narrative of the TRC is its own most important product' insofar as it created 'a single moral and political story out of this unruly multivocality' (2000: 138). The relation of the 'single story' to 'multivocality' in South Africa, and the tension between remembering and forgetting specific memories[2] in the context of the TRC's formulation of unity and reconciliation; and how these have affected the way South Africans are formulating their sense of themselves in the present, are focal points of this study. Although I draw on research material from many disciplines, my basic premise is the way performance has been central to these processes of negotiating memory in a number of ways: insofar as public events have been used to foreground particular memories and histories, in the way in which theatrical productions have supported or challenged these performances of memory, and in the way a performance lens can further nuance particular formulations of memory. This introduction proposes to suggest how and why I argue this role for performance.

Approaches to memory in relation to history

'Memory' is a difficult concept to define, as is evidenced by a dictionary definition which includes both 'the mind's ability to store and recall past sensations, thoughts, knowledge' either by a human brain or electronically, as well as 'the tendency for a material, or system, to show effects that depend on its past treatment or history [and] to return to a former state after a constraint has been removed' (*Collins English Dictionary*, 1994: 975). The wide-ranging nature of this definition illustrates the complexity of the concept: 'Memory' can refer to the formulation of an

1 For an analysis of this process, see Posel (2002).
2 For example, Brent Harris explores the tension between the TRC's role of 'uncovering' and 'reburying' the past, as opposed to 'revisiting and reinterpreting' it (2002: 162).

event, or to a process: the manner in which something is remembered. Significantly it suggests that because of the way in which this memory is stored in a material or system, be that an individual person, material or society, it will tend to resume the shape remembered more easily than a new shape. This implies that the way the past is remembered and recorded is both a response to previous events and memories, and may evoke *a priori* responses to future events. Memory is not a fixed or stable phenomenon, but more usefully perceived as a lens through which we view experience, and one that may be distorted. Thus both the content and the processes that have informed the formulation of South Africa's past will be analysed in terms of affect – both in the past and present, and in relation to the future. Time and space, history and geography are significant in this analysis, as often events are both narrated and embodied physically in a specific form and context.

The ancient Greeks and Romans anthropomorphised Mnemosyne (memory) as the daughter of ignorance, the mother of wisdom. This paradoxical positioning of knowing and not-knowing and its significance for history is articulated more explicitly by the French historian Philippe Aries, who pioneered research into commemoration and memorials in the 1970s. Aries argues that 'history deals with the horizon between the known and the unknown. It is memory that lures us to this horizon' (cited in Hutton, 1993: 168).

The psychologist Frederic Bartlett argues in 'Remembering: A study of experimental and social psychology' that

> remembering is not the re-excitation of innumerable fixed, lifeless and fragmentary traces. It is an imaginative reconstruction, or construction, built out of our attitude towards a whole active mass of organised past reactions or experience, and a little outstanding detail which commonly appears in an image or in a language form. It is thus hardly ever really exact, even in the most rudimentary cases of role recapitulation, and it is not at all important that it should be so (cited in Sacks, 1995: 173).

Here Bartlett argues for memory as a dynamic and imaginative process that is subject to many complex 'interferences'.[3] The concepts of 'construction' and 'reconstruction' are important for this study, and particularly to the processes involved in both.[4] However, it is worth reflecting

---

3 See Lowenthal (1997: 193–210) for more detailed discussion of the problems related to our ability to confirm memory, types of memory, forgetting, revision and reconstruction.
4 Munslow argues clearly for the difference between the past and history: that the past 'is what once was, is no more and has gone for good. History . . . is a corpus of narrative discourses about the once reality of the past produced and fashioned by

critically on Bartlett's suggestion that the inexactness of reconstructions is 'not at all important' in view of the potential role reconstructions may play when fed back into personal or, even more significantly, a national sense of identity, particularly through the historical or mythical narratives of a nation.

'Interferences' which may affect memory, and thus history, include: the context in which the event is being reconstructed, as opposed to its original context; the expectations of all involved, especially the historian;[5] and, of course, the lapse in time between event and its recreation, either in terms of a physical archive or commemoration, or a work of art referring to the event or person. These 'interferences' explain de Certeau's assertion that history is not objects in an archive, but what is done with and to them (1988: 20).

The time lapse particularly affects both content and how it is 'remembered', interpreted and encoded, or 'forgotten'. For example, the artist Robert Pope observes that much time, often an average of five years, might elapse between the original perception or experience and its artistic recreation.[6] He argues that the significance of this time lapse lies in the way it shifts the experience from the personal and transforms it into myth. Pope writes:

> During this gestation period the creative faculties act as a filter where personal opaque and chaotic data is made public, transparent and ordered. This is a process of mythologising. Myth and dream are similar: the difference is that dreams have private, personal meaning while myths have public meanings (cited in Sacks, 1995: 176).

---

historians.' He goes on to say that the past 'is a category of content (real events); second, that the significance of how it is told is crucial (the issue of discourse or narration of a story); and third, that history is a category of expression (varieties of narrative representation)' (2007: 9). In relation to the three dominant approaches to history, i.e. the reconstructionist, constructionist and deconstructionist, this study is most influenced by the approach to history viewed as narrative representation, in the light of the way that Hayden-White, Roland Barthes, and Paul Ricoeur refined our understanding of the processes of representation. I am indebted to de Certeau's view that the past is not translated but transformed into narrative construction, and that this process is what gives it meaning (1988: 6).

5 This has particular significance in relation to African historiography of the 1960s, when historians were expected to consciously write in such a way as to advance nation building, particularly in support of the Pan-Africanist movement (cf. Kapteijns (1977), Caroline Neale (1985) and Temu and Swai (1981)). On the way that the existent archive affects the way history is conceived and narrated, see Hamilton *et al.* (2002) and Hutchison (2010a: xi–xvi).

6 See Temu and Swai (1981) on the reconstruction of memory and the processes whereby we relate and reconstruct isolated scenes in a continuous sequence which is constructed (1981: 412–13).

Memory processes include ordering and interpreting the material. They also affect identity, insofar as we feed these 'meanings' back into our understanding of ourselves and into how we relate to these collective narratives of our worlds.

It is worth noting Charlotte Delbo's distinction between what she terms 'intellectual', or common memory and 'deep' memory (1990). Intellectual memory engages with what can be described and communicated in language, and thus, she argues, refers to experiences that have been processed emotionally and intellectually at some level. However, deep memory involves experiences that are visceral and leave physical imprints on the body; it operates outside of language, often because it is traumatic and unspeakable. This distinction is important when dealing with narratives that involve trauma, be they Holocaust narratives, which is what she is talking about, or narratives from the Algerian, Latin American or South African contexts.[7] The significance of this distinction is highlighted by the fact that often traumatic experiences cannot be narrated, but can be processed and/or expressed in representative forms, like performance.[8] This is particularly pertinent to the narrations of struggle and to the testimonies of the TRC.

Memory and nation building

Memory plays a specific role in nation building. The various theories and approaches to defining how a national identity is constructed are important for this study. The modernist approach to nation formation, which Nadine Holdsworth argues 'focussed on the specific economic, social and political material conditions of modernity, and industrialization in particular' (2010: 12), dominated the apartheid era, and are significant in contemporary South Africa insofar as these approaches to nation have become embedded both systemically and psychically in the country and its people. However, owing to various political and cultural counter-movements and the very fragmented lived realities of most South Africans both during and after apartheid, most individuals are aware of the more realistic constructivist nature of national identity, as formulated by Benedict Anderson in his concept of the 'imagined

7 Here I draw on Delbo on the Nazi Holocaust, Greene and Fanon on Algeria, and
    Diana Taylor on Latin America, where pertinent to the South African situation.
8 See Diana Taylor, 'Trauma and Performance: Lessons from Latin America' (2007b).

community' (2006: 6–7), and Homi Bhabha's formulation of the nation as being an ambivalent construct, engaged with competing discourses. In *Nation and Narration* he says, '[i]t is an ambivalence that emerges from a growing awareness that, despite the certainty with which historians speak of the "origins" of nation as a sign of the "modernity" of society, the cultural temporality of the nation inscribes a much more transitional reality'(1990: 1) This ambivalence is further exacerbated by people's experiences of exile, migration, transnationalism and globalisation which, for Bhabha, have led to the presence of hybridised identities characterised by splitting, doubling and mixing. In the post-colonial, or post-apartheid, context the issue of identity is made more complex both because of these movements of people and because of what Bhabha terms 'a dialectic of various temporalities – modern, colonial, postcolonial, "native" – that cannot be a knowledge that is stabilized in its enunciation' (1994: 218–19). He refers to Frantz Fanon's essay 'On national culture' which warns 'against the intellectual appropriation of the "culture of the people" within a representationalist discourse that may become fixed or reified in the annals of History' (*ibid.*, 218). This is especially important given the way discourses that were related to race, ethnicity and culture developed in South Africa, and how they continue to resonate in the present.[9]

I want to analyse examples of apartheid representational discourses and how they are being renegotiated performatively in the post-apartheid context, while bearing in mind Fanon's warning against creating alternative fixed national discourses. In doing so, I will consider how these representations of memory are formalised; I will also consider the relationship between national commemoration, where social structures are set up to 'remember' for a nation, and thus attempt to 'bring together the different fragments of the nation' (Mbembe, 2004: 404),[10] and theatrical representations, which are more local and individual. The processes of national commemoration involve making particular memories concrete through public art, most often sculpture, monuments and memorials, commemorative days, and by creating archives which reflect

9　Patrice Jeppson (1997) analyses the legacy of apartheid regarding the uses of these terms and the implications of this for public and people's historical archaeology.

10　Much has been written on memorials in South Africa and internationally. I have drawn on Sabine Marschall, Annie Coombes, A.M. Grundlingh, Nsizwe Dlamini, Ciraj Rassool and Leslie Witz from within South Africa. Bryant (2000) on post-1989 Czech history, Sicher (2000) on contemporary American post-Holocaust narratives, von Henneberg, (2004) on memory of empire in modern Italy, Linenthal (1995), Milton and Nowinski (1992) Schramm (2011) on the Holocaust, Hass (1998) on memories of Vietnam veterans, and J.E. Young (1993), J. Winter (1995) and D. Lowenthal (1997) on conceptualising the past.

the dominant, official national narrative. The formulation of the official memories of a nation often reveal more about the time in which they are constructed than about the period to which they refer. I will here be looking at how old monuments are renegotiated in the new context, for example the Voortrekker Monument in Pretoria, and how new monuments express central aspects of the new nation's sense of itself, and here I will be looking at Freedom Park. However, I will also consider how theatrical representations compare to these official formulations of national memory.

Nostalgia

Nostalgia plays an important role in any engagement with postcolonial history and memory. In tracing the development of nostalgia, Dennis Walder has suggested that the works of various writers 'represent the present as a place marked by a trail of survivors searching for their roots, for a home, in the ruins of history' (2011: 2). Hobsbawn's description of the 'twilight zone between history and memory . . . by far the hardest part of history for historians, or anyone else to grasp'; is what Walder calls 'postcolonial nostalgias' (*ibid.*), which involve both individual and collective attempts to redefine histories and identities in countries subject to the erasures of the past in an attempt to find new ways of defining and narrating their societies.

Nostalgia intrinsically involves 'longing', which Susan Stewart (1993) suggests has three possible meanings. The first refers to 'yearning desire' where the 'direction of force in the desiring narrative is always a future-past, a deferment of experience in the direction of origin and thus eschaton, the point where narrative begins/ends, both engendering and transcending the relation between materiality and meaning', despite the narrative's remaining subject to historical formation (1993: ix–x). The second meaning Stewart argues is related to the 'fanciful cravings of women during pregnancy', which she suggests 'takes us closer to the imagined location of origin, be it the transcendent with its seeming proximity to the immortal or the rural/agrarian with its seeming proximity to the earth; for it is with pregnancy that we see the articulation of the threshold between nature and culture' (*ibid.*). The third meaning of longing she calls 'belongings or appurtenances', which refers to the capacity of narrative to generate significant objects', including 'a significant other', and refers to point of view and how this effects the construction of individual and collective subjectivity (*ibid.*, xi). Stewart explores various narrative strategies by which people invent a realisable world, particularly through miniatures, souvenirs, and collections that reflect both a longing to return to a place of origin, and a desire to control space and time, relative to themselves. I shall consider these ideas not as they are manifest in objects, but as revealed in embodied repertoires.

I turn to Svetlana Boym's definitions and analyses of nostalgia.[11] She defines nostalgia (from *nostos* – return home, and *algia* – longing) as 'a longing for home that no longer exists or has never existed. Nostalgia is a sentiment of loss and displacement, but it is also a romance with one's own fantasy' (2001: xiii).

It is important to consider what losses, displacements and fantasies inform nostalgia in the South African context. Nostalgia is often discussed in relation to exile, which can be the result of physical displacement; or psychological, as in the case of people who are denied full citizenship in their own country, as was the experience of the majority during apartheid. Both experiences of exile are relevant to contemporary South Africa, where exiles and their families are returning to a country they have dreamed about, but do not necessarily recognise. The same sense of displacement may be the experience for South Africans who remained in the country, but now have to renegotiate their place and citizenship in the post-apartheid context. The period of transition in South Africa has certainly brought positive change, but it has also left many people uncertain about where they belong, particularly in relation to the dominant narratives that have come to represent the apartheid period.[12] It is thus not surprising that nostalgia features as an aspect of memory in contemporary South Africa. Boym argues that the nostalgia in a post-revolution context 'is not always for the ancient regime or fallen empire but also for the unrealized dreams of the past and visions of the future that became obsolete' (*ibid.*, xvi).

These 'unrealized dreams' are aspects of the fantasies that are intrinsic to nostalgia. The gap between how post-apartheid South Africa was imagined and the contemporary reality defines contemporary nostalgia, particularly insofar as this is perceived collectively. Unlike melancholy, which is confined to individual consciousness, nostalgia 'is about the

---

11 Although she focuses on metropolitan Europe, the comparisons are apt in the post-democratic South African context.

12 This is not only true for white South Africans for whom memories of the apartheid period are at best ambivalent, but for South Africans from diverse racial and ethnic backgrounds who are nostalgic for particular aspects of the apartheid past for various reasons. Some of these are analysed by Jacob Dhlamini in *Native Nostalgia* (2009).

relationship between individual biography and the biography of groups or nations, between personal and collective memory' (*ibid.*). Thus nostalgia often reveals the gap between the way in which the nation is narrated and represented and the memories of individual people who do not feel fully represented by these representations nor ascribe to the narratives.

Nostalgia highlights a specific tension that is central to contemporary South Africa: the tension between inclusion and exclusion, which are defined by collectively agreed terms of belonging. Boym argues that on the one hand nostalgic 'longing can make us more empathetic toward fellow humans, yet the moment we try to repair longing with belonging, the apprehension of loss with a rediscovery of identity, we often part ways and put an end to mutual understanding' (*ibid.*, xv). I shall consider how this tension is evidenced in specific historical moments in which South African as a nation was reconceptualised (1910, 1938/48–9 and 1994), by comparing the performance of nation with various theatrical engagements with these formulations.

In exploring different nostalgic engagements with memory I apply Boym's distinction between reflective and restorative nostalgia as 'this topology of nostalgia allows us to differentiate between national memory that is based on a single plot of national identity, and social memory, which consists of collective frameworks that mark but do not define individual memory' (*ibid.*, xviii). In this topology restorative nostalgia 'does not think of itself as nostalgia, but rather as truth and tradition. . . . [it] protects absolute truth, while reflective nostalgia calls it into doubt' (*ibid.*, xviii). Reflective nostalgia, at its best, critiques this position of finding absolute truth, it is more concerned with historical and individual time, and the irrevocability of the past; which we engage with through our imagination' (*ibid.*, 50). This form of nostalgia is more likely found in the context of critical engagements with the past.

Restorative nostalgia is characterised by a return to origins in an attempt to create a transhistorical reconstruction of the lost home, drawing on oral culture, collective pictorial symbols while blurring time frames (*ibid.*, 49). This is possible because, as French historian Pierre Nora argued

> places of memory do not have referents in reality. Or rather, they are their own referent: pure, self-referential signs. That is not to say that they are without content, physical presence, or history: quite the contrary. But what makes them places of memory is that, precisely, by which they escape from history. (cited in Greene, 1996: 118)

This attempt to escape from a particular historical time requires the conflation of memory, myth and history. This kind of restorative nostalgia is evident in much post-colonial writing, particularly in a newly independent nation's compulsion to rewrite its history and counter colonial constructions of its past (Neale, 1985). For the colonial immigrants who no longer feels at home in their mother country, and do not have a place in the newly independent land, often because the history of the indigenous people indicts them, 'History gives way to a remembered world in which time has stopped and the past has been absorbed into the present' (Greene, 1996: 18). Writing about the French colonials who had lived in Algeria, commonly known as the *pieds-noirs*, Greene argues that in the face of France's embarrassed silence on this history, the *pieds-noirs* experienced a confused sense of their own history, which they remembered with guilt and simultaneously as a golden time of honour, when the ideals of a colonial period 'functioned'. Thus the outlines of experience became blurred and memories moved inexorably into 'an atemporal zone . . . of private symbols and allusions, a mysterious world marked by displacements and the repetitions of dreams' (Greene, 1996: 106). It is noteworthy that in these circumstances the bleaker the present seems, the more glowing the sense of the 'lost paradise' of the past tends to be.

Some of the methods that narrators use to avoid confronting the realities of the past and/or present and to sustain the dream world include the transformation of history into myth, because myth invokes an unspecific symbolic world, which is often narrated in epic terms that suggests cyclic repetitions, without a precise chronology.[13] This private dream world is often signalled by the use of children's songs to suggest the internal, unreal world of the characters who recall an imagined time of lost innocence.[14] Nostalgic narratives are often elliptical, suggesting multiple and shifting perspectives and temporal gaps. This serves to disorient the reader or viewer, and denies them an ordered chronology which facilitates an historical overview. There may be a tendency towards a myopic concentration on the details of daily life, while the specific historical or political events remain hazy and confused. These narrative strategies reveal a world composed of primal moments of longing and desire rather than realistic presentations of an event or period, or even the 'official' version of history endorsed by those in power (Greene, 1996: 112–13).

---

13 Soyinka has also used ritualistic, epic dramatic forms to evoke a sense of pre-colonial communal coherence. Nevertheless, he too has been accused of limiting the socio-political effectiveness of his plays by the use of temporal myth and fantasy (Jeyifo, 1985: 97).
14 Stewart (1993).

I shall compare these descriptions of how nostalgic memories are experienced and narrated with ways in which specific cultural groups in post-apartheid South Africa have engaged with the past in the post-apartheid context.

The process of looking back is fraught because memory is coloured by emotion and so personal memory and historical events are often conflated. Boym argues that 'the notion of shared social frameworks of memory is rooted in an understanding of human consciousness, which is dialogical with other human beings and with cultural discourses' (2001: 52). The difference between the national narrative of history and individuals' recollections of the past reveals how diverse the experiences and memories are. If people keep negotiating these discontinuities there is more chance that a framework for a shared sense of the past and thus community may emerge in South Africa.

However, there is also tension between an individual or community's impulse to remember and to forget aspects of the past. In analysing this aspect of South Africa's engagement with its memories I want to evaluate the significance of Hamilakis and Labanyi's argument that 'all commemoration is about forgetting. While the material trace of past human practices evokes and elicits remembering, it could be argued that this is so precisely because it is a trace: a fragment evoking absence and loss' (2008: 12).

However it is employed, nostalgia is important as it signals pathology, a sense of dislocation, a longing for coherent identity that may no longer be possible in the contemporary transnational, global world which invites and excludes in the way it simultaneously opens and closes various literal and virtual borders.

Memory in the postmodern, increasingly globalised world

Pierre Nora argues that the decline of traditional, largely rural societies has resulted in a shift in the function of memory away from collective memory, which is linked to the nation-state and to its history, towards multiple individual memories (*les memoires particulieres*) which demand their own history (cited in Greene, 1996: 116–17). Homi Bhabha has argued that insofar as various social and literary narratives define a subject as a social entity, they undermine 'the linear equivalence of event and idea that historicism proposes'. Thus 'the locality of culture' is 'more *around* temporality than *about* historicity' (1994: 200–1). Increased mobility, through forced exile and migration, or because of travel and technology, has further fragmented and diversified communities, rendering unlikely a single communal consciousness or national memory. Michel de Certeau has suggested that 'what the map cuts up, the story cuts across' (1984: 129), suggesting a postcolonial world consisting of multiple transnational peoples with various diasporic affiliations whose experiences are formulated in diverse narratives.

Many people have responded to this increased fragmentation by identifying themselves more closely with a distinct communal group, which shares their memories.[15] Although South Africa has never had a single coherent national identity, the definition of nation during the apartheid years was very clear, albeit exclusive. Ironically, in countering the very narrow and prescriptive official definitions of South African identity, the counter-discourse often reinforced their apparent validity (see Witz, 2003). Thus the degree to which the current government, historians and artists engage with plural pasts, new histories, and local communities in relation to issues of gender, language, ethnicity and religion will determine the extent to which South Africa can really achieve 'unity in diversity', and create a 'rainbow nation' that reflects such diversity.

This fragmentation and multiplication of memory has affected the role of the artist. Fox suggests that whereas in the past

> the artist was a kind of priest, today's artist is something like an archaeologist of the soul, uncovering lost or hidden meanings. This is especially the case with the visionary artists of the New World, where indigenous history was unmade and the historical imperatives of the Old World were imposed by force and violence. (1986: 331)[16]

It is thus important to include an analysis of the role artists play in shaping a sense of a national identity, challenging official formulations of it, revealing the gaps, silences and disavowed memories, or imagining difference differently.

This reference to the term 'archaeologist' recurs often when reading about memory and history. 'Archaeology' and the concept of genealogy

---

15 In 'DissemiNation' Bhabha (1990) analyses how the diaspora and the movement of people has affected narrative, and discourses on identity and nationalism; see also Greene (1996) on the 'discontinuity' between past and present in complex societies; Hall (1996); Said (1994); Sorkin (1989) and Triulzi (1996).

16 Fox writes this in the context of analysing Walcott's approach to history as evidence of man's 'dis-ease' with his world and himself. This archaeological metaphor suggests something pre-existing that awaits discovery. It may be more useful to suggest the artist as someone who facilitates 'becoming' (Ingold, 2000).

are central to Foucault's writing on history,[17] which are particularly important insofar as he extended Nietzsche's interrogation of the subject and explored history as a metaphor comparable to the language model. In *The Archaeology of Knowledge* he argues that history consists of 'dispersed events – decisions, accidents, initiatives, discoveries' (1972: 8), which are arranged to suggest causality and continuity, and thus to maintain power structures. Here Foucault extends Nietzsche's argument that 'everything that exists, no matter what its origin, is periodically reinterpreted by those in power in terms of fresh intentions', during which process earlier meanings are necessarily destroyed, and new ones created (Nietzsche, 1956: 20). These two ideas are, of course related, as is evident in the way South Africans are rewriting the country's history, and thus its identity, in the post-apartheid context.

Within the context of fragmented, non-homogeneous, diverse worlds, which exist alongside one another, memory has become deeply psychological and private by nature. If one were to summarise the shifts in society and the corresponding shifts in memory, the movement would be from the historical to the psychological, the societal to the individual, the transmissive to the subjective. The ironic paradoxical result of this individuation of memory in contemporary society is that social memory is no longer unified, obvious, repetitive in a way that suggests continuity, but must be constructed, defined and preserved consciously, through repetitive performance. Often the individual's memory and sense of history must be untangled from a complex communal identity and context, a process to which the artist can contribute significantly. Reflecting on his own experience of negotiating his Caribbean cultural identity, and his education and life in the USA, Derek Walcott writes, 'Schizophrenic, wrenched by two styles,/ . . . I earn/ my exile' (*Castaway*, 1965: 61); as he straddles two worlds, he experiences 'dis-ease' with both, to borrow Fox's pun (1986).[18] This sense of confused identity is evidenced in many South African plays, and is clearly articulated by Ruth and Jakes in *Sophiatown* when they ask 'What the hell am I?' in relation to identifying themselves in terms of race, ethnicity, language, political sympathy and religion (Junction Avenue Theatre Company, 2001: 167).

17 In Foucault's 'Enlightenment' essay, he combines archaeology as a 'method' with genealogy as a 'design' (1984: 46). See Thacker (1997) for a detailed analysis of Foucault's uses of these terms in his attempt to write history, exploring 'archaeology' in terms of discontinuity and history as a discourse, and 'genealogy' in terms of a linguistic discourse, as applied in feminist histories and in the revisions of modern Irish history.
18 Although Walcott is writing from a Caribbean perspective, his experiences and exploration of the theatre's potential to engage with issues of history, memory and identity are apposite to this study.

Fanon, writing at the height of the Algerian war, documents the psychological reasons for the personal and cultural schizophrenia experienced
in colonial and post-colonial contexts at length in *Black Face/White
Mask* (1968) and *The Wretched of the Earth* (1963). This is an aspect of
the pathology central to nostalgia. Negotiating cultural dis-ease, and
plural senses of memory and identity are central to post-apartheid South
Africa's understanding of itself.

Yet 'amnesia' and myth-making need not always be perceived nega-
tively. In 'The Muse of History' Walcott defines history as 'amnesia'
(1974: 4), and suggests that the ability to make and remake one's history
through the imagination is what gives both the individual and his or her
society hope, insofar as both can be remade. Baugh quotes Walcott as
saying: 'We contemplate our spirit by the detritus of the past' (cited in
Fox, 1986: 337).

The artist can play a particular role in exploring the intersections
between history, myth and memory. During the apartheid years culture
was mobilised as a 'weapon' against the apartheid regime. However, in
1988, two years before the release of Mandela, Albie Sachs challenged
South Africa's cultural activists to rethink their definition of culture as
'a weapon of the struggle'. He argued that while this approach to culture
had been necessary, it had skewed the imagination and creativity of
South Africans, resulting in 'the multiple ghettos of the apartheid imagination' (1991: 187). He insisted that artists should shift from viewing
culture as something 'purely instrumental and nondialectical', to something more open, as an imaginative way to 'remake ourselves' (*ibid.*,
189). The new challenge, he argued, was to find a new aesthetic that has
the 'capacity to expose contradictions and reveal hidden tensions' and
finds a way of expressing a new sense of cultural diversity and political pluralism (*ibid.*, 188, 190–3). He called for the use of imagination
as a means to unlock a new way of thinking about cultural production,
which included the way South Africans saw themselves and their world,
perhaps echoing Walcott's call to 'contemplate our spirit by the detritus
of the past'.

Challenges to the reimagination of South Africa

This study will explore the place of memory in post-apartheid South
Africa by analysing state sanctioned-performances of the nation: by

way of the TRC, the modelling or remaking of specific memorials and museums, the Timbuktu Manuscript Project as an embodiment of Mbeki's African Renaissance, and the public performances-of-nation ceremonies at the 2010 World Cup; these features will be discussed alongside specific contemporary theatrical engagements with memory and identity. I will be exploring the potentials and limitations of both the 'white' museum space and 'black box' of theatre, drawing on Bharucha's challenge to 'get beyond the box' in 'problematising the "New Asian Museum"' (2000b), and Gerhard Marx's exploration of an object [here I substitute 'archive'] as both a noun and something which 'lapses into the verb' through 'performing the object', which 'introduces the possibility of myriad sentence constructions, meaning constructions' (2009: 226).

Since 1994 South Africa has seen a plethora of engagements with apartheid ranging from historical events and commemorations to iconic figures. The degree of complexity implicit in these memories is evidenced, for example, in the very ambivalent views and memories connected with Winnie Mandela. In *Winnie the Opera* (composed by Bongani Ndodana-Breen, 2011) she is a symbol of endurance and of tragedy, both a hero and anti-heroic figure; and in Aubrey Sekhabi and Paul Grootboom's play *Rivonia Trial* (2010), she is the haunting symbol of Nelson Mandela's love, longing and loss.

According to J. Brooks Spector, former USA diplomat and now acting head of Johannesburg's Market Theatre, '[e]very new country – or new political dispensation in an older one – needs such myths to make the regime seem right and fitting' (*The Daily Maverick*, 8 May 2011). However, the conceptualisations of iconic figures such as Winnie and Nelson Mandela in the new South Africa are not uncomplicated. In commenting on the centrality of memory work in contemporary South Africa, Verne Harris has taken issue with the terms in which this work has been defined and the consequences of this for the country. He argues that South Africa has 'underestimated the damage wrought by our histories – to individuals, collectivities and institutions', arguing that '[w]e were seduced by the possibility of a "quick-fix". (Madiba Magic would sprinkle salve on our wounds and we would emerge, quickly, as reconstructed "new South Africans")' (2011: 11). He also critiques the assumption in most post-apartheid memory work that 'the study of history [is] about learning from the past' (*ibid.*, 14). This, he suggests, allows for an unhealthy paternalistic reliance on experts and reduces general participation in 'creating new publics' (*ibid.*, 15–16). None of this is Mandela's fault, but rather the result of the nation's desire for a 'quick-fix', to escape the complexities of the past.

In view of this foregrounding of memory in contemporary South Africa, it is significant that many 'classics' of apartheid continue to be revived, as evident in the winter 2010 programme of the Market Theatre and the Wits Theatre's recent 'SA Season' under the banner of 'Honouring the Archive: Theatre, Memory and Social Justice'. Reporter Chris Thurman quotes academic Warren Nebe's insistence that 'staging these works in 2010 is not just about looking back but is, more importantly, about acknowledging their relevance today' (Thurman, 2010). I will discuss the significance of these revivals for contemporary South Africa in my last chapter.

These different engagements with memory raise the following questions: Why are certain memories foregrounded in the contemporary situation? How significant is context within which memory is evoked? How are the memories of various South Africans being included, interpreted or excluded from exhibitions, archives and museums, and to what effect? It is important to analyse how and why certain moments are prioritised as significant, either for the positive or negative impact the moment has had on the individual or group; so also should the processes involved in interpreting memories be analysed, because memory is transformed through them from being a personal code of meaning to becoming a shared public 'meaning'. This, in turn, shapes individuals' sense of themselves and their place in their societies.

The degree to which South Africans have become aware of the level of subjectivity involved in this process has been a particular challenge, in that the apartheid system had offered a relatively rigid and fixed construction of its history, ideologies and identities. The possibility of interrogating these constructions has created both a sense of possibility and caused intense anxiety for different South Africans.[19] If we consider the proposition that a 'particular recollection' of the past affects the way materials or systems tend 'to return to a former state after a constraint has been removed', and also that these responses are often multifaceted and layered, then a tendency to shift back into old familiar patterns of thought and social interaction, or automatically to resist new formulations, could have been predicted. Indeed, Daniel Herwitz has argued that South Africa understandably experiences these responses,

19 This is evident in a phenomenon commonly referred to as a 'family murder', where a parent takes his or her children's lives and then commits suicide. The HSRC investigated 12 cases over 18 months from 1 April 1989 to October 1990. M.C. Marchetti-Mercer revisits the issue in view of the fact that it continued to some extent in the new millennium. She concludes that this is a complex and multidimensional response to 'a period of social and political crisis as a result of its [South Africa's] transition into democracy' (2003: 91).

particularly in terms of its engagement with race as the cornerstone of apartheid ideology. He says that it

> is a profoundly overracialized society. It could hardly be expected to be otherwise, given the past. When race becomes a marker of every aspect of life, the rich languages, concepts, ideals, affiliations, and emotions people have about things are straitjacketed – as they would be by any singularity that cannibalizes the human mind, encroaching itself on our every thought and action. South Africa is racially obsessed. (2003: 107)

And this is as true a decade hence as it was when Herwitz made this statement. For many South Africans race is either 'an item of direct confrontation' or 'hostile silence' (*ibid.*).

I will explore the extent to which past essentialist positions on race, ethnicity, gender and history are being renegotiated, and how these revisions are affecting current thinking about identity, histories and geographies. It is worth noting here that place and space are critical to how we negotiate memory and identity. Harrison argues that physical spaces are 'metaphors for our social constructions of reality. . . . Places form landscapes and landscapes may be defined as sets of relational places and embody (literally and metaphorically) emotion, memories and associations derived from personal and interpersonal shared experience' (2003: 4–5).[20]

'Performance' is central to this analysis in a number of ways. First, I use it in the same way that Austin uses the term 'performatives', which suggests that 'to say something is to do something'; certain words or symbolic actions do not simply describe or represent actions, they are actions in themselves (1962: 6–8). This is obvious in ceremonies where lived realities are changed by uttering specific words and actions – a new nation is born, sentences are passed down, two individuals become a married couple. This study will explore the place and effect of official performative acts, as well as the place of performance in conceptualising, rehearsing and changing lived reality both in public forums and in fictional contexts.

However, I also use 'performance' in the sense described by Butler, to describe how we embody and enact social norms. Stets and Burke (2000) argue that identity formation lies in the process of identification, which requires a subject to acquire knowledge of the cultural texts, words, symbols and particular behaviours that define meaning in a specific

---

20 See Heidegger on dwelling (1958: 103), Yaeger on *Geographies of identity* (1996), Mbembe on the 'biopolitics of Johannesburg as a "racial city" and its transition to a metropolitan form' (2004).

context, and then enact these through the various 'roles' demanded of the individual by the culture. This has particular significance for individuals negotiating roles that are contested, because the way that they enact the roles contributes either to their reinforcing or deconstructing dominant discourses, including history. Butler's extension of Simone de Beauvoir's claim that 'the body is a historical situation' implies that when we understand the codes of a society and enact them appropriately, according to the dominant definitions, we are 'dramatizing, and reproducing a historical situation', that it is 'an act' that embodies particular cultural significations (Butler, 1988: 521, 524–8). This formulation of gendered enactment is significant insofar as it sets gender as a performative, a socially constructed set of behaviours, beyond biological predetermination. This concept is equally applicable to race, as Eliott Marshall so clearly demonstrates from a genetic perspective, demonstrating that race is not genetically encoded so much as socially defined (1998: 654), and Paul Gilroy has expanded in his analysis of racism, nationalism and ethnicity in Britain in the context of the African diaspora into the western hemisphere (1987, 2000, 2004). Thus, in Lyotard's terms, dominant cultural ideologies may be 'inscribed on human bodies and transmitted by those to other bodies' (Lyotard, 1977: 88).

The interaction between the dominant social systems and individuals within them is complex, particularly if individuals want to challenge these dominant cultural embodiments. Diana Taylor offers a powerful conceptualisation of the way in which externally formulated narratives of memory interact with embodied memories in her metaphors of the archive and the repertoire. This work emerges from Taylor's own experience of living between North America, specifically Canada, and South America, initially Mexico (2007a). Taylor aptly compares 'the *archive* of supposedly enduring materials (i.e. texts, documents, buildings, bones), and the so-called ephemeral *repertoire* of embodied practice/knowledge (i.e. spoken language, dance, sports, ritual)' (2007b: 19, her italics). In pursuing the comparisons between these various kinds of embodiments of memory, Taylor reminds us that it is important to consider the 'myths attending the archive': that it is 'unmediated . . . that it resists change, corruptibility and political manipulation'. Here the issues of hegemonic processes of mediation, those of 'selection, memorization or internalization, and transmission' (*ibid.*, 21), become profoundly significant in relation to issues of contested memories. Taylor argues that the repertoire 'enacts embodied memory: performances, gestures, orality, movement, dance, singing – in short all those acts usually thought of as ephemeral, non-reproducible knowledge' (*ibid.*, 20). These embodied performative forms are significant because they require the presence of those in whom the memory resides, which in turn suggests a greater potential for individual agency. Re-situating embodied practices as a system of knowing and transmitting knowledge breaks down old hegemonic binaries that have existed between oral and literary traditions, with the archive's perceived position as a repository of hegemonic power, and places these two systems of knowledge and memory in dialogue with one another.[21] Conquergood argues that a performance lens can 'open the space between analysis and action, and . . . pull the pin on the binary opposition between theory and practice' (2002: 145–6). Furthermore, it resists any attempt to define a single memorial account. This is especially important when the memories being generated are highly contested. In performance a dominant, official formulation of collective memory may be challenged and nuanced by alternative personal, local and fictional narratives and performances of memory. To this purpose, then, formal state-sanctioned performances of specific memories will be compared with theatrical productions throughout this study as representing dialectical discourses that together may suggest how we can bridge the gap between the oral and literary traditions, verbal and non-verbal, embodied and archived formulations of memory, and so engage with Sach's call for South Africans to formulate new ways of thinking about cultural production.

I begin at the rupture with the past symbolised by the release of Mandela and realised in the negotiations for full democracy in South Africa from 1990 to 1994, which heralded a period of transition, characterised publicly to a large extent by the TRC. The first chapter, entitled 'The TRC's Reconfiguring of the past: Remembering and forgetting', explores how the TRC archive was created, and what it means to contemporary South Africa. It begins by reading the TRC as a performance, exploring its dramaturgy, the roles of various interlocutors, performers, audiences, the media and how they all influenced the event as a travelling public performance of memory. It considers the significance of various silences and embodied, non-verbal aspects of the hearings, which were not included in the transcriptions, and how these omissions, and the way the extended TRC archives were constituted have affected the way in which the TRC was interpreted, particularly in the *Final Report*. It also asks what precedents have this national theatre of mourning set for South Africa?

The next chapter, 'Dramatising the TRC: The role of theatre

21 Conquergood argues that this is because 'the root metaphor of the text underpins the supremacy of Western knowledge systems by erasing the vast realm of human knowledge and meaningful action that is unlettered' (2002: 147).

practitioners in exploring the past', explores creative responses to the TRC. It examines individual narratives that have become iconic; asking why these have been chosen to represent the experiences of the broader majority. It analyses how contemporary cultural practitioners are particularly exploring various non-realistic, highly performative forms in conjunction with verbatim narratives to reflect on diverse lived realities in South Africa. Thematically it analyses how playwrights are engaging with specific disavowed aspects of the past, manifest in the repetitive images of ghosts and haunting in various plays, the exploration of the TRC's terms of justice, specific masculinities which are directly related to male identity being constructed in a conflict situation, and the legacies of violence which are institutional but were not deconstructed by the TRC.

I then analyse how iconic archives and memorials of the past have been renegotiated in the present in the chapter entitled 'Staging a nation: the Voortrekker Monument and Freedom Park'. The apartheid archives embodied particular narratives of South Africa, especially those that defined separate cultural identities, including their relative worth and histories. The way these archives of memory were constructed and controlled is important (Rokem, 2000), especially how they affected the social structure of the nation beyond apartheid legislation. The chapter looks at how moments of political crisis or transition have provoked the mobilisation of specific historical narratives to define national identities. It begins by looking at how South Africa narrated and performed itself in the 1910 South African Pageant of Union. It then considers how the Afrikaner struggle for independence and nationhood were focused in and around memories of the Great Trek and the Battle of Blood/Ncome River through the 1938 Voortrekker Centenary commemorations; particularly through the foregrounding of specific symbols and myths to create the sense of a 'shared community', which became the basis for conceptualising the nation in terms of Afrikaner-nationalism. I compare this commemoration with the inauguration of the Voortrekker Monument in 1949; with some references to the 1952 Jan van Riebeeck Tercentenary Festival Fair and the 1988 commemoration. It has been suggested that the extent to which the Battle of Blood River is celebrated serves as a reliable barometer of the historical, national and political thought of the Afrikaner (van Jaarsveld, 1979: 65–7), which suggests that this historical memory, and its embodied commemoration, has played an important role in formulating a history and national identity for South Africa. The chapter then goes on to explore the renegotiation of the Voortrekker Monument as a site of memory in the post-apartheid context, and compares it with Freedom Park, with which it is twinned, to explore the place of 'symbolic reparation' in South Africa's reinvention of itself.

Chapter 4, 'Performing the African Renaissance and the "rainbow nation"', analyses how Mbeki used the South Africa-Mali project (2005–08), alongside the New Partnership for Africa's Development (NEPAD), to embody his African Renaissance project. This project sought to deconstruct colonial and apartheid formulations of African 'backwardness', and reconnect South Africa with the African continent as a whole. Central to this analysis is a consideration of how Mbeki's key ideas regarding the African Renaissance and the 'rainbow nation' were embodied in the *Timbuktu Script and Scholarship* exhibition that toured South Africa between August and December 2008. I consider the extent to which this project mirrors many post-colonial African attempts to contest European colonial assertions regarding African culture and apparent lack of history without interrogating the assumptions underpinning the terms of 'civilisation' and 'progress' in colonial histories sufficiently (Neale, 1985). The chapter then shifts to compare this project with the way South Africa performed itself as a new nation in the public events that framed the 2010 World Cup; and to the Handspring Puppet Company's production of *Tall Horse* (2005–06), which was a South-African Mali collaboration that occurred at the same time, and was asking similar questions to Mbeki's project.

The final chapter, 'Post-apartheid repertoires of memory', explores contemporary popular performance and theatrical engagements with history and memory. It begins by looking at issues of embodied repertoires, particularly those that are contested, or strongly related to the liberation struggle narrative, and ask how these are being engaged with in the present, and what issues this raises for South Africa. It then shifts to explore how and why many South African theatres are restaging canonical protest plays, and how this relates to nostalgia. It analyses how and why memory and identity are still central issues for diverse communities in South Africa. As case studies it explores ways in which Indian and coloured South Africans are renegotiating their identities through mobilising specific memories and histories in particular ways, while remaining aware of the role nostalgia may be playing in these revisions.

Throughout, I am exploring how embodied repertoires engage with formal archives of memory, emphasising the importance of the embodied subject and the multiple ways in which we make and negotiate meaning collectively and individually.

1

The Truth and Reconciliation Commission's reconfiguring of the past: remembering and forgetting

We are charged to unearth the truth about our dark past, to lay the ghosts of that past so that they will not return to haunt us. And [so] that we will thereby contribute to the healing of a traumatised and wounded people – for all of us in South Africa are wounded people – and in this manner to promote national unity and reconciliation. (Desmond Tutu)[1]

Because of this very fullness, the hypothetical fullness, of this archive, what will have been granted is not memory, is not a true memory. It will be forgetting. That is, the archive – the good one – produces memory, but produces forgetting at the same time. And when we write, when we archive, when we trace, when we leave a trace behind us . . . the trace is at the same time the memory, the archive, and the erasure, the repression, the forgetting of what it is supposed to keep safe. That's why, for all these reasons, the work of the archivist is not simply a work of memory. It's a work of mourning. (Derrida, 2002: 54)

This chapter begins with the moment of rupture: with the release of Mandela in 1990 and the negotiations for full democracy in South

---

1 These words represented a key narrative of the TRC, often heard in opening statements of hearings, cf. the first day of the hearings in east London, www.justice. gov.za/trc/hrvtrans/hrvel1/mohape.htm, accessed 10/8/11. They are also used by Max du Preez in the SABC programme *Bones of memory*, see Kapelianis and Taylor (2000: vol. 1).

Africa to be achieved by 1994, followed by a period of transition, characterised publicly to a large extent by the Truth and Reconciliation
Commission (TRC), which sat from 1994–98. It will look at the role
the TRC has played, both as live event and as an archive produced
from oral testimonies, in the construction of a 'new' South Africa. In
analysing the archive, I explore its function, how it has been performed
and constructed, the various influences on these processes, and the
effect it has had on the memories of apartheid for contemporary South
Africa.

This exploration devotes close attention to specific issues raised by
Derrida in his engagement with the TRC: issues of context, both of the
live event and of the resultant archive, and how context has affected
the interpretation of key concepts like justice, reconciliation, forgiveness and culpability as South Africa negotiates emergent value systems.
The interpreters and the media played key roles in the TRC, both as
event and as archive. I want to evaluate especially the extent to which
they affected the creation of a single, coherent narrative of the 'rainbow
nation' (McEachern, 2002).

The chapter will then compare the TRC archive, as summarised in the
Final Report, to individual memories, and look at what the TRC means
for South Africa almost two decades later.

'Backstage' conceptualisations of the TRC

Kentridge's description of the TRC as 'exemplary civic theatre, a public
hearing of private griefs which are absorbed into the body politic as a
part of the deeper understanding of how the society arrived at its present
position' (1998: ix) begs the question of how our understanding of this
public event is affected if we read it though the lens of a theatrical event.
This would involve considering who wrote the script, how the production was conceptualised in terms of context, approach to the production,
performance and intended audience; and how this in turn influenced
the development of the final narrative.

In 1995 the Minister of Justice, Mr Dullah Omar, explained the
genesis of the South African Truth and Reconciliation Commission,
as being 'based on the final clause of the Interim Constitution'. The
Government of National Unity used the Promotion of National Unity
and Reconciliation Act, No. 34 of 1995 to 'help deal with what happened
under apartheid. The conflict during this period resulted in violence and

human rights abuses from all sides. No section of society escaped these abuses'.[2]

Although South Africa had successfully negotiated the handover to a fully democratic government, the country was uneasy, divided, without a coherent or consensual sense of the past. This needed to be redressed, insofar as the articulation of a shared past is central to the conceptualising of an 'imagined community' (Anderson, 1991) and the formulation of a nation (McLeod, 2000). Alex Boraine reflects that 'the ANC and civil society stressed that the past could not be ignored and that accountability was a prerequisite for human rights culture. To ignore the past is to perpetuate victimhood' (2000: 6). However, the form that accountability would take was uncertain, as criminal trials culminating in punishment were seen by many to be 'impossible or even dangerous for the country',[3] and 'blanket amnesty . . . was unacceptable' (*ibid.*, 7). Significantly, although the TRC was 'not a direct product of the negotiation process, it was deeply influenced by the process', so that it was finally decided that the TRC 'would hold in tension truth-telling, limited amnesty, and reparation' (*ibid.*), through the three committees: the Amnesty Committee (AC), the Reparation and Rehabilitation (R&RC) Committee, and the Human Rights Violations Committee (HRVC).

The script envisaged for the TRC is evident from its mandate, which was to promote national unity and reconciliation in a spirit of understanding which transcends the conflicts and divisions of the past by:

- establishing as complete a picture as possible of the causes, nature and extent of gross violations of human rights which were committed during the period from 1 March 1960 to the cut-off date [later set at 1994] including the antecedents, circumstances, factors and context of such violations, as well as the perspectives of the victims and the motives and perspectives of the persons responsible for committing such violations, by conducting investigations and holding hearings;
- facilitating the granting of amnesty to persons who make full disclosure of all the relevant facts relating to acts associated with a political objective and which comply with the requirements of the Act (Promotion of National Unity and Reconciliation Act);

2 See www.justice.gov.za/trc/, accessed 10/8/11.
3 This is clear when one considers the assassination of Chris Hani on 10 April 1993, and the slogan 'Kill the Boer' chanted by young ANC officials at his funeral; and the increased mobilisation of the 'bitter-enders' under General Constand Viljoen, who by June 1993 had recruited 150,000 secessionists, of which 100,000 were men-at-arms with experience (see Carlin, 2008: 121–43).

- establishing and making known the fate or whereabouts of victims and restoring the human and civil dignity of such victims by granting them an opportunity to relate their own accounts of the violations of which they are the victims, and recommending reparation measures in respect of them;
- compiling a report providing as comprehensive an account as possible of the activities and findings of the Commission and containing recommendations of measures to prevent the future violations of human rights. (*Justice in Transition*)[4]

A TRC pamphlet explained that the function of the Commission was to

- give a complete picture of the gross violations of human rights which took place and which came from the conflicts of the past;
- restore victims their human and civil dignity by letting them tell their stories and recommending how they can be assisted;
- consider granting amnesty to those 'perpetrators' who carried out the abuses for political reasons, and who give full details of their actions to the commission. (TRC Pamphlets, 1995)[5]

These aims formed the basic outline for the TRC script which was to break silences of the past by offering amnesty to perpetrators for full disclosure of previously disavowed perpetrations of human rights violations, invite individuals to speak of their own experiences, and thus establish a sense of the past that could be shared by the widest range of people in South Africa. The staging of the TRC as a public event was ideologically important as it attempted to restore public confidence in the legal system in South Africa, where previous inquests had resulted in the official denial of experiences of human rights abuses. The difference in the focus in the pamphlets and the formal Act, particularly in foregrounding victims' narratives in the former, compared with the broader aims of reconciliation and fact-finding in the latter, highlights the differences of emphasis for the public, as opposed to the government.

The centrality of this predetermined script for the 'new' South Africa is evident in the two particular ways in which this South African

---

4 See www.justice.gov.za/trc/legal/index.htm, accessed 10/8/11. Republic of South Africa, *Government Gazette*, 361: 16579, Preamble, African National Congress. 1996. *Statement to the TRC.*
5 Examples of these pamphlets for public information include: *The Committee on Amnesty, The Committee on Human Rights Violations*, and *Truth. The Road to Reconciliation* (see TRC pamphlets, 1995). Other formulations of the mandate are evidenced in the Promotion of National Unity and Reconciliation Act, 1995, ANC. *Statement to the TRC* (1996).

Commission departed from preceding Truth Commissions in other countries.[6] First, hearings were held in public fora, with extensive media coverage, including radio microphones and television cameras, which underlined the necessity for disseminating the TRC narratives widely. Secondly, it heard the testimonies of both perpetrators of human rights abuses and survivors. This blurred the distinctions between the various processes of producing sources, archives, narratives and a history,[7] particularly given the multiple interlocutors involved, and allowed the script to emerge from the hearings, as directed by the commissioners.

Posel and Simpson argue that the sense of direct retrieval of memories through live narratives 'became the basis for their collective authentication', especially through the mediatised close-ups which, they argue, 'confirmed the immediacy and veracity of the truths being told' (2002: 7). This in turn supported the TRC's presentation of itself as a 'fact-finding' body. However, this representation is misleading, as the TRC was actively shaping the material at every stage. It has been referred to as a 'founding theatrical event, a metaphysical "tournament of value"' (Taylor, 2008: 9), which was not presenting facts so much as defining a shared understanding of apartheid, while (re)defining concepts of 'truth', 'reconciliation' and 'forgiveness'.

This notion of the TRC as a national theatrical event makes for comparison with the so-called 'state-of-the-nation plays', which Dan Rebellato suggests are characterised by large casts, public settings, epic timescales and national venues (2008). Critics apply the term to works that explore the nation in a state of rupture, crisis or conflict. Holdsworth argues that

> in general terms, the state-of-the-nation play deploys representations of personal events, family structures and social or political organisations as a microcosm of the nation-state to comment directly or indirectly on the ills befalling society, on key narratives of nationhood or on the state of the nation as it wrestles with changing circumstances. (2010: 39)

What is significant here is that the state itself set out to stage a national public event to address these same issues, using individual stories to create specific coherent narratives about the past and thus to facilitate the growth of a coherent future nation. This involved outlining a script.

The scripting began with the Information Management System

---

6 See Priscilla Hayner's (1994) detailed account of 15 preceding commissions in other parts of the world.
7 For a useful discussion on these distinctions, particularly in relation to silence, see Trouillot (1995: 26).

(IMS)[8] used to collect and collate the data. Burr explores how the IMS set the parameters that not only facilitated the process for translating local, specific narratives into 'signs of gross human rights violations' that were 'superimposable' and 'combinable' (2002: 80), but also determined which narratives would be included. The parameters included a specific time frame, including specifically defined events or historic moments for consideration in the hearings,[9] spatial co-ordinates and definitions of categories which determined a specific understanding of the past, and a coherent time-line of past events that would ultimately become part of the 'new' national history (*ibid.*, 78). Thus we can argue that the history being offered for consensualisation pre-dated the first hearings, was implicit in the conceptualisation of the Commission, and was defined in part by the systems chosen to record its operations.

The next aspect of the 'backstage' events of the Commission was the process of selecting narratives for public hearings, both for the HRVC and the AC. The first direct contact between the Commission and applicants was with statement takers, some 40 persons in 1996 and 400 in 1997, many hired from community groups and non-governmental organisations.[10] Although some 20,000 applications were made by people wishing to testify to the Commission, only 10% of these were selected for the HRVC hearings by Commission staff. This is important because the transcriptions of all the applications and the testimonies finally heard at the various hearings form a significant part of the TRC archive, and thus provided the basis for the final narrative.[11] The selection process was based on 'the totality of the experience of that particular region or that particular city', fair distribution of race, gender, ethnicity, representing diverse political constituencies, and also on the need for stories that would 'resonant the most with people' (Cole, 2010: 9) The Commission also selected 'window cases': defined as cases that

8 The TRC database was designed and supervised by the American Association for the Advancement of Science. For an analysis of the implications of this system being imported, how it interfaced with the local, and was adapted by South African statement-takers, see Burr (2002).

9 These included the Sharpeville Massacre, Soweto Uprising and St James' Church Massacre, as evident in the Commission's publicity posters.

10 For details see Jaffer (1997: 1). The TRC *Final Report* (1998, vol. 5: 5) acknowledges that 'For thousands of people, statement takers represented their first and often their only face-to-face encounter with the Commission' (para. 19) and that they 'carried a heavy burden of responsibility and were the front rank of those who gathered the memories of the pain and suffering of the past' (para. 20).

11 Although the cut-off date for amnesty applications was 30 September 1997, many cases were only finalised in 2001, see Amnesty transcriptions, www.justice.gov.za/trc/amntrans/index.htm; there is an ongoing debate about whether or not to consider applications beyond this date. Application documentation is in a closed archive, not available to researchers.

could be representative of broader patterns of abuse.[12] This suggests a selection process that was both pragmatic and ideologically predefined in relation to the aims of the Commission, as set out by the African National Congress's *Statement to the TRC* (1996).

The repertoire: 'On-stage' dimensions of the TRC (1996–98)

The TRC's mandate was extraordinary. It involved accessing and researching people and backgrounds in widely diverse locales in South Africa, validating the approach to this event as a 'state-of-the-nation play which involved large casts, public settings, epic timescales and national venues'.[13] To achieve its mandate in the limited time available, hearings were held simultaneously in various parts of the country in various public spaces, school halls, community centres, etc. Cole describes such a hearing as 'a site-specific performance event' whereby

> the Commission took the process to people, moving throughout the country and invading particular communities for several months at a time. According to [Commissioner Yasmin] Sooka, there was usually an eight-week cycle in any particular location. This began with an advance team that briefed the community, made logistical arrangements, and organised the statement-taking process. A few days before the public hearings, the commissioners would arrive in the town to be briefed and to meet witnesses and community leaders. The eight-week cycle would culminate in the public hearings. (2010: 8)[14]

Each stage is important in assessing the extent to which the Commission was 'finding facts' and 'revealing truth'[15] in the positivist sense in which

12 See, for example, the statement on this by Dr Ally in Heidelberg on 4/02/1997, www.justice.gov.za/trc/hrvtrans/duduza/moloko.htm; other examples include BOP and Radio Freedom (www.justice.gov.za/trc/special/media/media01.htm), and the Guguletu Seven hearing.
13 For dates and places of HRVC hearings, see TRC *Final Report* (1998, vol. 5: 27–8); names of those who were considered to have suffered a gross violation of human rights, (*ibid.*, 29–107). For Amnesty hearings, see (*ibid.*, 122–7), and for later dates, see www.justice.gov.za/trc/amntrans/index.htm.
14 The cycle could last up to 10 weeks, including the post-hearing follow-up and referral phase (*Final Report*, 1998, vol. 1: 401).
15 It is perhaps worth noting that the Commission recognised four kinds of 'truths':

these activities were framed, as opposed to shaping material and the implications of these different approaches to the material.

We begin with space, the venues, which Commissioner Sooka has suggested were selected to 'performatively enact a new social order', insofar as they reclaimed spaces that had been denied to black South Africans under apartheid (*Ibid.*, 9). The significance of physical space in relation to conceptions of memory and identity is highlighted by Robert Harrison:

> Physical spaces are vital sources of metaphors for our social constructions of reality. Metaphors are not optional extras or embellishment to our ways of thinking and speaking. Our perceptions of reality are defined by metaphor: Places form landscapes and landscapes may be defined as sets of relational places and embodying (literally and metaphorically) emotion, memories and associations derived from personal and interpersonal shared experience. (2003: 4–5)

This underlines a strong relationship between an individual's sense of belonging and emotions generated by experiences that are attached to particular places and spaces. This is even more pertinent in cultures that have a strong oral narrative tradition, as argued by Hofmeyr, whose work has examined what happens when 'people lose access to the topography that helps to uphold oral memory' (1994: 160). One of the profound ways in which apartheid was enacted was through various laws that prescribed access to spaces, such as the ubiquitous Pass Laws, the 1950 Group Areas Act and the 1953 Separate Amenities Act. By reappropriating sites previously denied to South Africans for such an emotional recounting of the past, the Commission offered individuals the opportunity of performatively redefining their relationship with these sites, and thus their identities as South African citizens, to some extent. Here metaphor triumphed on both the narrative and non-narrative levels.[16]

In any theatrical event arguably the two central constituents are the performers and the audience. Both are to some extent affected by what I argue are dramaturgical choices, which affect the focus, script and conceptualisation of the whole production. I thus look first to the commissioners who were selected to facilitate these public hearings. Their backgrounds are important because each commissioner

---

factual or forensic truth, personal or narrative truth, social or 'dialogue' truth . . . and healing or restorative truth (TRC *Final Report*, 1998, vol. 1: 110–14). For a discussion of these see Posel (2002: 154–7).

16 See Ndebele (1998: 19–28).

brought a particular perspective to the hearings from their personal and professional lives, which in turn affected how they framed and interpreted the hearings for the public. For example, Cole analyses the way Commissioner Dumisa Ntsebeza contained and interpreted the shoe-throwing episode during the Guguletu Seven[17] hearing on 23 April 1996 in Heideveld (2010: 18–25). Desmond Tutu, although one of many commissioners, defined the terms and style of the Commission both ideologically and performatively, particularly in the way that all the hearings began and ended with hymns and prayer, which created a very specific dynamic for the forum, often one in conflict with the political context.[18]

The commissioners included persons who were, or had at one time been, practising Christian theologians: Archbishop Desmond Tutu, Reverend Bongani Finca, Reverend Khoza Magojo, Alex Boraine (also a politician) and Yasmin Sooka (also an advocate), who was President of the South African Chapter of the World Council on Religion and Peace. Commissioners with legal training included Dumisa Ntsebeza (head of the Investigative Unit), Chris de Jager, Fazel Randera, Sisi Khampepe, Wynand Malan (also a politician), Denzil Potgieter and Richard Lyster. Those with a medical background included Wendy Orr, Pumla Gobodo-Madikizela, Hlengiwe Mkize, Glenda Wildschutt and Mapule Ramashala; Mary Benson was a civil society activist, who had led the Black Sash. In accordance with the stipulation of the Act, Judge Hassan Mall was appointed chairperson of the Amnesty Committee.

After the statement-takers, who converted the initial narrative into a dataset, the translators were probably the most influential interlocuters at the hearings.[19] All three Commissions were heard with English

17 Refers to seven young men who were ambushed and shot at an intersection in Guguletu, Cape Town. They were said to be terrorists about to attack a police bus carrying senior officers, but these young men were untrained. Later the Commission heard how the group was infiltrated by 'askaris', informers, who gave the security forces information to set the ambush. The mothers heard about their sons' deaths on the television news. At the Amnesty hearing one of the women, thought to be sister of Christopher Piet, was so incensed at the video footage that had been used as propaganda and was reshown at the hearings that she took off her shoe and threw it at the men, hitting two policemen and disrupting the hearings. This shifted the horror of the event and the implications of its being filmed and televised to the presence of the women and their active role in these proceedings.

18 For analyses of the complexities of these competing fora see Audrey Chapman and Bernard Spong (2003), Deborah Postel (2002), Frederick van Zyl Slabbert, (2003). See also Zulu Sonkosi (2003) on 'Amnesty from an African point of view'.

19 There is some controversy as to whether it is correct to use the term translators as opposed to interpreters; I use the former to conform to the TRC terminology, while acknowledging related issues. I am indebted to du Plessis and Wiegand (1998) for details pertaining to the translation of the TRC hearings, particularly in distinguishing between the different issues related to the HRVC, AC and section 29 hearings (which were in-camera hearings focused on perpetrators' testimonies and

as the foundational language of translation; this meant that the witnesses spoke in their preferred language, while the translators sat in booths and simultaneously translated into English. This translation was then relayed to the other translators, who usually then translated into Afrikaans, the dominant language of the region and another language of the region. The translators worked in teams of two, where the one not translating would assist with notes, names, dates and idiom. The complexities of this process were exacerbated by a number of factors: the limited English-language competency of most of the African translators, compounded by their limitations with respect to regional variations of dialect and local idiom in a 'deep' use of a particular African language, translating taboo words or expressions and culturally sensitive matters, the very limited training they had had, the speed with which they had to translate, the fact that often there was more than one speaker, especially in the Amnesty hearings, where there was cross-examination, and the tension between translating words as opposed to emotional meaning. Also, simultaneous-relay translations were fast and often resulted in mistranslations being passed on to other translators, the commissioners and the wider public via the media. The stress experienced by the translators both in relation to what was demanded of them, and of having to translate highly emotive material in the first person, seems not to have been taken into account by the Commission's organisers, although the commissioners and media representatives, like Antje Krog, who had been invited to cover the hearings were given psychological support, but the interpreters were not.[20] Thus, although translation was key to the hearings, and the transcriptions of them formed the basis for the *Final Report*,[21] these factors were not acknowledged in the process. Yet each of these individuals and their own memories of life during the apartheid years shaped these narratives for South Africa and the world.

The next important performance aspect of the hearings is the non-verbal expressions that formed part of the testimonies – the cries, sighs, gestures and silences. Here I want to analyse what these non-verbal expressions added to the testimonies, as well as how they imply particular silences, denials, repressions and ambiguities associated with

---

their cross-examination); and to Lotriet (2002) on the training of interpreters; also to Yvette Coetzee of the *Truth in Translation* project for her insights into the processes [personal interview, 31/03/2011]. For background on translation see pp. 16–17 of Education material, www.truthintranslation.org/educational_materials.pdf. See also Yvette Coetzee's interviews with three translators (2006: 102–5).

20 See Cole on translation versus interpretation and related issues, (1910: 68–78, 190–1, footnote 17 on retranslation of material).

21 See, for example, the statement at the bottom of the page for accessing Amnesty transcriptions at www.justice.gov.za/trc/amntrans/.

the witnesses' remembering of the past. I consider this particularly important because these aspects of the hearings were not included in the transcripts or reports. The growing body of literature related to testimony and trauma indicates that language and memory are particularly challenged in the context of pain and horror, which in turn means that non-verbal expressions often substitute for, or reveal gaps in, the narrative. Christine Delbo, a survivor of Auschwitz, distinguishes between 'common' memory and 'deep' memory (1990). Common memory engages with experiences that have been processed rationally at some level, and thus can be described and communicated in language; 'deep' memory involves experiences that are visceral and leave physical imprints on the body. It often operates outside of language because the trauma is 'unspeakable'. This distinction is important when dealing with narratives that involve trauma. In analysing Delbo's fourth commentary on her experiences in Auschwitz, Lawrence Langer shows how the narratives interrelate:

> Deep memory tries to recall the Auschwitz self as it was then; common memory . . . restores the self to its normal pre- and postcamp routines, but also offers detached portraits, from the vantage point of today, of what it must have been like then. (1991: 6)

The intersection between deep and common memory often results in a frustrated, disrupted narrative, which evinces a disrupted sense of identity and memory.

Similar patterns of disruptions were evident in the testimonies of particular women at the TRC. Fiona Ross's (1998) findings support Langer's analysis of the way traumatised witnesses' testimony is often disrupted as they attempt to make sense of the past in relation to the present, arguing that this is manifested in repetitions, ellipsis and pauses, metaphor, tone of voice, gaps in information and fluctuations in narrative time. Ross suggests that the applicants drew on 'oral tradition and deep cultural echoes' as a way of managing the trauma. Here Ross makes an important distinction between the place of poetry in Holocaust survivors' accounts and survivors' use of poetry and song in TRC testimonies (1998: 175, footnote 4) which, she argues, is not 'aestheticising testimony' so much as a performance of memory, as individuals tap into oral forms that are implicitly related to the liberation movement in South Africa (see *Amandla!* 2002). These forms not only allowed for the expression of memories for which they may not have had words, but they also 'invited audiences to participate with them in the performances of memory and meaning, and drew audiences with them in the testimonial process' (*ibid.*, 35–8).

This may have had a two-fold consequence – it may support the claim that the liveness[22] 'became the basis for their [the narratives] collective authentication' (Posel and Simpson, 2002: 7) and it demonstrates how those testifying became a 'symbolic sign' for 'the nation's suffering', beyond individual experience (Burr, 2002: 84). This is important for consideration here, because either as a live or as a televised event, these narratives are contextualised in time and place, but also in dialogue with the past. This dialogue is complex insofar as it is constructivist: splitting, doubling and mixing time and experience. In a sense, then, the embodied repertoires being invoked in the testimonies interact with individuals' memories of the past in the context of the present, and thus affect the official archive insofar as it is being formulated from these live moments, but without conscious or critical engagement with the 'truths' being drawn upon in this formulation. I shall return to these ideas later in this chapter.

Veena Das proposes another way in which testimonies of trauma may go beyond words via 'an aesthetic of gestures' (2000: 211). These gestures may be physical, with the narrator bowing or holding her head, wringing her hands, or it may include other verbal gestures such as sighing or crying. These aural forms[23] differ greatly from written narratives, which tend to be synchronically formulated, with aspects associated with oral forms such as repetition or ellipses edited out. Ross notes that the emotive aspects of the testimonies were not confined to those testifying, but were often reciprocated by some of the commissioners and audience, in nods or even verbal responses, like Tutu breaking down in tears at the start of the hearings (1998: 38), which suggests the acknowledgement of a trace of something that is in fact absent, but 'which was present to contemporaries when they occurred' (Ricoeur, cited by Burr, 2002: 90, footnote 37). These gestures made up an important part of the event itself, and perhaps contributed to how more global aspects of the hearings were agreed upon by commissioners and the wider public. However, their absence from the transcriptions and *Final Report* does

22 I acknowledge the complexities around the notion of 'liveness' in relation to 'truth' (Auslander, 1999: 128–9) and its converse in the 'antitheatrical prejudice' which insists that that which is staged is inherently false. See Cole's (2010) analysis of the notion of 'liveness' in relation to audiences, not present but watching television broadcasts which '*was* the commission for this larger general audience' (2010: 94). Cole suggests that these were not '*equivalent*' representations of the live performance event, but were 'a performative iteration of the commission', which not only reported on the event, but analysed and 'performed it' (*ibid.*, 95).

23 See Coplan, (1995) who coined this term to refer to the complex product that emerged from speaking and listening to Basotho migrant labourers with whom he was working. See also Walter Ong (1982) and Duncan Brown (1998, 2006) on the complex relationship between oral and literary forms.

not allow for any engagement with this consensualising process, nor leave any traces of these gestures for future analysis, beyond videoed documents, which are directed and edited. This suggests an important gap between the embodied repertoire and emergent archive of this public formulation of collective memory.

Silence is another important aspect of testimonies not included in the written archives. It may signal the inability of an individual to articulate a trauma, as argued by Elaine Scarry (1985), or that witnesses are working out what should be said next. For example, when asked a question on a very emotional experience by commissioners, those testifying often paused for some time and looked as if they were mentally working out the 'least bad' response. The silences could also signal a choice, a refusal to speak. Das insists that silence is a legitimate part of the discourse on pain and that we have a personal responsibility to acknowledge it (1996: 69–71). She argues that as pain is usually situated in the body, the body is also the site in which silences are held. In the context of analysing Indian women's responses to the violations they experienced during the partition that separated Pakistan from India, Das argues that through their silence 'women converted this passivity [of being texts upon which men wrote] into agency', as they held 'poisonous knowledge' inside themselves (*ibid.*, 84–5). This is not to imply that they did not speak of their experiences, but like their South African counterparts, they engineered a particular kind of silence 'either by the use of language that was general and metaphoric but that evaded specific description of any events so as to capture the particularity of their experience, or by describing the surrounding events but leaving the actual experience . . . unstated' (*ibid.*, 84). Here memory is mobilised in a particular way: while acknowledging the violent event, the women refuse to generate future memories that could perpetuate victimhood and the legacies of the past, as an example of strategic forgetting.[24]

Comparable silences are evident in the TRC's engagement with specific aspects of the apartheid past, particularly in relation to gendered issues, as evidenced in the Special Hearings on Women. Early in the process Goldblatt and Meintjes predicted limited engagement of women with the Commission and highlighted that

> women have been subordinated and oppressed through socially constructed differences. Indeed, gender differences have meant that South African men and women have often experienced our history in different

24 This position is complex and suggests that, while women are choosing how they protect themselves, their reputations and men in their society, they do so at a cost to themselves.

ways. In South Africa, as in most societies in the world, women have been accorded identities [that] cast them in particular social roles [that] have restricted their civil and political status. Intersecting with gender are also race, class, and other identities, such as ethnic and religious allegiances. These form the basis of the 'public-private' divide, which has given the men the role of civil and political representative of the household, to the exclusion of women. (1996: 5)

It is important to recognise what these particular definitions of gender roles in South Africa have meant in terms of public memory and perceptions of gender and violence, both in relation to the past and present. In broad terms the TRC set out to create an authoritative, shared description and analysis of the history of South Africa.[25] It is important to note that while the Commission carefully analysed the 'context in which conflict developed and gross violations of human rights occurred' (TRC *Final Report*, 1998, vol. 2: 4ff), it did not include gender construction as part of its mandate. This may be because of the Commission's decision to limit its investigation 'to gross violations of human rights defined as the "killing, abduction, torture or severe ill-treatment" or inciting thereto' (*ibid.*, vol. 1: 29, also Ross, 2003: 17–26), which defined ill-treatment in physical, body-bound terms, as opposed to exploring the psychological aspects. These terms also failed to take into account cultural taboos related to sexual violence, and the *a priori* definition of women's roles in terms of the domestic sphere. Once again, it is important to acknowledge that the *a priori* conceptualisation of the Commission defined what memories would be included and excluded from this important public engagement with South Africa's past.

It is important to consider the implications of Ross's finding that 'sexual violence was represented in the hearings and in public discourse as a defining feature of women's experiences of gross violations of human rights', but that 'men were not called to testify about sexual violation' (2003: 24), although such acts were not restricted to women, nor indeed to the apartheid past. This is evidenced, for example, in some detail in the final report on the Special Hearing on Women (TRC *Final Report*, 1998, vol. 4: 284–317), which details 'gender-specific offences' committed by both male comrades in various ANC camps and South Africa's security police. However, the only specific engagement with male rape or sexual abuse is in reference to youths between the ages of 14–21, who belonged to the Bonteheuwel Military Wing (BMW) (*ibid.*, vol. 3: 484–5, vol. 4: 281–2). The *Findings and Conclusions* specifically

25 See Gibson (2010: 7).

highlights the abuses of women particularly in physical or domestic terms, related to their physical vulnerability or their roles as mothers (*ibid.*, vol. 5: 256), rather than as individuals engaged in a civic or political struggle. Considering the widespread sexual violence and rape of women and children in contemporary South Africa, and the ongoing institutional violence in prisons,[26] we are left with a question that Veena Das has posed about the relation between narrative truth and historical truth: 'Once violence has become a part of a system of representations which give form to memory, it seems to me that the crucial question is how it transforms the experience of violence' (1987: 12–13). This leads us to question whether the TRC in any way transformed South Africa's sense of the place of women and men in their societies, or furthered an understanding of the reasons for, and deconstruction of, the place of violence in a society which has long been defined by its presence.

One cannot analyse a public event without considering audiences. The TRC had two audiences: those who were physically present and those who experienced the hearings via radio and television, both nationally and internationally, with varying degrees of awareness of the details and backgrounds of the testimonies. For those actively involved, the event was defined largely by how their expectations compared to their experience of the hearings, for example, of how 'truths' were defined, what 'truths' emerged, and the extent to which individuals could or were expected to 'reconcile', etc.[27] In many ways these performances can be seen as rehearsals of an ideal state of the nation where truths are fully revealed, and reconciliation and forgiveness are enacted unreservedly. Of course, this was not the experience for most people, but like any rehearsal, it was aspirational and essential for stability, and as Foucault argues, the formulation of a clear history

---

26 South Africa has the highest per capita rape statistic in the world, see Anderson (1999–2000) on comparative statistics. A report published by the trade union Solidarity in June 2009 reported that one child is raped in South Africa every three minutes, with 88% of rapes going unreported (Smith, 2009). For an analysis of the relationship between past abuses and current levels of sexual violence see Moffatt (2010) and Gear (2005), who traces contemporary sexual violence and gendering in male prisons to rituals beyond the prison walls, particularly to mine compounds in South Africa.

27 For examples of these paradoxes see analyses by Piers Pigou on the limited truths revealed in the amnesty hearings related to 'The murder of Sicelo Dlomo' (2009: 97–116), Pamela Dube on the experience of Thandi Shezi at the TRC (in Posel and Simpson, 2002: 117–30) and Mtutuzeli Matshoba analysing 'The ordeal of Duma Khumalo', one of the Sharpeville Six, whose stigma for the murder of which he had been accused the TRC could not remove, nor could it assist him with the material consequences of his experiences under apartheid (*ibid.*, 131–44).

allows those in power to arrange and control power structures. It also allowed the widest possible audience to 'hear' the same story, as opposed to other Truth Commissions, such as the Truth, Justice and Reconciliation Commission in Kenya, which receives limited media coverage, and thus smaller but more varied 'audiences', which in turn raises questions around the processes of creating consensualising narratives of nation.[28]

Evaluating the mediated performances of the TRC is more complex, because there is almost no documented research on the reception of the TRC. Dayan and Katz explore the way media events are performed, in the Austinian sense,[29] and thus invoke 'an experience in its own right, different from the original, and probably more important' (1992: 79) The latter assertion is certainly borne out in terms of the more permanent record that newspapers, magazines and various radio and television programmes created of this event. Television in particular was able to give perspectives on the event not even available to those at the hearings, such as close-ups of people's faces and their reactions to specific testimonies, and cuts between speakers, audiences and commissioners. Television programmes were also able to select and edit what would be shown, and thus defined how the testimonies would be narrated and framed in news broadcasts, current affairs or documentary programmes, even editing in background information not included in the TRC hearings.[30] And perhaps most significantly, these programmes '*became* the TRC for millions of people' (McEachern, 2002: 30).

Although the role of the media in the performance of the TRC is highly debated and for the most part they have been criticised for their role in supporting the official narrative of nation building (McEachern, 2002; Posel, 2002: 7–9, 151–2; Saunders, 2007), their role was an important aspect of the revisioning of South Africa's past. Media had played a politically central role in apartheid South Africa, as seen in the

28 The Kenyan TJRC was established in 2009 to lead the inquiry into gross human rights violations and other historical injustices in Kenya between 12 December 1963 and 28 February 2008. It ended in April 2012; the commission has requested a further extension for the submission of their report. See www.usip.org/publications/truth-commission-kenya, accessed 14/8/11 and 4/9/12.

29 That is to say, in saying or representing something, we bring it into being (Austin, 1962: 6–8).

30 This background was part of the research for the TRC, preceding hearings, but not included in the 30 minute hearings. See du Preez's *TRC Special Report* for television examples (Yale Law School Lillian Goldman Library, www.law.yale.edu/trc/index.html; SAHA, in conjunction with the SABC, repackaged version of the series as an interactive product aimed at educational and outreach groups (launched December 2010, available 2011), see www.saha.org.za/projects/special_report_multimedia_project.htm.

legislation on public information and in the Special Hearings on the Media in 1997.[31] The South African Broadcasting Company (SABC) in particular had been complicit in assisting the state in its construction and legitimisation of apartheid South Africa. Thus after 1994 the media had to undergo a major transformation, as they were needed to communicate a wide understanding of what citizenship and democracy now meant, particularly for a nation with high levels of illiteracy (Teer-Tomaselli, 1995: 585). McEachern argues that one of the most important aspects of their role in this project was in 'imagining *the nation*' (2002: 20, her italics), because 'before 1994 people inhabited different nations', now 'the specific symbolic form of imagining was the telling of stories to make connections between people once understood to inhabit different spaces, different histories' (*ibid.*). Imagining simultaneity is an important way of imagining a nation (McLeod, 2000: 74–5).[32]

Cole takes issue with this generally critical position on the media, suggesting the need for a more nuanced analysis of their role, particularly Max du Preez's 87-episode weekly current affairs programme *Special Report*, broadcast on Sundays by the SABC from 21 April 1996 to 29 March 1998 (2010: 91–120). Cole demonstrates that this series contextualised individual cases in a way that the TRC hearings did not, and thus engaged with issues of systemic violence in apartheid South Africa, the consequences of economic and social inequality, and even the relationship between criminal and political violence, most of which was absent in the context of the TRC hearings and *Final Report*.[33] However, it must be said that although the programme enjoyed an estimated viewership of 1.2 million weekly (*ibid.*, 114), it is not characteristic of the dominant engagement with the TRC, and du Preez admits having a particular agenda and target (white Afrikaner) audience in mind. However, this analysis highlights Derrida's insistence that no archive is decisive, 'beyond interpretation'; so we have 'an ethical and political responsibility' (2002: 62, 46) to keep engaging with it, and thus continue

---

31 For detailed analyses see Teer-Tomaselli (1995) and McEachern (2002), transcriptions of the Special Hearings on the Media and the Findings in the TRC *Final Report*, 1998, vol. 4: 165–98.

32 For a more recent example, see the SABC series *Shoreline* (2009), which literally narrates the 'oneness' of South Africans by combining historic, biological and archaeological narratives with an exploration of South Africa's physical coastline.

33 Context was very much part of the initial statement, and also part of the investigative work done before the case, but not part of the public hearings. The contexts outlined in the *Final Report* also tend to be summative rather than specific and in line with the focus of the TRC, thus not focused on looking, for example, at gender, the relationship between criminal and political violence, or issues of apartheid systems.

to challenge the choices made before and during the hearings. To some extent the degree to which this is possible is affected by technology, which affects both content and access. [34]

This material has demonstrated two important factors in the way memories have been selected and shaped: the various interlocutors and the context in which memories are narrated. From the outset it was evident that the TRC had a clear agenda and mandate regarding definitions of truth, the kinds of memories to be foregrounded and the promotion of national unity by publicly performing reconciliation. This could be perceived as the storyboard for a production that is to be workshopped. Various 'players' then engaged with these ideas, from the statement takers and interpreters to the commissioners, who most overtly shaped the event through their selection of testimonies, the questions they posed during the hearings and their framing comments before, during and after each hearing; and of course the 'players' include those testifying. Each participant brought with him or her particular understanding of the terms of the Commission, which were then affected by their prior experiences and perceived role in the event. The latter was affected by the participants' particular expectations, and the degree to which they understood and agreed with the specific mandate of the TRC. In the live event, these aspects were negotiated through contextualised consensualisation, as the participants, and to some extent also the audience present, could articulate their questions, reservations or objections.

In some ways the TRC live event was like watching an improvised theatre piece, where all the participants have a sense of the basic plot outline and their roles, but what the audience see is being created before them. The mediated version was to some extent edited and interpreted, as we have seen. However, the transcriptions of this event formed the raw material from which the TRC script was written, as workshopped plays were often scripted after the plays had been created by an author. This is another process, which involves transforming the embodied event – which has negotiated various repertoires of memory – into a script, which then stands for the improvised, embodied event. For the TRC the 'script' that came to represent the performance was primarily the *Final Report*, but the analysis that follows considers this script in relation to other, related archives.

---

34 This is borne out by Cole (2010), who explicates not only the difficulty of accessing various TRC archives, but new sources via the internet.

TRC archives and embodied memories

The TRC archives are vast and include the material collated officially by the Commission and available in the public domain: some background information on the Commission, transcripts of the various hearings, some media reports and, centrally, the full *Final Report*.[35] There is the vast collection of unedited audiovisual recordings of the SABC, housed at the SABC and the National Archives; other significant recordings include media programmes such as the series *TRC Special Report*, directed by Max du Preez. The reflective books written by commissioners involved in the process,[36] and critical engagements with the TRC by public critics and academics from diverse disciplines constitute a substantial secondary archive. This section will look at both of these bodies of material. Other TRC-related material includes critical and creative responses to the TRC in novels, plays and films, some of which will be the focus of the next chapter.

However, there is an important archive that is not part of this analysis, because it is closed. It constitutes the bulk of the TRC archive, some three kilometres of print-out, and includes the statements made by unsuccessful applicants of the three committees, and the background research done by the TRC Investigative Unit on each human rights and amnesty case. Although the National Archives and Record Services in Pretoria is the official custodian of this archive, it is owned by the Department of Justice and Constitutional Development, who control access, even to researchers.[37]

I begin my analysis of the emergent TRC archive through the *Refiguring the Archive* project, which was originally conceptualised in 1998 by the University of Witwatersrand's Graduate School for the Humanities and Social Sciences in conjunction with the National Archives, the university's Historical Papers, the Gay and Lesbian Archives, and the South African History Archive. This project addressed the emerging questions on the definition, hegemony, methodology and

---

35 The report was published in seven volumes, see Truth and Reconciliation Commission of South Africa. 1999, and it is available at www.justice.gov.za/trc/. For *Fundamental Documents* see Doxtader and Salazar (2007), and Alexander *et al.* (2004–05) for select bibliography on the Truth and Reconciliation Commission Debate.
36 See, for example, Boraine (2000), Krog (1998), Sachs (2009).
37 For details on the struggle to access this database see Calland (2009) and Pigou (2009), while South African History Archive (SAHA) reports on the various aspects of this ongoing issue; see www.saha.org.za/.

various practices of archiving, and brought together theoretical and practice-based explorations of approaches to archives from African, European and North American perspectives (Hamilton *et al.*, 2002: 7–8). This was important because South Africa had been isolated from significant contact with the rest of the world since sanctions were imposed from the early 1960s. At the same time South Africa was of interest to the wider academic community insofar as it was renegotiating practices and archives in significant ways. Derrida's engagement with the TRC illustrates this, while at the same time it offers an important outside perspective on intensely debated and emotional internal issues. Political philosopher Daniel Herwitz argues that South Africa's neonatal state placed it in the situation where 'everything must be referred to the process of immediate critique or even withdrawal' (2001: xxv), and as such offered the potential for a complete revisioning not possible in systems that have developed slowly, over time. The uniqueness of the moment allowed archivists to explore how archives are affected by the way that a collection is physically added to or subtracted from, by technologies, and their dynamic relationships to their physical environments, organisational dynamics and political imperatives (Hamilton *et al.*, 2002: 7)

The *Refiguring the Archive* project framed its distinctiveness from similar projects such as the 1999 Subaltern Studies project as being to challenge 'the claims of the archive to constitute the record, provide evidence and act as a source' (*ibid.*, 9). It was strongly influenced by Foucault's view 'that archives are often both documents of exclusion and monuments to particular configurations of power' (*ibid.*). Thus this project focused on trying 'to understand the circumstances of the creation of the archival record in general, and of specific collections in particular" (*ibid.*). This is of particular interest here in that the Wits Archive project has drawn heavily on the circumstances of the production of specific oral archives, to explore the implications of the various attempts to 'fill the gaps' in South Africa's previous archives by turning to literature, landscape, dance, art, the human genome as archive, and the significance of new technologies in the politics of archiving. This resonates with Diana Taylor's (2007b) exploration of the intersection between the archive and repertoire, or embodied remembering.

There is much debate about the relationship between memory and archive. The director of the Archival Platform,[38] Jo-Ann Duggan has suggested that:

---

38 A research, advocacy and networking project in South Africa, initiated in May 2009 and formally launched in November 2009, which aims 'to promote public

The act of exteriorising, or sharing, shifts memory from the private realm of the individual into the public domain. But, this does not necessarily mean that it enters the archive. As with records, memory enters the archive when it is both exteriorised and deemed to be of archival value. Deemed memories enter the archive because they are considered to be potentially valuable to us when we think about the past. As valued resources, they demand preservation so that they can be accessible to others, in the present and in the future. (2011)

The significance of this for the TRC suggests that simply narrating a memory in the public domain does not guarantee it a place in the archive; something more is needed: it must be 'deemed to be of archival value', that is, more widely 'considered to be potentially valuable to us when we think about the past'. This suggests that the relationship between memory and archive is profoundly affected by external hegemonies. Derrida refers to these hegemonies as being 'the social and political power of the archive, which consists in selecting the traces in memory, in marginalising, censoring, destroying, such and such traces through precisely a selection, a filter', including 'the limitations in time and space' (Derrida, 2002: 44). In this statement the agent remains unspecified, possibly because it is not singular. As stated earlier, the TRC interlocutors were many: the Government of National Unity, which set the terms of the Commission, the statement-takers, the commissioners who selected the cases for public hearing and mediated the proceedings and *Final Report*, the translators and the media. So the first aspect is to consider which memories are available to the general public through, for example, the official website, and which are not. The second aspect worth considering is what the degree to which the state is or is not willing for these archives to be accessed and reviewed says about the government's need to control the archive in order to maintain power (Foucault, 1972: 8). It is also worth considering how long an archive should be kept closed and how soon one can effectively 'read' an archive.[39]

To some extent these questions relate to Ricoeur's suggestion that '[h]istory continues to be born from this taking of a distance which con-

---

engagement with and investment in the archive through networking and information sharing'. It is supported by the Nelson Mandela Foundation and the University of Cape Town (UCT) Archives and Public Culture Programme, and funded by the Atlantic Philanthropies (Deacon, 2009: 1).

39 See www.saha.org.za/ on the debate on the proposal by ANC members of the Ad Hoc Committee on the Protection of Information Bill, commonly referred to as the Secrecy Bill, which overrides the provisions of the Promotion of Access to Information Act (PAIA). As of 31 March 2012, The National Council of Provinces has delayed pronouncement on the adoption of the Protection of State Information Bill to 17 May.

sists in the recourse to the exteriority of the archival trace' (2004: 139), an idea which Derrida formulates thus:

> The archive does not consist simply in remembering, in living memory, in anamnesis; but in consigning, in inscribing a trace in some external location – there is no archive without some location, that is, some space outside. Archive is not a living memory. It is a location – that's why the political power of the *archons* is so essential in the definition of the archive. (2002: 42)

This suggests a provocative relationship between the 'living' or embodied memory and the archive, which, while locating memory, can only do so partially, as a 'trace'. Distance from the experience and location are important for an archive, as they allow the individual and society to 'forget', precisely because the event is officially 'remembered'. However, while the memory appears safe in the archive, its externality simultaneously renders it 'vulnerable', because of 'the relation between the absence of the thing remembered and its presence in the mode of its representation' (Ricoeur, 2004: 57–8); in other words, the representation of the memory is vulnerable to various interpretations when disconnected from the individuals that experienced the event, or even to being forgotten. On the other hand, if something is not officially remembered for a particular community, it is likely that they will actively seek to keep their memories alive, often in ways that lead to particular readings of the past being passed down through the generations.[40]

This shift from the embodied memory to the archive is important because, as Derrida argues, 'in the strictest sense of the word, there is no private archive. An archive has to be public, precisely because it is located' (2002: 48). However, its public nature renders it subject to the agendas of the wider socio-political milieu. What was at stake in South Africa was the power to (re)define 'truth', 'reconciliation', forgiveness' and the past. Derrida argues that 'the very actions in which the TRC is shaped from the beginning is a linguistic intervention', vis a vis the translation of concepts which may have distinctive cultural meanings, for example, forgiveness or reconciliation (*ibid.*, 66; see Sonkosi, 2003). This suggests a process that involved more than creating a consensual understanding and/or perception of the past in the present; or even restoring victims their human and civil dignity by letting them tell their stories. It was also initiating engagement with profoundly complex and contested concepts. Ironically, though, it seems to have chosen to 'fix

40 See examples of this discussed in the final chapter.

knowledge' of the past and thus 'guarantee the veracity of the history it produced' (Harris, 2002: 161–77) rather than keep open the exploration of ambiguity and complexity.

To develop issues related to an archive being open or closed, I return to the issue of the externality of the archive, how this facilitates 'the possibility of the destruction of the archive' and how this affects an archive's ability to help people remember and forget. I want to ask how these opposing impulses to remember and forget affect 'the work of mourning', which Mark Sanders (2007) discusses in his chapter 'Remembering apartheid', arguing that

> when a witness makes a request of the commission, he or she asks it to join materially and affectively in the work of mourning. This enlistment instantaneously multiplies through dynamics of substitution and transference – the extent that the commission represents the national public, an assortment of victims, bystanders and beneficiaries – and indeed stands in as proxy for the perpetrator who refuses to come forward and make good the violations he or she has committed. Testifying on behalf of the deceased 'victim,' the witness before the commission invites condolence. (2007: 40)

Sanders argues that the requests made to the Commission were both material, in requesting help to find the bodies of victims and support funeral rites, and psychic in 'mournful commemoration' or the 'official and public acknowledgement' of the loss of individuals and of what apartheid withheld from them, namely 'a massive refusal to mourn the dead of others' (*ibid.*, 49) Thus both in the live event and through the archive both the survivors and perpetrators of apartheid can potentially mourn the past. However, the relationship with this process and forgetting is problematic because there is conflict between the state imperative to forget and the individual's need to remember. How then do we evaluate the function and efficacy of the TRC and its archives?

Efficacy, memory and the performance of truth and reconciliation

This question raises the wider issue of the relationship between narrative truth and historical truth, or as Gibson terms it, 'the microtruths, of what happened to specific loved ones, and dealing with the macrotruths about the nature of the struggle over apartheid' (2004: 13). It is very evident that one cannot summarise the emergent narrative of the TRC easily, as most analyses are usually made in relation to specific individual stories (Posel and Simpson 2002; Sanders, 2007; Krog *et al.*, 2009; Cole, 2010). However, as many critics have argued, there is tension between these two truths. So I pause to consider what memories and sense of the history of apartheid have been widely established by the TRC, and what aspects are contested; I also ask how and why particular narratives have entered the public sphere as iconic macro truths.

However one sees the role of the media, or indeed the Commission itself in representing and translating the past, the TRC's first engagement with memory occurred in live time as commissioners, testifiers and the audience engaged with specific events in the past. In the 30 minutes allocated each testifier; an attempt was made to discover 'the whole truth', by a process of dialogue between people sitting in the same space. This goal is ambitious given that, often, forgetting is part of the process of remembering: when analysing public memory, researchers often refer to forgetting, or selective amnesia. Gil Eyal[41] suggests that the 'crisis of memory' has less to do with 'the diagnosis of too much or too little memory' so much as with 'a historically specific *will to memory*, a constellation of discourses and practices within which memory is entrusted with a certain goal and function' (2004: 6–7). This 'will to memory' may take two forms:

> in one version, memory is the guarantor of *identity* and maintains it through time – it is the mechanism of *retention* responsible for the experience of being a selfsame individual moving through time; in the other version, however, memory plays a role in overcoming psychic *trauma* and the processes of dissociation it sets in motion. Individuals are healed by remembering that which was repressed. (*ibid.*, 8)

The distinction between these ways in which memory can work is interesting in the context of the TRC where, on the one hand, people saw the process as healing; insofar as disavowed memories could now be acknowledged. On the other hand, for individuals facing Amnesty hearings, the memories they were being asked to recall would challenge their sense of identity, because the values that defined the past were being challenged. This exemplifies the paradoxes intrinsic to the TRC's mandate to create a common identity through a sense of a shared history and unity of time and space. Eyal goes on:

> For the trauma to cease to exercise its pernicious effect, and for individuals to recover their moral responsibility, the trauma and the whole

41 In the context of analysing discourses and rituals of collective memory in the Czech Republic and Slovakia after the fall of communism.

chain of moral complicity that ensued from it had to be *confessed* and *witnessed*, rather than simply remembered and told. This was the peculiar *mnemonic operation* of this will to memory. To tell the truth about the past did not mean simply to recover an event that was lost or censored, but to own up to its significance; to recognize that one has denied it in the past and to accept responsibility for one's moral complicity; or at the very least watch somebody else do that, and through identification with the negative hero of the confession drama overcome one's trauma as well. (*ibid.*, 23)

This explains the TRC's insistence on the whole country's engaging with, acknowledging and accepting some level of responsibility for its past. Although some people did refuse to engage with the Commission,[42] this was difficult because there were broadcasts on radio stations and television news every day. The TRC *Final Report* noted:

16. Between April 1996, when hearings commenced, and September 1996, extensive news and current affairs coverage was supplemented by a weekly 'wrap-up' of Commission activities on all language stations, as well as live coverage of hearings on Radio 2000.
17. Financial constraints forced cancellation of the weekly summary programmes and the live coverage from 1 October 1996. However, the Commission secured a grant from the Norwegian government which enabled it to contract SABC Radio to restore these two features on a full-time basis from June 1997. (1998, vol. 1: 356)[43]

Accepting responsibility for one's moral complicity and acknowledging memories that had been denied official recognition were important aspects of the Commission. But I return to the metaphor of the TRC as a state-of-the-nation play to explore another possible effect: while Michael Billington (2007) suggests that it allows a society to reflect on itself and so provoke social transformation, Jill Dolan argues that its power lies in the exhilaration created by a sense of connection with others evoked by the performance; this allows the audience to 'share experiences of meaning making and imagination that can describe or capture fleeting intimations of a better world', can create a wider sense of 'community' and even of 'humankind' (2005: 2). This is evidenced in the invocation

---

42 See various reports on 'white indifference' to the TRC process; for example, see SAPA report, 30 December 1996a; also Ndebele on 'the bleeding heart English-speaking liberal' who, he suggests, 'proposes one of the greatest dangers to the TRC hearings' (1998: 26–8). It is also worth noting that many black South Africans did not engage with it because they did not accept the terms of the Commission, particularly regarding amnesty and the discourse of forgiveness.

43 For full details on media coverage see TRC *Final Report* (1998, vol. 1: 357–61).

of *ubuntu* both during and beyond the TRC.[44] *Ubuntu* is a concept founded on the notion of common humanism, rendered as *umuntu ngumuntu ngabantu* in Zulu, and in SeSotho *motho ke motho ka batho* (I am because we are), or 'a person is a person through other persons' (Ramose, 1999: 49ff, 2002), It is driven by values related to truth, justice and compassion (Motsei, 2007: 10), and associated with African formulations of humanism and socialism which claim that all people, whatever their class, race or status, must be accorded equal dignity and personhood.[45] This concept was aligned with the Christian message of forgiveness in the Commission, thus redefining the promotion of forgiveness at the Commission for wider acceptability, particularly insofar as it tapped into the African traditions of consensus (Coplan, 2000: 139; Louw, 2001: 19–23; Sonkosi, 2003). It is referenced in many ways, for example, by the term '*Simunye*', a Zulu word meaning 'we are one', used by the SABC as a catch-phrase between programmes,[46] and it has also been deployed beyond the remit of the TRC, for example, as a 'management concept' in Southern Africa (Karsten and Illa, 2001).

However much one may speculate as to the effect of the TRC, it would be useful to be able to evaluate to what extent the terms of the TRC's mandate have been accepted by the majority of individual South Africans. For this analysis I am deeply indebted to James Gibson's (2004) quantitative research undertaken in 1996 and late 2000–01 in South Africa. First, it is worth acknowledging a general ambivalence in South Africans' engagement with the TRC, which is caught between generally agreeing on the need to 'learn from the past, in order to avoid repeating mistakes', and the view that 'it's better not to open old wounds by talking about what happened in the past'; a view subscribed to by roughly 75% of the white and coloured people and those of Asian origin, and 60% of the black South Africans interviewed (Gibson, 2004: 46).[47]

---

44 *ubuntu* is referenced in the Explanatory Memorandum to the Parliamentary Bill, www.justice.gov.za/trc/legal/bill.htm. Amy Biehl's father refers to *ubuntu* in his closing statement in the amnesty hearing on the murder of his daughter, case AC/98/0030, www.justice.gov.za/trc/decisions/1998/980728_ntamo%20penietc.htm.

45 For a discussion of this concept in the wider African philosophical context see Dani Nabudere (2002).

46 There are various community and cultural projects with the same title in South Africa; see www.ifagiolini.com/projects/simunye/, 'We Are Together' (*Thina Simunye*), this is part of the Agape orphanage project, which includes a CD and film (2006, dir. Paul Taylor), see http://wearetogether.org/, www.youtube.com/watch?v=wsakg-9JPtk, accessed 1/9/11.

47 These racial categories are used by Gibson and are still widely used in South Africa. See Herwitz (2003) on the limited deconstruction of racial categories in post-apartheid South Africa.

Gibson suggests that the history of apartheid generally agreed by the TRC was that

- apartheid was a crime against humanity and therefore those struggling to maintain that regime were engaged in an evil undertaking;
- both sides in the struggle over apartheid committed horrific offences, including gross human rights violations;
- apartheid was criminal because of both the actions of specific individuals (including legal and illegal actions) and the actions of state institutions (2004: 72–3).

Not unsurprisingly, the degree to which individuals have accepted these 'truths' has been affected by their level of group identity, their previous experiences in terms of the harms or benefits of apartheid, varying levels of engagement with the Commission and trust in the forum (for summary of 'truth determinants' see Table 3.5 in Gibson 2004: 112–13). However, overall Gibson found that the TRC was successful in moderating the majority of South Africans' views that 'apartheid was a crime against humanity' (94.3%), and that 'both sides did unforgiveable things' (76.1%). However, only 57.3% accepted the TRC's challenging the view that 'the struggle to preserve apartheid was just', and most saw the abuses being caused by individuals, not institutions (only 35.1% agreed that this statement was false) (Table 3.2, 2004: 96). The latter issue is probably the result of the TRC's focus on individuals, as opposed to institutions, despite the specific institutional hearings. Gibson notes that

> these findings strongly suggest that the activities of the TRC did indeed contribute to greater acceptance of the truth about the country's apartheid past among whites, coloured people, and those of Asian origin. . . . For many the TRC seems to have challenged the basic legitimacy of apartheid, thus moderating their view of the past.
> Black South Africans are another matter. (*ibid.*, 98)

The reason for the latter statement is that there seems to have been widespread resistance to the TRC's aims, particularly to amnesty. However, Gibson argues that as a result of black South Africans' experiences of apartheid, and awareness of gross violations of human rights, ultimately the truths promoted by the TRC were more shared than not, and that the TRC's truth is a balanced truth, moderating previously held views (*ibid.*, 115). This may be so regarding individual atrocities related to human rights violations, but less clear when exploring equivalence or complicity. Bhekizizwe Peterson (2009: 21) reminds us of Primo Levi's cautionary insights after reflecting on his experiences at Auschwitz, which acknowledge the complexities involved in any attempt to understand the relationship between victims and persecutors, while unequivocally rejecting attempts to create equivalences, saying that 'to confuse them [murderers] with their victims is a moral disease or an aesthetic affectation or a sinister sign of complicity; above all, it is a precious service rendered (intentionally or not) to the negators of truth' (ibid., 33). This argument about moral relativity is potentially harmful, requiring arguments of relative victimhood to be carefully contextualised.

What of now? The SA Reconciliation Barometer Report of 2010 (Lefko-Everett et al.) largely support Gibson's general findings.[48] On historical confrontation, the data showed that 'most South Africans agree that apartheid was a crime against humanity and feel that they would like to forgive those who hurt them during this period and move on with their lives. However, many also feel that more work remains in prosecuting perpetrators of apartheid crimes and supporting victims of rights abuses' (ibid., 5). This suggests that the broad narratives pertaining to perceptions of apartheid created by the TRC have entered the generally accepted view of South Africa's past, becoming formalised as history. With respect to encouraging greater tolerance, we see that almost half of South Africans believe that race relations in the country have improved since 1994, but cite 'socioeconomic inequality and political party membership' as the greatest sources of social division, and economic issues as being the greatest current concern in South Africa. This underlines the significance of the TRC's failure to engage with institutional culpability in the hearings, and emphasises the importance of organisations such as the Khulamani Support Group to provide ongoing personal engagement with issues highlighted by the Commission.[49]

48 This is a nationally representative public opinion survey that has been conducted by the Institute for Justice and Reconciliation annually since 2003.
49 Formed in 1995 by survivors and families of victims of the political conflict of South Africa's apartheid past in response to the pending Truth and Reconciliation Commission by victims who felt the Commission should be used to speak out about the past to ensure that such violations never occur again. Today the Group collaborates with various civil, government and professional organisations and individuals to assess ongoing needs nationwide and then structures projects and initiatives at the local level. For example, Arts & Culture Khulamani has produced four theatre productions, and supported the film Zulu Love Letter (2004). It has also acted on behalf of victims of apartheid beyond the TRC. It continues to lobby the government and has brought a lawsuit against eight US-American, European and German corporations for their part in aiding and abetting international human rights violations committed by the South African government under its policy of apartheid; see Alien Tort Claims Act Lawsuit, filed in the USA in 2002, heard in Appeal in 2006, and which offers a complex angle on retributive justice; see analysis of outcomes in Saage-Maaß and Golombek (2010).

Thus, despite the TRC's failure to engage with the effects of the systemic iniquities of apartheid, particularly in terms of their economic and social impact, there is ongoing evidence to support the view that the broader narratives of the TRC regarding the apartheid past and related discourses of tolerance have entered into a broadly shared consciousness among the majority in South Africa. It has also created a wider history that incorporates events and narratives of more groups within South Africa than the histories published during the apartheid period.

The *Barometer Report's* findings on the perceived importance of the rule of law are particularly significant in that they reference the TRC's original mandate to 'nurture a culture of human rights and democracy within which political and socio-economic conflicts are addressed both seriously and in a non-violent manner'(TRC *Final Report*, 1998, vol. 5: 435). Gibson cites valuing the rule of law as central to establishing a robust human rights culture, but he concluded from the results of the surveys he undertook in 1996 and 2001 that 'a culture deeply respectful of the rule of law has not yet been established in South Africa' (2010: 191). He argues that this was the result of general experiences of official institutions under apartheid, and possibly exacerbated by the way the TRC was established outside the traditional framework of the law, particularly in relation to the granting of amnesty.[50] This signals that much of the work of the TRC has been effective to some degree beyond the hearings themselves, and that the macro truths have created a basis for consensualising a sense of the apartheid past. This in turn has allowed South Africa to move forward socially, politically and economically.

However, this came at a cost. As Grunebaum and Henri have highlighted, the irony in the TRC's being set up as a 'testimonial space (which is both public and visible) [is] that a reconciliatory discourse of nation-building, underpinned by the notion of a collective and redemptive healing comes to be enacted' (2003: 102–3). What resulted was a conflict of interest between the initial concept of hearing and healing the effects of violence and silence on the peoples of South Africa, and the state's need to create a consensual understanding of the past in the present and formulate a coherent and 'reconciled' narrative for a stable future. Thus South Africa is caught between the need to forget and move on, and to continue mourning and processing an unspeakable past. Most contestation occurs around the terms set by the Commission – particularly for amnesty, and how these terms have created precedents for the future.

---

50 For detailed analysis of this see Gibson (2010, Chapter 5). See also preceding footnote for an example of perceived failure at law.

The significance of the terms of the TRC is outlined in Verne Harris's[51] Alan Paton lecture entitled 'Madiba, memory and the work of justice', in which he argued that the post-apartheid project has been overly reliant on 'two interlinked figures, or symbols: "the new South Africa" and "Nelson Mandela"' (2011: 4). This has caused a 'determination to build new metanarratives' (ibid., 5), resulting in 'a totalising agenda' where too many sub-narratives have been squeezed out, too many counter-narratives ignored' and 'loose threads too often have been seen as threats to a seamless narrative rather than an opportunity for richer, complex and more textured weaving' (ibid., 6). This 'totalising agenda' is evident in the terms of the TRC and its *Final Report*. Harris suggests that the metanarrative of reconciliation, as opposed to forgiveness, has provoked a political 'crisis of legitimacy', which is exacerbated by the fact that too few 'can access the instruments of democratisation' (ibid., 12–14). Many of these criticisms are supported by the findings of Gibson and the Reconciliation Barometer survey. Some of the unexpected consequences of much of post-apartheid's memory work, Verne argues, are 'opacity' and 'deafening silences' (ibid., 8), and 'sensitivity around access to information' (ibid., 9).[52] He critiques the 'assumption that remembering brings with it healing' (ibid., 10); we need to accept that it can retraumatise, or simply open new hurts.

Whatever the complexities, the challenge is to deepen engagement with memory without deploying it in the service of new metanarratives, but instead to effect the 'decolonisation of our memory institutions' (ibid., 19). In speaking to Yvette Coetzee, the TRC translators, Nomusa Zulu, Angela Sobey and Khetiwe Mboweni-Marais, reflect on the strengths and weaknesses of the TRC, agreeing that it was important, 'a beginning' of a process. Angela Sobey says, 'It made me appreciate where we have come from and the fact that we are still standing. We may be battered, but we are not broken' (in Coetzee, 2006: 104). For Khetiwe Mboweni-Marais it has meant reflecting on the meaning of forgiveness, which in Sotho (*tshwarelo*) literally means 'hold this for me'. She says, 'The implication is that if I am asking for forgiveness, I must give something back that I have taken from you' (ibid., 105): a challenge for each individual emerging from a conflict situation.

The implications of the issues arising from the TRC continue to be

---

51 Head of the Nelson Mandela Foundation's Memory Programme. All references here are to his 2011 lecture.
52 See, for example, the debate on the controversial Protection of Information Bill (POIB), particularly around definitions of national security, which it is argued will challenge the terms of the Promotion of Access to Information Act (PAIA) approved by Parliament in February 2000 and came into effect in March 2001.

debated in and through the law, academic research and performance in South Africa. It is clear that the live event presented various repertoires of memory, which were selected, interpreted and represented in formal archives, most notably in the *Final Report*. The engagement between repertoire and archive goes on; the next chapter explores specific creative explorations and adaptations of material from the hearings and how these 'perform back' to the TRC archive.

An appropriately ambiguous place to both end this chapter and introduce the next is with Antje Krog's *County of my Skull* (2006), as a source cited by most critical and creative works related to the TRC. In this text Krog foregrounds aspects of specific testimonies, interpreted through her own experience as a white, Afrikaans-speaking South African. Many of Krog's reflections on key moments of the TRC have become iconic images of the Commission, which have been reiterated in literature and performance, because consciously or unconsciously this text became a primary source for many artists and researchers. This is understandable, given the overwhelming volume of material that the TRC generated, and the immense difficulties involved in accessing its archives.

Krog clearly states that *Country of my Skull* was her own 'highly personalized version of the experiences of the TRC, . . . NOT a journalistic or factual report of the Commission' (Krog, 2006, emphasis in original). She refers to her book as a 'quilt' that patches together various perspectives that tell 'the story I want to tell', and so should be read as 'creative non-fiction' (1998: 170). However, as Cole has noted (2010: 81), despite these statements many researchers continue to refer to Krog's text as if it is an authoritative verbatim transcription of the hearings. This demonstrates the powerful impact that creative interpretations of a public event can have on the public consciousness of it, insofar as these creative engagements can seem so familiar that they are easily transferred into personal memories.[53] It seems to me that Krog's text is one of the first creative engagements with the TRC, translating and shifting material from the Commission through her own subjective consciousness into something new and fictional. This shift calls for us to view the material as we would other creative engagements with the TRC, requiring analysis of the processes of selection and interpretation of particular narratives from the vast amount of material that is the TRC archive.

These include the testimonies of the family members of the Cradock Four: Matthew Goniwe, Sparrow Mkonto, Fort Calata and Sicelo Hhlaudi, who were abducted while returning to Cradock from Port

---

53 For this reason Cole (2010) calls for a return not only to the transcripts, but a re-reading of the visual archive for wider analysis of the TRC and its significance.

Elizabeth and assassinated by an apartheid hit squad in 1984.'[54] Their murders became notorious and provoked a turning point in the resistance movement, which in turn triggered the call for a state of emergency. Six years later Mandela was released and South Africa began to move towards democratic rule. The Commission chose to begin the HRVC hearings in East London with the testimonies related to the Cradock Four.[55]

Other iconic testimonies include the Guguletu Seven hearings, where four of the victims' mothers 'told their emotional stories to the commission . . . often breaking down' (SAPA, 1996b). These include the narratives of Eunice Miya, Cynthiqa Ngewu and Ms Konile, which highlight the mothers' indescribable feelings of loss and the ongoing experience of police harassment by victims' families at funerals and later at the mothers' homes. This story is repeated, I argue, because it characterises a particularly horrifying aspect of the past that many experienced and recognise.

Lucas Baba Sikwepere's testimony (HRVC, Heideveld, 25/6/96)[56] is often quoted as an example of the efficacy of the TRC. Although he lost his eyesight while being tortured, he testified that symbolically he feels as if he regained his sight through being able to speak at the Commission and be heard. While his narrative is moving, it also exemplifies the kind of narratives that were foregrounded in the face of the complex and diverse criticisms brought against the Commission, because it highlighted the potential efficacy of this commission for healing.

I argue that these and other similar testimonies have come to stand for the 'macro truths' that have emerged from the TRC, of the suffering of traumas that are unspeakable, but which can be shared through empathetic engagement with both the verbal and non-verbal expressions of memory. These memories are used both to critique the state-of-the-nation in terms of the legacies of apartheid (Billington, 2007) and suggest the possibility of imagining a different nation (Dolan, 2005), one where previously antagonistic people are reconciled and can work together for a common future. The next chapter explores creative engagements with the narratives that emerged from the TRC, as well as offering additional narratives that were absent, repressed or ambiguous at the Commission hearings.

54 Documentaries include *The Cradock Four* and *The Cradock Murders*, see www.thecradockfour.co.za, www.shadowfilms.co.za.
55 See Alex Boraine's opening comments, HRV hearings, East London, CASE: EC0028/96 - EAST LONDON, day 2, www.justice.gov.za/trc/hrvtrans/hrvel1/calata.htm, accessed 21/8/11.
56 See www.justice.gov.za/trc/hrvtrans/heide/ct00508.htm, accessed 21/8/11.

2

Dramatising the Truth and Reconciliation Commission: the role of theatre practitioners in exploring the past

Throw a clatter of memories at the mirror of your life and watch the pieces scatter on the ground. There's no pattern. They glint in the shadows, demanding inspection as you hesitate to choose which one you'll pick up first. Some pieces choose themselves, however much you try to avoid them. (Hugh Lewin, 2011: 17)

The end of apartheid brought with it many changes, including changes to the memories with which we engage. The TRC and arts practitioners have played different roles in piecing together fragments of memories: in reconstructing a sense of a shared past and thereby formulating a narrative for the new 'rainbow nation', or by challenging the silences in official histories. This chapter focuses on the contributions of the performing arts in these processes.

During apartheid many artists, such as Athol Fugard, saw their role as 'just to witness as truthfully as [they] could' the experiences of South Africa (Fugard, 1983: 172). However, as the TRC facilitated people speaking for themselves, the inevitable consequence was that 'the TRC emasculated many storytellers. Their fiction could never compete with the real-life theatre that was unfolding every night to millions of viewers' (Mda, 2002: 279). The TRC forced theatre to move from 'bearing witness' to hidden atrocities to critically frame the use of verbatim text, particularly insofar as the testimonies were the means by which the issues of truth, justice and reconciliation were being negotiated. Artists also began to engage more consciously with the implications of 'performance' in the production of 'truth'. They also had to resist a widespread tendency in South African society 'to erase the past in order to reconstruct a new collective identity' (*ibid.*, 280).

This chapter will explore how theatre has responded to the TRC, various macro and micro truths and memories that have emerged or been denied, and will try to determine the significance of various performance aesthetics for engaging with South Africa's experiences of the past.

The TRC has generated a vast body of material, both in terms of volume and emotional impact. Njabulo Ndebele (1998: 20) asserts that it provided a forum where 'an elaborately constructed intrigue of immense size and complexity' could be exposed incrementally. He suggests that this incremental engagement with South Africa's apartheid past may facilitate both some understanding of this past, and a different conception of the future as the 'resulting narratives may have less and less to do with facts themselves and with their recall than with the revelations of meaning through the imaginative combination of these facts. At that point, facts will be the building blocks of metaphor' (*ibid.*, 21). This point may be the place where South Africa can imaginatively renegotiate a different South Africa, as suggested by Albie Sachs (1991: 187). Metaphor is key to understanding the microtruths that emerged from the TRC, where the many narratives that comprised the TRC hearings were subsumed into a few stories, usually representative of some particular barbarity or expression of human emotion.

Literary forms played a central part in framing the public's reception of the hearings. For example, the SABC broadcasts of the hearings were often narrated by poets such as Antje Krog, using the pseudonym 'Samuel', and included poetry by South African oral poets Gçina Mhlophe, Jeremy Cronin and Mongane Wally Serote, and the exiled Chilean Ariel Dorfman. Literature was important because many of the stories were unspeakable, and the frame allowed both distance from and a means of making sense of these stories.

Another important contribution of the arts in South Africa to this process has been to challenge the claim that 'the narrative of the TRC is its own most important product' insofar as it created 'a single moral and political story out of this unruly multivocality' (Coplan, 2000: 138). These challenges have been made in fiction and non-fiction prose as well as in performances, which to date include Mike van Graan's *Dinner Talk* (1996) and *Green Man Flashing* (first performed 2004), Pieter-Dirk Uys's *Truth Omissions* (1996), Paul Herzberg's *The Dead Wait* (1997), Walter Chakela's *Isithukuthu* (1997), Nan Hamilton's *No. 4*

(1997), André Brink's *Die Jogger* (The Jogger, 1997), Jane Taylor and the Handspring Puppet Company's *Ubu and the Truth Commission* (1998), the Kuhlamani Support Group's *The Story I am About to Tell* (1999), Antje Krog's *Waarom is die Wat Voor Toyi-Toyi Altyd so Vet?* (Why are those who toyi-toyi in front always so fat?, 1999), John Kani's *Nothing but the Truth* (2002), Yael Farber's *Molora* (Ashes, first performed 2004), and three collaborative testimonial plays: *A Woman in Waiting* (1999), created with Thembi Mtshali, *Amajuba: Like Doves we Rise* (2000), created with the North West Arts Council's resident actors, and *He Left Quietly*, with Duma Khumalo (2003) (all in Farber, 2008a). Feature films and documentaries by South Africans include Bhekizizwe Peterson and Ramadan Suleman's *Zulu Love Letter* (2004) and Ian Gabriel's *Forgiveness* (2004); David Forbes's *The Cradock Murders: Matthew Goniwe and the Demise of Apartheid* ([2003] 2010), *Red Dust* (Hooper, 2006) was a UK-SA production. *In My Country* (Boorman, 2005, based on Antje Krog's *Country of my Skull*) was an American directed and produced film. Other recent creative engagements with the TRC include Philip Miller's *Rewind: A Cantata for Voice, Tape and Testimony* (2006), and the project *Truth in Translation* (2006–09), created collaboratively by Michael Lessac, Paavo TomTammi, Hugh Masekela and Colonnades Theatre Lab. I will be considering some of these creative responses in detail later in this chapter.

These works engage in complex ways with the four modalities of 'truth' outlined by the TRC in its hearings: factual or forensic truth, personal or narrative truth, social or 'dialogue' truth, and healing or restorative truth (TRC *Final Report*, 1998, vol. 1: 110–14). These modalities suggest a complex relationship between establishing fact, setting up specific questions related to the veracity of a narrative, and acknowledging the personal, subjective nature of these narratives. The way social truth is defined implies that 'truth' is arrived at through a dialogic process of consensualisation,[1] which can then be a basis for healing. As Tutu and others have stated, 'all we ask from them is an acknowledgement that these things were done and they happened, and that they're accountable'.[2] These works explore the complexities of these different

---

1 For a more detailed discussion of how this relates to verbatim theatre in South Africa and the place of the witness in pre- and post 1990s theatre see Hutchison (2009, 2010b). See also Greg Homann's (2009a) exploration of how these modalities inflect back through pre- and post-apartheid theatre, particularly regarding violence.
2 Archbishop Tutu, quoted in the SAPA media report 'Applications Flow in as Amnesty Deadline Looms', Cape Town, Sept 30. See also the statements of people on the Register of Reconciliation, for example, Colleen Matthews, 3/2/1998, Johannesburg (p. 12). This phrase occurs often in volume 1 where the *TRC Final Report* outlines the conceptualisation of the TRC.

ways of telling various truths, and underline the necessity for dialogue and negotiation at a personal level for the potential reconciliation of people with conflicting memories.

The creative engagements with the TRC that I have chosen to analyse are from different genres and moments in time. They focus on issues raised by the TRC, but that were not necessarily addressed by it directly. My analysis begins by exploring self-consciously performative selections and stagings of specific TRC narratives and their effect in facilitating a further understanding of the Commission and the ways in which we engage with the past. It then shifts to look at more realist theatrical engagements with themes either vaguely referred to, absent from, or that emerged from the TRC hearings. Referring to *The Dead Wait, Nothing but the Truth* and *Green Man Flashing*, I explore how these plays engage with the themes of exile, ghosts and hauntings, issues related to masculinity, and the tension between justice and compromise in the context of the TRC; thus reflecting some of the unresolved issues of the Commission. I end by considering how *Molora* brings together the exploration of what constitutes an appropriate performance form when engaging with ongoing socio-juridical questions in the post-apartheid South African context, and the place of the wider community in completing the social action begun by the TRC.

Performative framings of the TRC and its narratives

I want to begin by looking at how the overt signalling of the performance frame has been used both to question the way the TRC used narrative to create macrotruths and to facilitate ongoing engagement with emergent issues in a safe and nuanced way.

Ubu and the Truth Commission (1998)

Jane Taylor and the Handspring Puppet Company began working on this play during the TRC hearings. Taylor's involvement was informed by her project *Fault Lines,* which explored the role art might play in addressing human rights issues, and which had toured Germany, Chile, Israel, Sudan and Zimbabwe. The mode in which this play engaged with the TRC was important, insofar as the Commission had just begun its work. Taylor outlines her intention in engaging with this material:

Primarily, I wanted to foreground the role that artists could play in facilitating debates around the Truth and Reconciliation Commission. . . . it is my
feeling that through the arts some of the difficult and potentially volatile
questions, such as why we betray or abuse each other, could be addressed
without destabilis[ing] the fragile legal and political process of the TRC
itself. (1998: iii)

Here Taylor acknowledges the fragile position of the TRC and her
commitment both to the Commission and to exploring the issues that
emerged from it in a spirit of cooperation, but without compromising a
critical perspective.

Although verbatim testimony is included in the play, it is not its
central focus. Notably, it inserts TRC narratives without identifying
the sources of the testimonies. The first and third testimonies show
parents being called upon to identify their children's bodies, which are
so badly damaged that they cannot be easily identified (Taylor, 1998:
11, 13, 31, 33).[3] A nameless mother narrates her fight for her son's life
after he has been necklaced[4] (ibid., 23, 25) in the second narrative. The
last testimony is The Scholar's Tale, an amalgamation of testimonies
about seeing a child murdered (ibid., 47); the narrator asks how people
could be treated worse than animals, saying, 'even a dog . . . you don't
kill it like that, even an ant, a small little ant' (ibid., 49). This latter
fragment of testimony recurs as a theme piece of Miller's REwind
Cantata.

Ubu and Truth Commission addresses the issue of the Amnesty
Hearings in the narration of the 'tubing' technique for torture, which
simulated suffocation (ibid., 43); it is very similar to the 'wet bag' technique which was so controversially re-enacted by Jeffrey Benzien at his
Amnesty Hearing, and is included verbatim in REwind (Hamba Kahle:
The Bag). Both performances highlight the worst kinds of abuse and
dramatise the conflict of granting amnesty to perpetrators like Benzien
simply for telling 'the whole truth'. However, this play differs from the
cantata because all the TRC narratives are anonymous, which shifts
the audience's focus from an individual's suffering to a more abstract
engagement with a system that facilitated this kind of abuse. This forces

3 All subsequent references are to this published version of the play.
4 Necklacing refers to a form of lynching whereby a victim is restrained in a tyre
   doused in petrol, which is then set alight. It was used in the townships to punish
   suspected police informers. More than 900 people were reported as having been
   murdered in this way between 1984 and 1989 (Final Report, volume 6, section 3,
   chapter 2, p. 272, online). However, the SADF gives different figures for the same
   period; see Ellis (1998: 272, footnote 42). Monaghan (1999: 16) suggests that a further
   500 were necklaced between 1990 and 1994.

an audience to ask questions about agency, culpability and the implications of reconciliation at the expense of justice.

The critical distance created by presenting anonymous narratives to engage with macro meanings is also evident in the way Ma and Pa Ubu are juxtaposed to puppet figures and multimedia back-projections. These performative frames are important aspects of the way this play engages with the archives and repertoires that were emerging from the TRC.

Taylor suggests that

> while the TRC has had the two-fold purpose of documenting the cases of victims and hearing the amnesty applications of perpetrators, it effectively has also been instrumental in creating a context for interrogating how and why such human rights abuses could occur. (1998: vi)

Taylor here argues that the TRC shifted human rights and trauma discourses from the realm of the inexplicable to a place where we can consider the implications of unspeakable acts collectively. This play, it seems, pushes this space even further. Pa Ubu is both a crass cartoon figure, particularly in the violence of the language he uses throughout the play, and a psychologically realistic man filled with self-doubt and fear. This characterisation transforms the play from being a potential burlesque to a more disturbing critical engagement with apartheid. As a perpetrator of human rights abuses, Pa Ubu is faced with the problem of whether or not to engage with the TRC on his own terms, or hope to evade the law. His torment and vulnerability are dramatically emphasised by his performing in only his vest, underpants and shoes, and by the ways in which he is tormented by the puppets and the documentary material.

The puppets function in two ways in the play: they allow us to engage with particular kinds of abuse without overly individualising the experiences to emphasise the centrality of institutional violence and culpability in apartheid; while simultaneously allowing us sufficient distance to consider how narratives are being mobilised in the present. Two kinds of puppets are used in the play to facilitate these critical engagements. The first are symbolic of the collective forces surrounding and linked to Pa Ubu, including Niles the Crocodile, the Dogs of War and the vulture cawing Pa Ubu's doom. These puppets strongly foreground the institutional nature of violence and abuse in apartheid South Africa, thus shifting our sense of the perpetrator from specific individuals, like Jeffrey Benzien or Dr Wouter Basson,[5] to the institutions that

5 Also known as 'Dr Death', Basson headed the chemical and biological warfare
   programme of the apartheid government during the 1980s and early 1990s. In

facilitated and perpetuated systematic and systemic violence. Although institutional responsibility for apartheid atrocities was addressed in the Special Hearings of the TRC, as evidenced from Gibson's report, it was inadequate because the overwhelming preponderance of abuses were narrated in terms of individual culpability. Thus, the dominant contemporary perception of apartheid is that individuals rather than institutions were responsible for these abuses.

Rough wood-carved human puppets are used to represent individuals who testified at the TRC, and they speak in their mother tongues. Their manipulators are visible and the translator stands in a booth – ironically the same booth that Pa Ubu showers in to wash off the evidence of his grisly deeds – and translates the verbatim testimony into English. The dominant effect of this device is that it allows an audience to engage with these harrowing accounts, while simultaneously noting the artifice of the puppets as they demonstrate that they are being 'spoken through' and manipulated by their puppeteers. These dramatic performances of trauma testimony poignantly capture the complex relationship between testimony, translation and documentation not explicitly acknowledged by the Commission. Despite the mediation, the puppets are presented with dignity and convey a great sadness. As we hear the stories we feel their emotive impact, but are not so overwhelmed by the particular stories that we lose sight of the issues that underpin them, as may have been the experience of attendees of the hearings or if the stories had been emotionally dramatised by actors.

The third performative aspect of this play is the use of back-projections, which act as a distancing device and critical commentary on the Commission. As already noted, the media played a profound role in translating the TRC and creating iconic images for the public. This play uses documentary, newspaper and cartoon clips in the back-projections to frame Pa Ubu's narrative against broader historical events and alternative memories, and thus implicitly challenges the terms for amnesty. It also asks how the 'the whole truth' can be measured against complex and contested memories by highlighting the way in which evidence can be manipulated by frames and juxtapositions. This raises questions about how evidence and documentation related to the TRC has undergone similar selection and interpretation, particularly in the *Final*

September 2011 he was once again defending himself from charges brought against him by the Health Professionals Council of South Africa (HPCSA) for his 'unethical conduct'. Material related to Dr Wouter Basson is available at SAHA in the following collections: The Freedom of Information Programme Collection (AL2878), The Chemical & Biological Warfare collection (AL2922), The Sally Sealy collection (AL2924).

Report. The only narratives not challenged by back-projection in the play are the survivors' testimonies. These could not be challenged both because the HRVC hearings were designed to create a space in which those silenced for decades could be heard, and because they are personal memories, which cannot be contested as they stand as narrative truth. However, this raises the question of how South Africa can move from narrative truths to negotiate consensual and healing truths, particularly in the case of memories of extreme violence?

Testimony is used to raise and frame issues at the heart of the play. Pa Ubu's confession is juxtaposed to the survivors' testimonies, particularly as it frames the way the Christian agenda of confession and forgiveness, which underpinned the TRC, could be manipulated by the perpetrator, in this case Pa Ubu, who insists that 'the blood of the Lamb sets me free' (*ibid.*, 69). Just as his testimony is used to critique the terms of reconciliation in the context of justice, so these anonymous survivors' verbatim testimonies reveal how their narratives have been used to conceptualise unity and reconciliation for the nation. At the end Pa and Ma Ubu sail off into the sunset with impunity, leaving the audience confused about the cost of reconciliation and the implications of this 'deal' for the future.

The Story I am About to Tell (1998)

In this play, facilitated by the Khulamani Support Group, three survivors, Catherine Mlangeni, Thandi Shezi and Duma Khumalo, retell the testimonies they gave at the TRC. The play moves between the victim's personal testimonies and an imaginary minibus journey to the hearings, during which the actors offer fictional arguments about the status of white applicants, the evaluation criteria and compensation for Amnesty Hearings, and ultimately the problems of reconciliation and justice.

The spatial arrangement on stage replicates the TRC setting, with the witness telling his/her story downstage centre, which makes the audience intensely aware of the vulnerability of the witness. A commissioner translates the narratives from Sesotho or Zulu into English. The relationship between the real and the fictional was both powerful and problematic for the audience, who are aware of the very real and personal trauma of these individuals as they retell their experiences and (re)embody their distress. Duma Khumalo wrung his hands as he narrated his memories of death row, of hearing the daily marches to the scaffold and the sound of chains as he awaited execution for a crime he had not committed; Catherine Mlangeni rocked back and forth as she told of how she crawled back into the room where the shattered body and head of her son lay, blown apart by a booby trapped Walkman; and Thandi

Shezi covered her face with her hands as she remembered the shame of her rape by security policemen. The verbatim text here is both 'real' and 'not-real' testimony. Both we and the performers are aware that this is a scripted and rehearsed performance, even the TRC narratees spoke of 'learning' and 'forgetting' their lines. This suggests that in the performance process even the verbatim testifiers find some distance from their personal story, so that these narratives became emblematic of something more abstract and general.

This juxtaposition of stage and TRC contexts is both interesting and problematic. First there was the issue of the potentially damaging effects the reiteration of narratives of victimhood may have on the narrator who is not an actor,[6] as well as the complex implications of highlighting aspects of manipulation and potential performance for people telling their own stories. At one level, the fictional frame of the play makes the trauma narratives bearable insofar as the frame distances the audience and the narrators from the actual event; but, at the same time, it has the potential to facilitate a perception of these narratives as fictional, and thus not worthy of serious attention at best, or as being lies at worst. The issues of the effect and status of theatrical testimony in theatre in the context of trauma are complex and the subject of ongoing debate.[7]

It is significant that the Amnesty Hearings are presented differently from the HRVC Hearings in this play. The Amnesty applicant in the play is not an actual TRC applicant, but is performed by an actor in the role of a former Defence Force conscript. His narrative of being forced into the army and his struggle with both his past and present is highly provocative and contested in South Africa, an issue to which I shall return later in this chapter. This may suggest the limits of what could be embodied as 'real' in South Africa at this time. It also indicates the theatre's role in staging imaginary conversations that may not be possible in everyday life, while asking important critical questions related to the

6 See Butler (1997: 9) on the power to injure through reiteration of violent narratives, also Ross (1996); Schaffer and Smith (2004), although the performers denied this, see Thandi Shezi in dialogue with Pamela Dube (in Posel and Simpson, 2002: 117–30).
7 See Wake on 'false witnessing', which she argues is what an actor does in the absence of the 'primary witness' (2009: 9). I argue that the context frames the audiences' awareness of the play's intention and their expectations more fully than Wake suggests. Responses to the performances at the Tricycle Theatre, London (1999) differed substantially from those of the audience at the Market Theatre, Johannesburg (1997), where many in the audience were from the townships and had experienced similar violence, and perhaps felt more able to engage with the harsh socio-political realities being presented. This difference was also evident in the responses to *Ubu and the Truth Commission* in South Africa (1998), Germany (1998) and the UK (1999); see Hutchison (2009, 2010b).

veracity of personal narratives, and the consequences of some narratives not being included in the TRC.[8]

In analysing the controversial use of verbatim text by the survivors themselves, it is important to consider how participants experienced these aspects of the play. Thandi Shezi told Pamela Dube that, although she has been very damaged by her prison experiences,

> the play has given me the opportunity to confront my demons. There are times when I realise that I am not a victim any more. Through the play, I have been able to give a voice to thousands of women who have been raped but could not 'come out'. (In Posel and Simpson, 2002: 126)

Dube notes the ambivalent attitude of many members of Khulamani to the TRC:

> For the victims and survivors of brutality, the TRC was a platform on which to share painful memories, for Thandi [one of the founding members of Khulamani] and many others it did not necessarily hold out the prospect of healing. In the play, Thandi says, 'I am not going near the TRC, thank you very much. Because they will talk about reconciliation and forgiveness. How can I reconcile and forgive when I am no longer a woman? She still finds it painful to relive her appearance before the Commission. (*ibid.*, 128)

Similarly, Shezi acknowledges that it 'was a victory' to speak at the TRC, but also that she felt 'exposed' and 'abused all over again', that 'it felt like all they wanted was my story. I felt used' (*ibid.*). The complexities of agendas and competing discourses made the TRC a contested forum. The responses of people like Shezi suggest that the initial narrating of traumatic memories at the TRC resulted in their feeling 'heard', but it did not necessarily bring emotional relief from the trauma. Theatre may be a more effective way of processing trauma insofar as it involves a relatively extended process, which Shezi calls 'a process of reconnecting body to soul' (*ibid.*, 129). This is an important formulation because often trauma causes people to disembody, particularly in the context of sexual violation.[9] This suggests the importance of community-based theatre for facilitating a process of bringing together narrative or 'intellectual'

---

8 The SADF were very reluctant to testify, and very few individuals came forward to speak about this aspect of apartheid history. I will analyse some of the implications of this later in this chapter.

9 This is a classic symptom of post-traumatic stress disorder (PTSD), see interview with members working in the Trauma centre in Cape Town on responses to rape, and other forms of violence (Mengel *et al*, 2010: 75–102). This collection of essays also explores specific limits of the American Psychiatric Association's definition and approaches to treatment of PTSD in the South African context.

memory and embodied or 'deep memory', what Young calls 'integrated historiography' (2000), and which may allow the former to become the latter. It emphasises the importance of the TRC in facilitating public engagement with complex and emotional experiences and memories, but also highlights the need for public engagements with these issues to continue in forums, like the Khulamani Support group.[10]

REwind: A Cantata for Voice, Tape & Testimony (2006)

Philip Miller's *Cantata for Voice, Tape & Testimony* moves us forward to the 10th anniversary of the establishment of the TRC. It premiered on 16 December 2006, the Day of Reconciliation, suggesting that the discourse of the Commission continues more than a decade later. It also engages with verbatim testimony from the TRC and explores the potential implicit in performatively juxtaposing archive and the repertoire of memories.

The move from a theatrical to a musical engagement with the TRC is significant, because it represents a shift from the individual speaking voice to multiple singing voices, exploring dialogue between individual soloists and the choir, and thus offering us ways of experiencing layers of witnessing and engaging with memory, both from the Commission and our own repertoires. It also draws on repertoires of music inherent in South African culture, both on an everyday level and that which is specifically related to the Struggle, as evidenced in *Mapantsula* (1988), *Have You Seen Drum Recently* (1998) and *Amandla! A Revolution in Four-Part Harmony* (2002). The protest songs, Christian and African hymns, and the rhythm of the toyi-toyi trigger memories that individuals and groups carry within their bodies. Christine Lucia illustrates this in her analysis of Abdullah Ibrahim's music and use of memory, which she suggests he uses to 'generate a space – for himself and, more importantly, for his listeners – in which anything, including a utopian future, could be imagined' (2002: 127).[11]

The importance of the oral repertoire was recognised by the TRC,

10 Formed in 1995 by survivors and families of victims of the political conflict of South Africa's apartheid past in response to the pending Truth and Reconciliation Commission by victims, who felt the Commission should be used to speak out about the past to ensure that such violations never occur again. See note 49 in Chapter 1 for details about its ongoing work in South Africa.
11 Ibrahim is a South African jazz composer born in Cape Town in 1934, whose work has been influenced by his own experience as a man classified as coloured during the apartheid years. Lucia's article focuses on his 1970s' music and how it fostered an 'awareness of identity with place and the need to develop a notion of South Africa as "home"' (2002: 127).

which began every day with a hymn. The SABC broadcasts interjected testimonies with hymns and songs, which were used to indirectly contextualise references through wider communal memory. The oral memoir of the TRC collated by the SABC (Kapelianis & Taylor, 2000) begins with *Bones of memory*, the first of five volumes of testimony, and include 'Thula Sizwe' sung by Lele Magudulela, and 'Bones of Memory', written and sung by Gcina Mhlope. It ends with the old and new South African anthems, 'Die Stem' and 'Nkosi sikelel' iAfrika', recorded from the HRVC hearing in Athlone, Cape Town on 22 April 1996. Miller's cantata draws on these repertoires, but also makes them strange and new through the multiple layering of the performance.

On stage there is a transparent gauze screen in front of which stand the soloists – mezzo, soprano, bass, tenor – and a string octet; and behind them the choir stand, which is at times visible and other times semivisible or invisible, like ghosts.[12] Videoed photographic sequences of text and images, directed and designed by Gerhard Marx, are projected onto the screen and mediate the libretto. Marx's images are metonymic fragments: a chair, a bed, a loaf of bread, a glass of milk, the fronts of houses; which Jessica Dubouw argues go beyond visual referencing as they 'exceed all explanatory frames. Like the content of a traumatic dream, the literalness of his photographic images, their nonsymbolic insistence . . . don't so much align the visual sign to the traumatic event, but question the nature of what this (curative) alignment might be.' She goes on to suggest that the way the images speed up, slow down and 'refuse to settle . . . speak to the incompletion of history, to the collapse of its boundaries, its beginnings and ends' (2010: 93).

The cantata is a musical composition that traditionally has at its centre a sacred text, comprising recitatives, arias and choruses. The combination of solos and choral song creates a dialogue between different discourses and positions, between speaking and hearing, witnessing and bearing witness. The implicit reference to a sacred text in this cantata may allude to the spiritual framing of the TRC, particularly in Judeo-Christian terms, with Anglican Archbishop Desmond Tutu as chair, and the ritual opening of each session with song (hymns) and prayer. This choice of form also implies questions concerning the status of the TRC archive as sacred text.

The taped testimony of victims and perpetrators is moderated by other sounds layered over the music: the breathing or cries of testifiers, the voices of translators discussing how much they can hear,

12 In the South African premiere the choir consisted of the 65 members of the Gauteng Choristers.

background negotiations of language, the sound of microphones being knocked, feedback on the sound system, or the sound of a tape rewinding. The way in which this soundscape is constructed, layered and juxtaposed with the images implicitly highlights complexities around the transmission and making of meaning during the Commission. It explores the unspeakable experience of engaging with the past and of living on a decade later, where trauma continues to be narrated in the present tense.

I now want to examine how Miller has engaged with the TRC by looking at specific fragments and ghostly images from his work. The cantata, like the Commission, begins with the swearing of an oath 'To speak the truth/ And nothing but the truth/ So help me God', repeated in Xhosa, Sotho, Zulu, Afrikaans, Venda and Shangaan. This oath evokes questions related to evaluating the veracity of testimony and what constitutes the 'whole truth'. The significance of this issue is signalled in a number of ways in the cantata: by drawing attention to the mediated experience as microphone feedback grates on nerves because of the high pitch; of the layered experiences as voices verifying that testifiers and translators can hear one another, or negotiate in which language they will speak, is simultaneously heard over the testimony. The piece ends with 'Siyaya', a slogan in the rhythm of the toyi-toyi, which is part of the embodied repertoire in South Africa signalling a call to arms in the struggle for change, reminding all of the violence that preceded this negotiated event and that was perhaps the reason for its existence.

Many of the testimonies included are iconic and the programme cites most of the dates and places of the hearing of these testimonies, referencing the verbatim nature of the text and the veracity of the material. However, Miller does not stage each testimony as a singular text, often he layers the texts and, as in the case of Mrs Miya, he abstracts sound. So, in his titular piece Miller repeats Mrs Miya's gasp for breath and the sound of the tape rewinding, which shifts us away from a literal narrative to a more visceral response to it. These sounds comment on the fact that this testimony is taped and the material is archived. It seems to ask: What happens when we rewind the past? Will this allow any greater understanding of inexplicable events? The juxtaposition of Jeffrey Benzien's demonstration of the wet bag torture technique and the incredibly beautiful sound of the soprano, tenor and choir singing 'Hambe kahle mkonto/ Wem khonto weSizwe', which literally means 'go well', or 'go safely Spear of the nation', viscerally underscores the contrast between the realities of apartheid and individual or communities' hopes and dreams, the most basic being one's hope that loved ones will return safely. This piece dramatises a range of human emotion

– from deep care to brutal inhumanity, beyond the specific, personal experience.

Sometimes the images that accompany the soundscape convey inexpressible feelings invoked by the narratives. Often these images involve stripping. For example, in the testimony of Edward Juqu on the death of his son Fuzile Petros Juqu in February 1985, we see the image of a chair being stripped of its covers and inner filling. In the testimony of Jann Turner on the assassination of her father, and Nomonde Calata on the death of her husband, the accompanying image is of a bed being stripped. A bed is a very personal place, often related to safety and intimacy, but here it is a mnemonic for the violent deaths and absence of the loved ones. Similarly, as Ethel Nobantu narrates the death of her 10-year-old son Luthando, in the accompanying image the bread crumbles and the milk he had had for lunch drains away, representing his lifeblood draining from him as he lay in the street. All these images are of everyday things with which we don't necessarily consciously engage. Here they become images of emotional loss, suggesting how memory continues beyond the narration of the event, and perhaps asking how one forgets, or reduces the pain of this remembering? These images illustrate how trauma narratives often remain visceral, linked to unrelated objects, as the memory remains trapped in the temporal collapse of the traumatic moment.

Other images are more obviously symbolic and may indirectly imply criticism of the TRC process. An example is the image of the goat which accompanies the almost incoherent testimony of Notrose Nobomvu Konile, the mother of one of the Guguletu Seven. The goat references the premonition of Mrs Konile of the death of her son Zabonke.[13] However, within the Judeo-Christian frame of the TRC, the goat can also refer to sacrifice and the scapegoat that in Judaism was used to carry the sins of the people into the wilderness.[14]

'Offering of the Birds' evokes a similar religious reference to the Jewish Law for the poor who, if they could not afford a bull or lamb as a guilt offering for sin, could bring two turtledoves or two young

13 For a detailed discussion of this testimony which reveals unacknowledged assumptions that underpin research related to the TRC see Antje Krog, Nosisi Mpolweni and Kopano Ratele, *There was this Goat* (2009).
14 Under Jewish law the goat served as a sacrificial animal which could be presented as a burnt offering (Lev. 1 v10; 22 v18, 19), a communion sacrifice (Lev. 3 v6, 12), a sin offering (Ezra 8 v35), and a guilt offering (Lev. 5 v6). At certain times goats were sacrificed as sin offerings for the whole nation (Lev. 23 v19; Numbers 28). On the Day of Atonement, two goats were used. One was sacrificed as a sin offering for the 12 non-Levitical tribes, and the other was designated for the nation and was sent away into the wilderness (Lev. 16 v1–27).

pigeons instead (Leviticus 5 v7). Here the law acknowledged economic constraints, while insisting on symbolic reparation for error. This image appears on the scrim during the testimony of Bayeni Ennie Silinda on the necklacing of her son, Frank Silinda, in September 1986, and the Amnesty Hearing of security policeman Jacques Hechter regarding his murder of ANC activist Harold Sefola. However, this image could also be referencing Picasso's dove of peace, dead here, which may imply a negative comment on the peace process in South Africa. The ambiguity of the image allows for multiple engagements with the debates on reparation, reconciliation and peace.

The cantata moves through literal and symbolic sounds, including the testimonies themselves.[15] We hear Tutu's summation of the TRC experience: 'We have been moved to tears. We have loved. We have been silent and we have stared the beast of our dark past in the eye and we have survived the ordeal'; we also hear survivor van Wyk's call for forgiveness. But the non-verbal expressions of grief seem to dominate the piece, appearing near the start and the end of the cantata. Eunice Miya's gasp for breath before her narration of her finding out about her son's death on the television news is the central motif for Miller's title piece *REwind*. The last piece is *The Cry of Mrs Nomonde Calata*, and refers to the widow of Fort Calata, one of the Cradock Four. During her testimony Nomonde Calata broke down and gave a heart-rending cry, which was broadcast live on radio and television throughout South Africa and internationally. Boraine says that

> It was that cry from the soul that transformed the hearings from a litany of suffering and pain to a deeper level. It caught up in a single howl all the darkness and horror of the apartheid years. It was as if she enshrined in the throwing back of her body and letting out the cry the collective horror of thousands of people who had been trapped in racism and oppression for so long. . . . many people told me afterward that they found it unbearable and switched off the radio. (2000: 102–3)

Krog concurs, saying that 'that sound . . . will haunt me for ever and ever' (1998: 42). Both Krog and Boraine remember not just the sound, but the movement of Nomonde Calata's body. This cry and other non-verbal expressions of grief, anxiety and embodied memory have become iconic, because they express more than the transcribed narratives; they encode the unspeakable experience of the traumas behind the specific narratives, with which anyone could relate.

15   This includes P.W. Botha, who refused to appear before the Commission, and Winnie Mandela, whose testimony was controversial.

Finally, the cantata draws us back from the unspeakable horror of trauma and ends with the lullaby 'Thula Sizwe' (Quiet Nation), which is an evocation of a peaceful community.[16]

This is a rich and provocative text which signalled that the TRC had accomplished much in facilitating public engagement with complex memories and that despite much reservation, artists and public alike are still engaging with these a decade later. Miller has created a form that acknowledges the fragmentary nature of memory and engaged with emotional truths, particularly in his use of sound and visual images to convey inexpressible loss and pain. He also engages critically with the TRC, indirectly questioning the religious frame and asking whether we have paid appropriate reparations for the sins of the past, while asking about the place of these memories in the present. This work deals directly with the dilemma of memory for a nation that is still profoundly divided, one which needs to remember and also to forget in order to move on.

Truth in Translation project (2006–09, ongoing)

This play is difficult to analyse because it evolves and changes as it travels and interacts with audiences. It is comparable to Miller's *Cantata* insofar as music is at its heart. Hugh Masekela draws in some of the same iconic narratives heard in other performances, which are merged with the memories and personal experiences of the interpreters and actors, thus becoming a collective memory of the event. Its uniqueness lies in the perspective of the translators, who are centre-stage here, acting as a chorus commenting on the TRC.

The project was conceptualised as multifaceted, with the South African narratives in dialogue with back-projections in spaces of memorial significance within the context in which the play was being performed. It premiered at the Amahoro Stadium in Rwanda (5/08/06), where some 12,000 people took refuge during the 1994 genocide, and the Bosnian performance took place at the Mostar Bridge (20/09/08). These interactions between performers, memories and spaces are important: Schramm argues that 'the memory of violence is not only embedded

16 At a performance of this cantata at the Southbank Centre in London in 2010 I was struck by the responses to the cantata, at times hushed, some laughter at P.W. Botha's 'Who's laughing?', and quiet crying at times. However, when 'Thula Sizwe' was played at the end, the audience spontaneously joined in singing and even toyi-toying in the aisles, marking not only the hopefulness of this ending, but also the weight of remembering evoked by the rest of the cantata. I was reminded of the many warnings against mourning for too long.

in peoples' bodies and minds but also inscribed onto space' (2011: 5). Situating this play in significant spaces highlighted parallels between South Africa's story of violence and processes for negotiating the past within these other contexts. It also challenged official conceptualisations of the past, suggesting that there may be no single narrative; that the narratives and landscapes of violence are always emergent, constantly being reproduced by the different people who are engaged in memory work in these spaces (*ibid.*). These layered, contested and embodied memories formed the basis for post-show talkbacks and reconciliation workshops with local communities facing comparable issues of conflict and contested memory, in collaboration with local NGOs, before and after the show. The impact of this play has been phenomenal:

> To date, the production has performed for 55,250 people, facilitated workshops for 10,545 participants and has played in 26 cities, in 11 countries on 3 continents. From Rwanda to Northern Ireland, Zimbabwe to the West Balkans, South Africa to the United States and beyond, this theatre piece has been performing to audiences from very different cultures, who have experienced conflict in very different ways. Every place reveals its own story of struggle and its own process of healing and coping. Since 2006 (the 10th anniversary of the TRC) when we opened in Kigali, Rwanda, we have been filming the diverse and often conflicting reactions provoked by this controversial production. (www.truthintranslation.org/, accessed 25/02/2011)

The work goes on, with 10 new theatre productions being envisaged in different conflict zones over the next 10 years (2010–20).

The play has been criticised for its somewhat 'laissez-faire structure', owing to the 'devised nature of the script',[17] and for the potential (re-) traumatisation of performers and audiences, although the play negotiates this issue consciously and carefully, particularly with the talkbacks and workshops.[18] It has had a phenomenal impact, both within and beyond South Africa, providing an important model for how theatre can make a significant contribution in the context of trauma and memory work. It mirrors many of the best aspects of the Khulamini Support Group, and its strength lies in using theatre as a platform to facilitate real dialogue for negotiating memory, identity and conflict, with reference

---

17 Mark Fisher 'Truth in translation', *Variety Review*.
18 See Max du Preez's analysis, 'A hard act to follow', *Mail & Guardian*, 1 September 2006, www.mg.co.za/articlePage.aspx?articleid=282840&area=/insight/insight_africa/, accessed 25/2/11; see also the responses to the play in Rwanda, the Balkans and Ireland, at www.truthintranslation.org/index.php/v2/press_responses/, accessed 14/2/11.

to the work of Paolo Freire and Augusto Boal. If the TRC provided the catalyst for imagining reconciliation, this play suggests how theatre can engage with lived realities within a fictional frame to create a safe space within which to imagine real conflict resolution.

What the works discussed above have in common is the way in which they have used performance to engage an audience actively with TRC testimony, creating distance to delay a purely emotive response. This in turn facilitates critical reflection on how memories may be mobilised both to understand the past and challenge particular formulations of it, thus keeping such formulations fluid and open to including diverse, even contested conceptions of the past.

Haunting tropes of the past

I now turn to plays that are less overtly performative, more tradition-ally text-based, and which address particular issues of silence related to the TRC. The first is Paul Herzberg's *The Dead Wait*, arguably the first play to engage with the TRC, written in 1995, a year before the Truth Commission began its hearings, and premiered at the Market Theatre in 1997. It was substantially reworked and performed in Britain in 2002. I will be analysing both the 1997 and 2002 versions of this play. Both John Kani's *Nothing but the Truth* (2002) and Mike van Graan's *Green Man Flashing* (2004) premiered at the Grahamstown National Arts Festival. Although these plays were written by men of different ages, cultural and racial backgrounds, they are comparable in a number of important ways. The first two plays draw overtly on autobiographical experiences, and all three plays deal with returned exiles, interrogate specific formulations of masculinity, and address the TRC directly.

The Dead Wait is written as a memory play, with Josh Gilmore, a white South African returned from exile in London to Cape Town, as the protagonist. The plot-line focuses on Josh's experiences in the army in Angola where his commanding officer made him carry George Josana, a badly wounded high-ranking ANC operative, for days on his back and then execute him. This narrative is set against his background as a privileged white South African and a talented sprinter.

Sipho Makhaya, the Assistant Chief Librarian of a small public library in Port Elizabeth is the protagonist of John Kani's *Nothing but the Truth*. He lives with his daughter Thando, who is a teacher and 'interpreter at the Amnesty Hearings of the Truth and Reconciliation Commission'

(Kani, 2002: 2).[19] The action of the play focuses on the return of Mandisa, Sipho's niece, born during her father's exile in England. She is bringing the remains of her father, Themba, who is Sipho's brother, for burial in South Africa. This event brings Sipho's personal issues with his past into dialogue with South Africa's public engagement with its past through the TRC.

Green Man Flashing explores the contradictions, complexities and ironies of a nascent non-racial, non-sexist new democracy. The plot involves a white activist lawyer, Gabby, who is raped by her boss, the incoming President, just before an election. She is strongly urged to forfeit her legal right to press charges for the greater good by her ex-husband, Aaron, who is now 'one of the political party's major trouble-shooters' (2006: 173).[20] This play focuses on exploring various ways in which the past continues to impact on the future on both the personal and national level.

All three plays are set in the present, but engage with the past. The later version of *The Dead Wait* engages much more specifically with the Angolan war and the TRC than the 1997 version. The shift into the past is signalled by the marimba and sounds of war. Kani's play is in two acts, separated by Thando and Mandisa's attendance at the Amnesty Hearings, which shifts the play from focusing purely on issues of personal memory to the wider context of defining 'truth', 'justice' and 'forgiveness' for the country. *Green Man Flashing* is described as 'filmic', as the narrative unfolds though a variety of disparate scenes. Despite their naturalistic styles, the narrative structures of these plays suggest the subjective unreliability of memory in the way they play with time, narrative and confession.

Perspectives on exile

The term exile can be used in a number of ways: broadly it refers to someone living as an outsider, either physically or as the result of social and political exclusion. The majority of South Africans lived as internal exiles under apartheid, where they were refused the rights of full citizenship. However, here I am engaged with literal exiles: people

19 All subsequent references will be from this version of the play, signalled by page numbers only.
20 All subsequent references will be from this version of the play, signalled by page numbers only.

returning to South Africa from abroad, and the issues arising from their return.

The Dead Wait explores the return to South Africa of Josh, a liberal white South African, and his memories of the Angolan war, which prompted him to live in exile in London. The 1997 version of the play deals with his return in far more detail than the 2002 version, in which his dying father and sister do not appear. The earlier play explores Josh's disconnection from his family and past, suggesting that relationships are hard to sustain without shared memories. His sister expresses a real bitterness at his liberal sense that he 'fought some unique battle to topple the state in the streets of Earl's Court' (1997: 27), while she was left to cope with their parents. The later version chooses to focus on the war and exclude these issues of exile and family, perhaps to reduce the number of thematic foci.

Nothing but the Truth has the fraught status of exiles and their children in post-apartheid South Africa as a central concern. Sipho's first words in the play are: 'Typical. Just like him. Always not there to take responsibility' (2). Like Tina, Sipho feels that he always paid for his brother: materially, insofar as he paid for his university education, and 'everything else' (33). He believes that Themba cost him his son, whom Themba had recruited into the Struggle (20); their father's funeral, which was turned into a political rally (46); his wife, with whom Themba had had an affair; and consequently potentially his daughter, whose paternity is uncertain (49–50).

The image of the returning hero is challenged by Sipho's memory of Themba as a selfish man who 'was in the Struggle, but on his terms. He got what he wanted from the Struggle – money, women, fame' (48), while Sipho, who had paid for much of Themba's life, is not even Chief Librarian (51). His contention is that while he 'might not have been on Robben Island' or left the country, he 'suffered too', and also deserved 'some recognition' (52). Both of these plays address the complexity of defining a liberation hero or indeed a culprit in absolute terms; they also deal with the issue of the thousands of South Africans who 'suffered' but have not been officially recognised in the national memory, because of the terms set by the TRC. It asks what happens to these men and women who were 'not too old to put them [the new government] in power but then suddenly [are] too old to be empowered?' (51).

Lily, in *The Dead Wait*, and Mandisa, in *Nothing but the Truth*, represent the condition of the children of exiles who have grown up in England, but for whom it is not home (2002: 16). When Mandisa comes to South Africa, however, she does not understand her father's culture: she has brought ashes instead of a body and does not understand the expectations around mourning (19, 39); she does not speak Zulu fluently (24–5), and does not understand the TRC at all.

Lily's position is different because she knew her father less well than Mandisa knew Themba, and lost him many years before. Ironically, she shares her memories of her father with Josh, who killed her father:

> He was very loving. But he was always fighting . . . I spent my life waiting. And then one day he stopped coming. [*Pause*] Many people loved him. But I didn't have a chance to do that, because he was married to the struggle. There were times I hated him for making that choice. For delivering himself into your hands. Now you know. There's nothing more we can say to each other. In time, I'll decide how I will approach this thing. (1997: 101–2)

In the 2002 version she is less angry about her father's choices (68–9) and more able to communicate with Josh, despite his part in George's death and his having watching her for 'twenty years' without speaking to her (1997: 98, 2002: 57). This suggests how shared memories can connect people, even adversaries.

Rather than focusing on the insider-outsider experiences of apartheid, *Green Man Flashing* critically reflects on racial politics in post-democratic South Africa. Gabby is a white woman from a liberal family, who at the age of 24 left South Africa with her partner Aaron Matshoba, because of the harassment they faced as a mixed couple. They settled in East Germany and continued actively participating in the struggle. After 12 years in exile they returned to South Africa together, but then Aaron seemed 'embarrassed about having a white wife in the new South Africa', so he avoided taking her to social functions or introducing Gabby as his wife (188). Later Gabby tells Anna that 'so many of the couples we knew in exile split up after they came back' (191). This play suggests the limited impact of the TRC, which was not able to effectively reconcile the nation; memories about the past continue to polarise people racially to the extent that relationships are less able to survive in post-apartheid South Africa than they were during apartheid.

These plays show how the macrotruths of the TRC are complicated when placed alongside the 'microtruths' of the everyday lived experiences of individual people. It suggests how important it is for their loss and suffering to be acknowledged before healing can begin. They also challenge the simple positioning of people as victims, perpetrators or heroes, nuancing the relationships and culpabilities in ways impossible in a public space in the half an hour assigned at the TRC for giving testimony.

Ghosts, haunting and justice

All of these plays include references to ghosts and haunting. Ghosts are traditionally figures that haunt the present because their past remains unresolved, often because justice has not been done. 'Haunting' is also a term used when discussing survivors and perpetrators of trauma, because their lives are inextricably bound with the traumatic event, especially when they are called upon to recount and sometimes re-enact it.[21] This repetition often causes retraumatisation (Schaffer and Smith, 2004). However, haunting need not only be associated with external references to an event. Dominic LaCapra writes that the traumatised subject is 'haunted or possessed by the past and performatively caught up in the compulsive repetition of traumatic scenes – scenes in which the past returns . . . the tenses implode, and it is as if one were back in the past reliving the traumatic scene' (2001: 21). This explains why images of 'haunting' often predominate the histories of trauma and loss, especially where the facts that relate to certain kinds of traumatisation are excluded from politico-juridical processes. Because these aspects of trauma have not been acknowledged, they continue to haunt the subject. These plays suggest how the 'unspeakable' may be heard through exploring the relationship between ghosts, a haunting past and justice.

Both versions of *The Dead Wait* have ghosts at their centre, signalled by the sounds of gunshot or the marimba, which herald the ghosts of Josh's memories of Angola. In *Nothing but the Truth* Themba haunts Sipho's life, particularly with regard to undisclosed memories. The issue of haunting in *Green Man Flashing* relates more to the TRC and its legacies than to an individual haunting, although Gabby and Aaron are significantly affected by their teenage son's murder.

Haunting is important for these plays because, as Jacques Derrida outlines in his exploration of 'hauntology and its attendant ethics' in *Specters of Marx* (1994: xix), spectres move us to consider the occlusions of post-traumatic politico-juridical processes by collapsing the oppositions between life and death, presence and absence, and by implication past, present and future. Wendy Brown suggests how this may work:

---

21 For example, at the TRC perpetrators were called on to narrate in detail how they performed a violent act. The most controversial testimony was that of police agent Jeff Benzien, who was asked to demonstrate the 'wet bag' torture method on one of his former victims (see McEachern, 2002). Many women narrated graphic details of acts of humiliation and rape in prison (see Ross, 2003).

> Ghosts may be redemptive insofar as they offer us intangible sites for imagining a future beyond discredited modernist narratives of progress and a violent exclusionary metaphysics of presence. Spectrology, in this sense, is postprogressive history relocating historical meaning to an 'other space and idiom'; it imagines political justice in a world that is 'contingent,' 'unpredictable,' and 'not fully knowable'. (2000: 144–5)

Brown here suggests that hauntings create a liminal space in which protagonists can have impossible conversations with figures from their past, imagine alternative relationships or decisions, and reconcile with the dead and perhaps themselves. However, in order for these things to happen in real time and space, the world must change and we must consider how to effect the change. Sipho is clear on what socio-political changes would enable him to contemplate amnesty for his son's murderer. He is able to forgive Themba because he, Sipho, finally acknowledges the complexities of his memories and his own place in them, including his sense of loss and resentment at his 'dullness', which may have contributed to his wife's unfaithfulness.

The haunting in *The Dead Wait* is specifically focused on the silences of South Africa's involvement in the Angolan War, which began in 1975 and is described by Herzberg in his preface as 'South Africa's Vietnam' (7). This later version explicitly refers to places in Angola, the military power of the Cubans, and how conscripts had to pledge silence about their experiences in the army and sign an affidavit that they were not South Africans, in the event of their death or capture in Angola (49). Memories related to these aspects of South Africa's past have been largely overlooked, primarily because of 'the army's reluctance to reveal its secrets' (55), but also because of the ambivalent status of white, ex-South African Defence Force (SADF) conscripts. As Mbongiseni Buthelezi, coordinator of the Archival Platform's Ancestral Stories, has commented, although there is a growing literature on the Border War,[22] there is not much engagement with the conscripts' experiences, which he argues 'seem to be a crucial part of reckoning with South Africa's past in the reconciliation process' (2011). Thus plays like *The Dead Wait*, Anthony Akerman's 1980s *Somewhere on the Border*, revived at the Grahamstown Festival of 2011,[23] Greig Coetzee's *White Men with Weapons* (premiered 1996), and Deon Opperman's new musical *Tree*

---

22 See *The Theatre of Violence: Narratives of Protagonists in the South African Conflict*, edited by D. Foster, P. Haupt and M. de Beer (2005), Tony Eprile (2004), J.H. Thompson (2006), and Steven Webb (2008).

23 For responses to this play see www.nationalartsfestival.co.za/events/event/309 and on Angolan memories see 'Paul's blog http://angolajourney.blogspot.com/2011/07/ways-of-remembering.html, accessed 15/2/11.

Aan! (Act! 2011)[24] show the important role theatre is playing as it creates spaces for people to explore disavowed memories such as these, which must haunt thousands of South Africans.

Josh is haunted by George and his commanding officer Papa Louw. He does not understand why Papa Louw is obsessed with him, nor his place in the conflict. Later he says to Papa: 'Your voice . . . little ways. Never left me.' (61). He journeys to lay the ghosts of both of these men. Lily has also been haunted by a father she barely knows; and ironically she is the one who tells Josh to stop running and speak to her father. She says, 'Pick up your burden and carry it like a man' (69). This burden is explained by George's ghost, who remembers asking his mother 'Will there ever be justice for the dead, Mama?' and she replied, '*No one . . . can stop what must be*' (69, italics in original). He then recalls how she talked with her ancestors and asked for peace, but 'then . . . she asks . . . for more. She asks them . . . to leave a *burden*, a burden in the hearts of those who killed the innocent. A burden *so heavy*, that from its weight . . . there can be no escape . . . *but justice*' (70, italics in original). This image of the past as a burden is explained at the end with the image of George on Josh's back, disappearing into the distance, but instead of being a haunting burden, Josh now carries a past he understands and chooses to bear.

Justice and the legacies of the TRC literally haunt *Green Man Flashing*, but before discussing this I want to pause to consider another controversial issue related to the operations of the TRC and which is important to all three plays – the issue of gender and violence.

Constructions of masculinity, sexuality and violence in apartheid South Africa

---

Construction of masculinities in any context is complex and multifaceted, as can be seen by the work of Connell (1995, 2005a), who particularly opened out the analysis of the relationship between the constructions of masculinities and institutions. He also highlights the significance of context, both geographic and historical when discussing such gender constructions. Robert Morrell has outlined key issues

---

24 Compare Andile Mngxitama's response to this play, 'Hoe durf julle?' (How dare you) (http://kaganof.com/kagablog/wp-content/uploads/2011/06/0237.jpg), with Leopold Scholtz 'Opnuut 'n groot wroeg' (A great wrestling anew), http://kaganof.com/kagablog/wp-content/uploads/2011/06/0236.jpg, accessed 16/11/11.

related to constructions of masculinities in the Southern African context (2001; Ouzgane and Morrell, 2005), particularly highlighting how the transition from apartheid to the post-apartheid context has created competing agendas that influence how masculinity is defined and performed in South Africa. These include South Africa's reintegration into the global political and economic context, rising unemployment, violence, and HIV-AIDS. When discussing masculinity in the context of conflict, or post-conflict, the question of how to engage with men whose identities have been framed in and around conflict situations arises. The TRC demonstrated how gender-defined roles during the apartheid era affected behaviour, particularly related to violence. While it is clear that to express regret over some of this behaviour is to negate the sacrifice and suffering made on all sides in the struggle, but to avoid renegotiating the terms of this identity formation is to accept the perpetuation of masculinities that cannot accommodate the implementation of the terms of human rights outlined in the recommendations of the TRC.

These plays are important insofar as they define specific tropes of masculinity, and contextualise them in particular experiences of apartheid. Krueger rightly traces the difficulties of exploring issues of masculinities in South Africa without being essentialist, or reducing descriptions of masculinity to accounts of destructive behaviour (2010: 53–61). He offers a useful way forward by suggesting a shift in focus from trying to define what a man is to what he does, drawing on Butler, Goffman and Austin. I thus seek to explore what issues of masculinity are being addressed in these plays, and how these relate to disavowed memories in contemporary South Africa.

I begin by considering how apartheid impacted on socially constructed norms related to the performance of gendered identity. For example, Robert Morell explores how in the period following the 1976 Soweto uprising young men in Natal disrupted traditional male hierarchies, and justified this disruption by virtue of their involvement in political action. He traces this trend throughout the 1980s and early 1990s in Natal (2006: 16–17). Erlank (2003) traces the significance of the ANC liberation discourse between 1912 and 1950 being formulated in terms of the need to reassert a denied manhood, how this shifted previously held values, and explains the relatively marginal position of African women in the liberation narrative, despite their very significant contributions to it. Ramphele (2000) traces how the status of 'Comrade' became the social leveller between men and boys, so that the role of urban warrior became a dominant defining factor of masculinity, as it still is in many urban black and coloured communities in South Africa. Ironically, this became an equally compelling marker of white

South African men, for whom military conscription was compulsory from 1967, with harsh penalties for refusal: a jail sentence,[25] or leaving the country. Many white South African families ostracised men who refused to do their military service (Baines, 2008: 215). Debbie Epstein has argued that 'South African masculinities have been forged in the heat of apartheid and the struggle against the apartheid state' (1998: 49), and that as 'masculinities (and femininities) are historically specific and not fixed, then those constructed during the apartheid era will, inevitably, have to change, be remade in new and unpredictable ways within these changing material realities' (ibid., 50). Class, race and ethnicity all impact on the way that gender was perceived and performed during apartheid, and for change to occur there must be some conscious engagement with these formative norms.

Tropes of masculinity that recur through these plays include the father and military figures who are sexually potent men. If, as we have seen in the few references above, the discourse of struggle of both those seeking to keep control of South Africa and those fighting for liberation, has dominated definitions of masculinity in South Africa, then it is important to consider whether the past and its ghosts have been interrogated to the point that 'alternative versions of masculinity, which normalise opposition to violence, racism and misogyny may be possible' (ibid.). Sexual violence and its relation to gendered roles in the ANC, for example, were acknowledged at the TRC, but the underlying reasons for these constructions of masculinity and the forms of gendered violence were not analysed. The recurrence of these images suggests the need for further engagement with the relationship between constructions of gendered identity and apartheid history. As we have seen, there has been little official engagement with the role of ex-SADF national servicemen in South Africa, and as Baines argues, neither silence nor ignorance is conducive to coming to terms with the legacy of the 'Border War' (2008: 226).

In *The Dead Wait* Josh's father, Henry Gilmore, is his trainer, 'the best thing' in Josh's life (32). The training includes more than athletics; he teaches Josh how to 'be a man'. The particular kind of masculinity being advocated is evident in Henry's response to Josh's confessions regarding Angola. In the 2002 version Josh tells the Commission, 'I told the truth. To my father. In the stadium. After Angola. Before my race. [Pause] He hit me. [Pause] That was then. He was what he was' (16–17). In the 1997 version he tells his sister, 'he struck me in the face. Twice. Hard. The

---

25 This ranged over time from between two to six years, depending on the length of the period of conscription.

hardest blows I can remember . . . and in a voice I didn't recognise . . . he told me . . . to . . . be a man...' (45). In both cases the response is without compassion and is physical. To be a man is to show no weakness or fear. The characters in the play are affected by their parents – Josh by his father, Lily by her absent father, Papa Louw by the death of his mother. Masculinity and fatherhood are inextricably linked, either literally, as we see from Papa, in the early version he aspires to be the youngest father in South Africa (1997: 53), and in the later version he is a teenage father (2002: 63); or in psychological terms, as the men fight for the land, which is often spoken of in feminine terms in colonial discourses: 'virgin territory' which must be 'taken'. The fight for South Africa both internally and in the surrounding countries is enacted in terms of a violence which is often sexualised. This is evidenced in Papa's behaviour towards Josh and George.

Papa bullies Josh, calling him a 'poes' (1997: 58), translated 'cunt' (75), and cruelly makes him watch the illegal torture of George. Josh says to Lily, 'There are things you know: scrotums . . . hacked off and cured for gear levers. Ears . . . pickled in meths. Field telephones to shock nipples and cocks. Babies . . . flung onto open fires. And there are things you don't. We went . . . over the border' (17). This last comment is ambiguous; it could be literal or metaphorical, going beyond what is even admitted. George is shot through his stomach and a testicle (17). Papa tries to get information from George by booting him in the groin (30), and squeezing his testicle until he faints (35). When Josh protests the cruelties, Papa accuses him of having had a homosexual relationship with George (2002: 50–1), which was a serious allegation in apartheid South Africa, where such a relationship was illegal both in racial and sexual terms, but not dealt with by the TRC.

Apparently natural familial relationships are all challenged by the violence, as is evidenced in the encounter between these soldiers and a Wambo woman walking with a child on her back. She is afraid and both Josh and the audience assume that it is because of the threat of rape. However, when Papa examines the child, he sees that it is dead, and has been cut from its stomach to neck, and it is full of grenades (42). Josh's horror is shared by the audience. It also explains the high number of men with post-traumatic stress disorder who have not been treated, because they may not speak of these experiences since they have not been officially recognised.

These older men transform Josh: he learns fear, but also humanity. Ironically, it is through his close contact with 'the enemy' that Josh discovers a real sense of shared humanity as he 'came to know him [George], in a way I will never know another human being again' (1997: 45). In the

2002 version he says, 'In a few days I knew him, I learned about living' (17). This narrative deconstructs simple binaries of racial and ethnic difference and suggests that personal engagement with another person as a human being facilitates growth, dialogue and a shared humanity, which extends beyond the brief and formal encounters of people at the TRC.

Similar stereotypical markers of masculinity are evident in Kani's play, with Themba's identity being closely associated with his physical power and sexual performance in contrast to his brother. Even as a child he bettered Sipho, demanding and then breaking his wire bus (10). As an adult Themba 'had an anthology of every beautiful woman who ever walked the streets of New Brighton', and later took Sipho's wife, though he had many women. Sipho, in contrast, had a low sperm count and struggled to father a child (36–7). While Themba is a hero of the ANC, Sipho is humiliated at work, called 'Sifo, a disease', and dependent on white women like Mrs Meyers and Mrs Potgieter for his job at the library, despite their acknowledging his contribution (31). All of these markers both reflect and reinforce the dominant construction of masculinity in South Africa.

All the issues already discussed, issues of gender, violence and justice implicitly engage with gaps in the TRC. These plays also have characters who explicitly comment on the TRC.

The TRC evaluated

The debates raised regarding the TRC suggest that the issues are not yet resolved, memories cannot be laid to rest, and so the debates continue beyond the Commission. Both Mandisa and Lily reject the terms of the TRC. Lily says that Josh's submission to the Amnesty Commission 'will achieve nothing. You purge yourself and your colleague walks free. What is that?' (2002: 57). She admits her own pain and anger at a father for his choices, and says, 'what I sense you're really asking for, I can never give you. Nor can any Commission of *Truth*' (2002: 69, italics in original). Lily cannot reconcile with Josh as she has her own ghosts to lay to rest. However, she is able to speak with him as a human being and they share their memories of George with one another, which suggests that perhaps what the TRC achieved was to begin the process whereby individuals can share memories and thus create a shared sense of the past, which could facilitate the negotiations for a better future. It also indicates the limits of the Commission in terms of justice and reconciliation.

Thando and Sipho offer counterpoints to these outsiders' perspectives on the commission. Thando has lost her brother to the struggle,
but has chosen to work as a translator at the Commission and strongly
counters Mandisa's attack on the TRC, citing those who have been
denied amnesty:

> No, your anger is selective. We, who stayed here. We who witnessed first
> hand the police brutality. We who every Saturday buried hundreds of our
> young brothers and sisters shot by the police, dying in detention, dying
> because of orchestrated black on black violence, accept the TRC process.
> You have no right to question that. Mandela spent 27 years in prison. Is
> he asking for someone to be sent to Robben Island to spend years there
> as payback? If all those who suffered can forgive, then so can you. If our
> president can ask us to work for a better life for all of our people, so can
> you. (*ibid.*, 29–30)

When Mandisa insists that it all looks 'too easy', Thando explains that it
is not 'generosity' but 'ubuntu', an 'African humanity' (30) that underpins the work of the Commission. There is a sense of ownership, of redefining the past on their own terms, which empowers those who remain.
For Mandisa *ubuntu* is about the subject's humanity, defined by how he
or she sees another human being.

Sipho has refused to attend the hearings (21). He insists that this is
not a personal matter, but that 'it's about justice', which for him means
for Luyuyo's case to be re-opened and the man who killed him to be
identified, charged and found guilty of murder, and experience the
humiliations of prison before he can apply for amnesty, 'because he "has
disclosed all"' (53–4). This suggests that more than acknowledgement
of guilt is required, that there must be some kind of reparation by the
perpetrator. It is significant that Sipho differentiates between the terms
he sets for justice for the unknown murderer of his son and for his
brother, whom he says he forgave years ago, but was waiting for him to
ask forgiveness (56). In this case, acknowledgement seems to be all that
is necessary. This implies the need to distinguish between personal and
political injustices and processes for negotiating forgiveness; it seems
that the Christian terms for requesting and receiving forgiveness are
appropriate in the case of his brother, but that legal justice is required
for the murder of his son.

The two versions of *Dead Wait* differ most in terms of their engagement with the TRC. The 1997 version preceded the Commission, and
suggests ambivalence with the forum. The later version engages much
more fully and positively with it. Instead of saying that he will make
an application, Josh appears before the Commission and is granted

amnesty. He is acknowledged as both a 'victim . . . and a perpetrator' (2002: 55).

However, he is obviously disappointed at the Commission's limitations in bringing men like Papa to justice. He says, 'I don't think the truth can be commissioned. It's like asking a vulture to puke up its prey' (60), but later says, 'They [TRC] may not be perfect, but for the moment they're all I've got' (67).

Papa Louw offers a very cynical perspective on the Boer position: adamant, almost proud that what they did in the past was deliberate and carefully thought through:

> We defied the world, we denied the left their day of reckoning. . . . *We're here! we're still alive! and in the end we didn't get a hiding.* . . . IT WAS A FUCKING WAR, YOU FUCKING FRAUD. WHAT DO YOU THINK IT WAS? *I did what I did in the bush and I had to do it. And no forum, no tribunal, no commission is going to find otherwise: in camera, or on the end of a fucking rope!* (2002: 64, emphasis in original)

Josh's distress mirrors that of millions of South Africans for whom reconciliation has meant that people like Papa can walk away free. Josh says, 'You knew [what you were doing]. And if I didn't, I should have' (*ibid.*).

The Dead Wait traces Josh's journey towards acknowledging culpability for his part in the abuses committed during the apartheid period. Like *Nothing but the Truth*, it also suggests that this is only the beginning, that justice must be done, though this play does not suggest what this justice should include. Both plays insist that silences can and must be broken, and that the burden of decades of abuse cannot, and perhaps should not, be so easily lifted. They suggest that societal structures and patterns of behaviour need attention: between fathers and their sons and daughters, men and women, as well as between races in South Africa. While these two plays do not deny hope, they are not utopian, particularly in the perspectives they offer on the personal and psychic complexities entailed in any engagement with memory and the past of apartheid. One of the important contributions of both plays is deconstructing simple binaries and stereotypical roles, especially of victim, perpetrator and hero. They also begin an important engagement with women's roles in South Africa, particularly in terms of self-determination.

Green Man Flashing looks at the implications of the compromises of the TRC for individuals in the post-apartheid context. The significance of the TRC resonates into the twenty-first century, as in *Green Man Flashing* Mike van Graan explores the implications of the 'deals' made by the Commission that haunt contemporary South Africa. The conflict between personal rights and wider historical and political imperatives is signalled in the moral dilemma that van Graan constructs around the image conjured up in the play's title, and vividly illustrated in the discussion between Aaron, Gabby and her lawyer Anna:

> AARON: Anna, if you were standing at the traffic lights, and the green man's flashing in your direction, whose right of way is it?
> ...
> GABBY: It's hers. So?
> AARON: But there's a taxi coming down the road at eighty kilometres an hour and it's not going to stop, despite the traffic lights being red and the green man flashing in your favour. Would you still cross the road?
> ANNA: Of course not.
> AARON: But why not? It's your right to cross the street!
> ANNA: And your point is? That Gabby can give up her right to seek justice and live. Or she can exercise her right, and risk getting wiped out in the process. (206–7)

In the context of this illustration, both Gabby and Matthew must forfeit their personal rights for the sake of personal survival. This may seem extreme in a context where resisting theft or bringing criminal charges against an individual does not pose a personal threat to the complainant. However, the weightiness of the issues raised is highlighted when one considers the response provoked by the charge of sexual assault brought against Jacob Zuma, president elect in 2005, a year after this play's premiere. Although the court dismissed the charges, the controversies surrounding the trial highlight the pertinence of the gender issues raised in the play. The trial was highly publicised and politically charged, with strong support from the ANC Youth League, who strongly condemned the complainant, calling her 'Lucifer', and protesting outside the courts with placards demanding 'Burn the bitch'. Amazingly, there was no official reaction to this public abuse of women, given that an equivalent racial slogan would have led to an arrest. In a lengthy analysis of the trial and the politics of rape, Mmatshilo Motsei argues that this trial both 'presented a crisis for the nation', and offered 'the potential to take us to a place of new discoveries' (2007: 90). She reiterates much of the critique raised by Ross regarding the failure of the TRC to 'create a safe space for healing women's sexual wounds' (*ibid.*, 75–6), particularly in the way they defined human rights abuses.

However, Motsei also suggests that the naming of the complainant 'Lucifer', intended as a pejorative term, is ambivalent. The word literally means 'bearer of light' and Motsei contends that in bringing the charge, the complainant was forcing South Africa to look at its own approach to women, sexual politics and HIV/AIDS. The public reactions to this trial raised a question about whether it is possible for a woman to take action against a male comrade in South Africa, or whether she will inevitably be labelled 'mentally ill' (Motsei, 2007: 148–51), as having 'asked for it' (*ibid.*, 151–3), or simply viewed as property. This trial forced South Africans to reconsider their views on women, sexuality and power.

The play interrogates the implications of the precedents set by the TRC. Aaron argues that the concept of 'justice as a deal' stems from the TRC:

> ANNA: The point is that a woman has been raped. The point is that this woman, my friend, your ex-wife, Gabby, has a right to justice!
> AARON: I agree. A hundred percent! But life's a little more complex than that. Sometimes . . . sometimes justice has to be sacrificed for the greater political good.
> . . .
> AARON: Anna, you're a lawyer. You represented victims at the TRC. Did you throw up your hands then?
> ANNA: That was different.
> AARON: Was it? How many perpetrators of human rights abuses were brought to book? How many victims whom you represented got justice? None. Not a single one. Justice had to be sacrificed for the greater political good. The TRC was a deal, Anna. It wasn't about justice. You know that. (2007: 201)

This critique on the 'deal' made at the TRC for South Africans is made more dramatically explicit by having Gabby's statement of her experience inter-spliced with police inspector Abraham's TRC testimony of his seeing the abuse and rape of Mrs Dhlamini during the apartheid years. He expresses his appreciation for the TRC process, while explaining his previous silence: 'It wasn't appropriate for coloured officers to lodge complaints against their white colleagues.' He also expresses his deep shame 'for being silent. For doing nothing.' (*ibid.*, 196).[26]

This juxtaposition of Abraham's statement with Gabby's current dilemma suggests that, without intervention, these abuses continue. It highlights the interconnectedness of justice, gender and power issues, and asks the audience to consider the implications of elevating reconciliation and political stability above justice, especially for the individual.

The play ends ambiguously: we do not know what Gabby has decided about the deal she has been offered as she is about to give evidence by video link in Australia. This ending allows an audience a context and space in which to debate fraught and taboo issues, to voice deeply personal and

---

26 Hamber (1998) supports this argument.

potentially controversial views on gender, sexuality and violence in contemporary South African society without their being too personal.

Molora (Ashes)

I end this chapter with an analysis of a creative engagement with the TRC that brings the thematic issues and performative experimentation together. Yael Farber's *Molora* was first performed in 2004. (This play followed three other plays, *A Woman in Waiting, Amajuba, He Left Quietly,* published in *Theatre as Witness,* which echoed the TRC testimonies.) Farber has described this play as 'the journey back from the dark heart of unspeakable trauma and pain' (2008b: 8). She uses the various narratives surrounding the *Oresteia* to explore how the dispossessed of South Africa can contemplate reconciliation, forgiveness and healing. Adaptations of Greek drama have played an important role in South Africa's negotiation of its place in relation to the European canon and post-colonial resistance.[27] The *Oresteia* is of particular significance as it marks a symbolic shift in Greek politics from cycles of violent vendettas towards justice framed by democratic process, paralleling some of the issues central to South Africa's move from an apartheid to a post-apartheid context. *Molora* draws on Aeschylus's *Agamemnon* and *The Libation Bearers,* and Sophocles's and Euripides's *Electra.* In comparing different approaches to the *Oresteia* (2010: 210–11, 285–8), Edith Hall suggests that Aeschylus 'portrays how society changes in response to the things people suffer' (*ibid.*, 211); while Euripides is more critical, demonstrating the political compromise in the play's resolution and thus highlighting that 'real life cannot be controlled like a literary narrative' (*ibid.*, 287). *Molora* explores the paradoxical need for social stability, alongside the impossibility of principled reconciliation in the face of embodied memories of past violence.

The focus of the play is split between the protagonists in conflict, Klytemnestra, Electra and Orestes; and the chorus, who are men and women from the Ngqoko Cultural Group of the Transkei who worked with Farber on this play, and who here convene as the jury. Half of the chorus sits facing the audience, spatially replicating the TRC hearings; while the other half sit opposite, amongst the audience, who initially also include Klytemnestra, Electra and Orestes. These three characters

27   For details see van Zyl Smit (2008, 2010).

all testify; Klytemnestra as a perpetrator, who represents those who submitted applications to the Amnesty Committee, and Electra and Orestes as victims at the HRVC. *Molora* brings the committees together, and the spatial arrangement draws the audience in, dynamically implicating them in the actions and judgments of the play.

The play begins with the lament 'Blood has been spilt here', sung in Xhosa by an old woman over a grave, reminding us of the unresolved issues of the past. In the next scene Klytemnestra, a middle-aged white woman, and Electra, a young black woman, each testify about their pasts, with the main points being translated into English or Xhosa, as appropriate, again dramatising the experience of being at the Commission. The next scene shifts from narrative to re-enactment, as Klytemnestra and Electra move from the testimony tables at opposite sides of the stage to enter the centre 'where memory / the past will be re-enacted' (2008: 19).[28] This dramatises their commitment 'to the process of unearthing the past' (*ibid.*, 25). The spatial arrangement and song both reference the TRC and shift away from it, as it moves away from Christian forgiveness and reconciliation to focus on images of mourning, lamentation and a sense of unresolved conflict. Musical instruments used traditionally in Xhosa communities of the Transkei, such as the mouth bow, calabash bows, mouth harps and milking drums, along with split-tone singing (*umngqokolo*), draw the audience into a deeply emotional exploration of betrayal, revenge, loyalty, duty, filial relationships and ultimately justice and retribution. The performance includes long, uncomfortable silences, which force reflection on the testimony, particularly on the disparity between the verbal formulation and the embodied re-enactments of past violence.[29]

Farber believes in 'testimonial theatre' as a 'genre wrought from people bearing witness to their own stories through remembrance and words', which she believes has a 'capacity for healing through speaking, hearing and being heard' (2008a: 19). Klytemnestra is more than a monster, she is an individual whose violent acts are explained, and who dreads Orestes's return and vengeance (35, 48); she mourns the death of her daughter Iphigenia (39), and her first husband and child, who died violently at Agamemnon's hands (44). Here Farber shifts from

28 All future references to this version of the text.
29 Compare Klytemnestra's account of her murdering her husband (22–3) and her re-enactment, including 'covering her expressionless face, arms and hands in blood' (26), which she washes off at the end of the scene (28), or her torture of Electra to reveal the whereabouts of Orestes, as she re-enacts ubiquitous torture methods referred to at the TRC – simulated drowning (48) and cigarette burns to her palms and neck.

stereotypical imaging of South African violence as being predominantly masculine, with Klytemnestra speaking the rhetoric of the biblical legitimisation of apartheid theology (32–3), and Electra warning against 'a law for men' defined in terms of 'blood for blood' (45). Despite this warning, Electra insists that she 'will do what must be done', and thus risks turning into her mother, who in turn is responding to previous violence done to her. This highlights the paradoxes involved in defining someone as a victim or perpetrator of violence, as often they are both, as the previous plays also demonstrate. It is Orestes who perceives the emptiness of revenge (84), which the play clearly presents as 'a choice' (80). Significantly, it is the chorus of women who overpower Electra, restraining and cradling her until she 'finally breaks down, weeping for every injustice of the past' (85), and the diviner praises the ancestors in Xhosa, praying for success in their work to stop crime and killing, and in speaking truth (86). This seems to suggest a need to go back to community and a sense of spirituality in order to mourn the past, before one can forgive and move on.

The play juxtaposes two positions: the first presented by Electra in her opening statement that 'while the guilty pay not with blood for blood- / Then we are nothing but history without a future' (25), and Klytemnestra's epilogue, which suggests that 'by grace alone' we are still here, with the day dawning and the chains falling from a house that, 'For too long . . . has lain in ash on the ground' (87). The performance, though, does not present a polemical binary, but rather dramatises the complexities of moving from the first to the second position. Images of water, blood and ashes highlight the high price of ending violence, and demonstrate how wide the gap between ending violence and moving towards forgiveness and reconciliation is in reality. Glenn Odom outlines the significance of these issues in the context of Farber's using tragedy as a frame for this play. He argues that

> tragedy and reconciliation contain contradictory impulses: tragedy requires a universal space, whereas reconciliation tends to emphasize a specific, monumentalized space; tragedy removes individuals from community, whereas reconciliation subsumes the individual story within the communal; tragedy involves the expiation of emotion by means of catharsis, whereas reconciliation requires both the expiation of emotion and the creation of new emotion; tragedy requires closure, whereas reconciliation is explicitly continuous. *Molora* sanctions neither alternative. (2011: 47)

This play highlights the tensions of the TRC, which was caught between the imperatives of justice and reconciliation; and our engagement with them as witnesses and judges. In her Foreword Farber insists that it was not the gods – nor any *deux ex machina* – that delivered us from ourselves. It was the common everyman and everywoman who, in the years following democracy, gathered in modest halls across the country to face their perpetrators across a table, and find a way forward for us all. (2008b: 7)

The everyman/woman is represented in *Molora* by the chorus, who, in the spirit of *ubuntu*, engage with the ghosts of the past that haunt the living and the returning exiles, who are caught between their memories of a violent, disenfranchised past and a desire for a peaceful present. It is they who facilitate the rituals of mourning and initiation, important transitional moments in life. These rituals introduce a controversy central to trauma studies and remind us of the long debates on evaluating ritual in the context of drama (see Finnegan, 1970). Both contexts wrestle with the difference between presentation and representation, particularly as regards the place and expectations of an audience, who are witnessing this event.

The TRC has been analysed in terms of Turner's model of 'redressive social action' (1982: 10) in which, by combining juridical or religious ritual, those in power sought to 'divin[e] the hidden causes of social conflict', offer a 'therapeutic ritual (involving the exorcism of malefic spirits and the propitiation of "good" ones)', and then perform 'a major ritual celebrating the values, common interests, and moral order of the widest recognized cultural and moral community, transcending the divisions of the local group'. Bozzoli argues that the TRC ritual created only a partial bridge between the personal and social realms, but in a way that replaced individual representations with collective briefs that were 'new myths' (2004: 257–62). The use of the chorus in this play seems to suggest that we, the community, must complete the social action begun by the TRC. However, Odom argues, citing Ricoeur, that this is complicated insofar as the audience are ambiguously placed 'at once inside and outside the community – witnesses to the testimony, but not actors in the narrative' (2011: 54). We are witnesses and potentially judges, which is problematic because 'testimony only becomes complete when, through judgment, it "transcends experience and history" . . . [which] must displace the individual within his or her community' (*ibid.*, 55). This separation may be partially addressed by alternating testimony with embodied re-enactments of violence, which shift an audience between their role as judges and their subjective experiencing of the narratives. However, the extent to which this facilitates catharsis and rebalance, a requirement for a ritual experience, is uncertain.

Despite, or perhaps because of, these paradoxes *Molora* demonstrates the effect that performance form may have on thematic exploration, as the audience experiences the paradox of being both inside and outside a community, shifting between judgment and emotion, without easy resolution. This play, alongside Farber's three other testimonial plays, highlight that the past is not yet past, 'a country [we] would never have to visit again' (2008a: 97, 175), but rather we have to find ways of facing these painful pasts and find hope. These plays, like those discussed earlier in this chapter, engage with ghosts and haunting, various kinds of exile and the renegotiation of gender roles in South Africa, in ways that are layered and complex, revealing fault lines rather than offering simple solutions. This may facilitate meaningful reconciliation insofar as it is open, explicitly continuous, requiring ongoing debate and re-evaluation. What is clear is that none of these plays formulates or supports the coherent narratives and myths of 'truth', reconciliation or forgiveness proposed by the TRC, and they thus constitute important counter-narratives to these metanarratives of the past. The plays suggest that particular issues and memories continue to haunt South Africa because they have not been dealt with sufficiently in the TRC. The plays highlight both the achievements of the TRC, insofar as it has articulated key issues sufficiently for other forums to be able to expand on them; and the weaknesses of the TRC, where particular memories have been disavowed or not sufficiently interrogated. They invite individuals to extend beyond hearing the stories to engaging with what these mean for renegotiating identities and communities, while being critically aware of the precedents set both by apartheid and the TRC for contemporary South Africa.

3

Staging a nation: the Voortrekker Monument and Freedom Park

The past is never dead. It's not even past.
(William Faulkner, *Requiem for a Nun*, Act 1, sc. 3, p. 85)

The inherited apartheid archives embody particular narratives of South Africa, especially those that defined separate cultural identities, with their relative worth and histories. The way these archives of memory were constructed and controlled is important (Rokem, 2000), especially insofar as they affected the social structure of the nation, beyond apartheid legislation. This chapter looks at how at moments of political crisis or transition, specific narratives of history, from particular cultural perspectives, have been performed in public spaces to define national identities. It begins by looking at how South Africa narrated and performed itself in the 1910 South African Pageant of Union. It then explores how the Afrikaner struggle for independence and nationhood was facilitated through particular commemorations of the Battle of Blood/Ncome River to establish symbols and myths, drawing on their history from the nineteenth century, and conceptualising Afrikaner nationalism in and through the 1938 Voortrekker Festival and the inauguration of the Voortrekker Monument in 1949; some references to the 1952 Jan van Riebeeck Tercentenary Festival Fair and the 1988 commemoration of the Great Trek will supplement this analysis.

The chapter then compares the renegotiation of the meaning of the

Voortrekker Monument as a site of memory in the post-apartheid context with Freedom Park, which is twinned with this Monument. In particular it looks at how the past is being redefined, how new and formerly marginalised symbols and memories are being incorporated into South Africa's re-narration of itself; analysing the effect these formulations of memory are having on our understanding of and engagement with diverse historic narratives and a sense of complexity in South African identities.

Performing memory spatially[1]

In my introduction I argued that historical and cultural encoding occur primarily in two ways: either linguistically through narrative, both written and oral; or spatially through architecture, gardens, public sculptures, monuments, museums and exhibitions. The chapters preceding this one demonstrate the complexities of selecting, interpreting and formulating diverse experiences of the past into a coherent narrative, as well as of disseminating the formulated narratives as widely as possible. They traced the importance of engaging with and controlling the archives which underpin and verify a specific formulation of a nation's history. However, performing these narratives in public spaces, in forms accessible to the broadest public audience possible, involving the public wherever possible, is equally important for a nation in transition – either when a narrative of nation is being formulated, or it is being desegregated and reconstructed through reinterpretations of history. These performances highlight particular moments in history as worthy of commemoration, either as national holidays, or by embodying them spatially in memorials and monuments; or by renegotiating the cultural position of previously dominant memorial moments or figures.[2] I begin with performances of national commemoration, and then look at how these ephemeral narratives are made more permanent in visual archives, such as museums.

Museums have played a significant role in these processes, traditionally giving material form to authorised versions of the past, which have in turn become institutionalised as public memory. This process

---

1 This section draws on earlier research on the District Six and Robben Island
   Museums (Hutchison, 2004).
2 Mbembe argues these are attempts to 'bring together the different fragments of the
   nation' (2004: 404).

includes shifting memory from the realm of the personal to create public memory by ordering and interpreting experience; this, in turn, shapes our understanding of ourselves and our world. Museums play a large role in this creation of public meaning and are significant because they are often part of the Cultural Ideological State Apparatus (Althusser, 1993: 15–22), which David Meltzer argues 'represent[s] the ruling class ideology, and [is] unified by political and class identity' (1981: 115). Museums traditionally standardise and fix a narrative or image of the dominant group visually, and in doing so interpret and marginalise 'Others', whose experiences lie outside the dominant narrative. Thus, in recent years museums in South Africa have been criticised for being 'mausoleums' in need of deconstruction and redefinition (see van Tonder, 1994).[3]

The possibility for such deconstruction and redefinition, I argue, is defined by the strength of the museum's *a priori* narrative and the degree to which it can facilitate dialogic interaction with alternative memories and identities. Although it is true that museums tend to act as state apparatuses, particularly insofar as they are dependent on state funding for their continued existence, I believe that they are potentially significant spaces in which people can both actively recover and collate memory, and negotiate stories and identities for themselves, outside the formalised historical narratives of nation building, or the divides of their historically and geographically segregated communities.[4]

Understanding the traditional role and place of museums is impor-tant when exploring how these spaces may be mobilised relative to memory, because both the curators and visitors to the spaces bring with them assumptions about the function and construction of exhi-bitions, and also at times their own memories of the events being represented. South Africa has a long history of commemoration of the dominant European, primarily Afrikaner, hegemony, as is evidenced in the Voortrekker Monument in Pretoria, the Taalmonument (Language Monument) in Paarl; the South African Museum in Cape Town, the former Africana Museum in Johannesburg; Durban's Killie Campbell Local and Natural History Museums.

Thus, when attempting to redefine the place of museums, I consider the history of the space alongside the ideologies that have defined it, which to some extent define some of the assumptions which visitors

---

3 Other important explorations regarding the transformation of museums in the twentieth century include Dubin (2006), Karp, *et al.* (2006) and Bharucha (2000a, 2007).

4 For details on the background to this argument, see Hutchison (2004).

may bring with them when visiting these spaces.[5] I look at how the museums 'perform' particular versions of history, both spatially in the exhibits and their accompanying narratives, and directly through theatrical performances in and about the spaces, paying particular attention to the potential for dialogic spaces where the public can engage with alternative memories and histories. I write this from a performance perspective, aware that a number of scholars from different disciplinary backgrounds are currently conducting research in the field of public memorialisation and heritage in relation to memory; I have drawn on their work to inform my perspective.[6]

The performance of national identity

As outlined in the introduction, national identity is conceived of, imagined and performed in various ways. This chapter draws on Benedict Anderson's concept of nation as an 'imagined community' (2006) that is unified by particular symbols, narratives and unities of history, while drawing specifically on Hobsbawm and Ranger's concept of the 'invention of tradition' (1983) to explore how source histories, myths and genealogies have been used to support the dominant discourse of identity in South Africa at different moments in its history. These constructions are often ambivalent and opaque, given the number of competing discourses (Bhabha, 1990). South Africa is now in the position of a post-colony, which means that the state must disentangle itself from colonial and imperial configurations of culture and politics (Said, 1991, 1994; Mbembe, 2001). This process is particularly complex in South Africa because, despite South Africa's gaining official independence in 1910, the configurations of white cultural, political and economic hegemony persisted until 1994. So there are a number of key historical moments, and more than one 'nation', that must be acknowledged when considering the performance of memory and identity in South Africa.

The history of South Africa has been a history of struggle: against

5 For a discussion on problems related to the reclamation and redefinition of the Africana Museum, now the Museum Africa in Johannesburg, see Hamilton (1994). For a discussion on the controversial attempt to challenge past versions of representations of the /Xam or San people by Pippa Skotnes in 1996, see Jackson and Robins (1999), Patricia Davison (1998) and Martin Hall (1998).
6 These include Sabine Marschall, David Bunn, Annie Coombes, Nsizwe Dlamini, Ciraj Rassool and Leslie Witz, along with international scholars referred to in the introduction that focus on Holocaust, Vietnam and other war memorials.

the elements and wild animals, while various ethnic groups both from within and beyond South Africa have fought one another for autonomy and control of the country's rich natural resources. These were often the reasons for migrations to and within South Africa, and the cause of most of the wars within it and against outside powers. However, exploring which of these struggles are officially 'remembered' and commemorated, when and by whom is the central focus of this chapter.

When I think back to the history I learnt at school, the moments that were emphasised included the establishment of the Cape as a Dutch settlement by Jan van Riebeeck in 1652, the arrival of the settlers from the United Kingdom at the Eastern Cape in 1820, and the various migrations from the Cape, particularly the Great Trek in the 1830s, the discovery of diamonds in Kimberley in 1867, and gold in the Transvaal in 1886, which led to the Anglo-Boer, or South African War in 1899–1902. The end of this long and bitter struggle between English and Dutch-speaking South Africans officially ended with the declaration of the Union of South Africa in 1910, as a dominion of the English crown under a coalition government. Apart from the two world wars, the next most significant date in South African school history was 1948, when the National Party (NP) under D.F. Malan came into power and began to implement apartheid as the dominant ideology politically, economically and socially in South Africa. Here I pause to consider how South Africa arrived at this moment, and how both ideology and performance were mobilised in the conceptualisation of apartheid.

1910 Pageant of the Union of South Africa

It is important to note that until 1910 'South Africa' did not exist. This was the moment that two independent Boer republics and two British colonies were amalgamated into a state called the Union of South Africa, following the bitter Anglo-Boer War (1899–1902). In his article on the 1910 Pageant of the Union of South Africa, Peter Merrington outlines this moment of 'reconciliation' between the English- and Dutch-speaking South Africans[7] as a moment that was 'a political and

---

7 This conflict began with the Dutch and British governments struggling with one another to control the Cape, and later British hegemony provoked many Dutch settlers to migrate from the Western Cape, and later from the Eastern Cape in search of independence from British rule. The conflict culminated in the Anglo-Boer Wars (Botha, 1938).

cultural configuration that was both national and imperial' (1997: 1), and which set many of the terms for later configurations of the South African nation. These configurations included the conceptualisation of various 'ethnic types' of South Africans, as well as the reconciliation between the two dominant white settler groups. These representations illustrate Lyotard's formulation of *mise en scène* as 'a complex group of operations' through which a rhetorical idea is translated so that it may be 'inscribed on human bodies and transmitted by those to other bodies' (Lyotard, 1977: 88), which in this case, Merrington suggests, is a performance of a putative national and racial identity (1997: 5). I want to explore how these ideas were staged in the 1910 Pageant of Union, and the implications of this event which provided a model for imagining and performing the nation for later historical commemorations, which I will expand later in this chapter.

Frank Lascelles was the Union Pageant master, and he followed Louis-Napoleon Parker's formula for the so-called 'new pageantry' in England.[8] Usually a Pageant was a two- or three-day event in an open-air setting, where about nine historical episodes were staged in chronological sequence, followed by a dramatic monologue or masque. Dialogue was kept to a minimum, but orchestras, narrative and dramatic verses and laudatory verses were often included. It usually involved several thousand performers, drawn from local communities, who provided their own costumes and properties. Parker also insisted that 'the executants must include every class of the community, both male and female. . . . A Pageant is absolutely democratic. That is one of its many merits' (1928: 283–4). Although people were in different social positions in the pageant, it emphasised cooperation between different groups in a community and enhanced local arts, crafts and heritage, which suggests the role of the pageant as constitutive of communal identity.

In a later article Merrington explores the implications of Lascelles's argument that 'The critic must not murmur if persons and events are found in a juxtaposition for which there is no absolute warrant in the chronicles, or if fancy sometimes bodies forth possibilities which may never have been realities', suggesting that this comment 'can be applied not only to the superficial expediencies of theatrical production, but also to more radical questions of identity and politics' (Merrington, 1999: 245). This exemplifies Austin's performative speech act, which brings something into being; in this case the pageant narrates

8 See Merrington's analysis (1997) of the significance of 'New pageantry' as typifying the imperial and national idealising imagination between 1900 and the late 1930s. See Parker's formulation of the key elements and perceived efficacy of the 'new pageantry' (1928: 279–86).

a particular version of history in order to constitute particular conceptualisations of the nation, with the concomitant relationships of the people subject to the particular ideologies and structures being presented. For example, Darnley describes the pageant as presenting an apparently unified South Africa:

> Hottentots, Basutos, Zulus, Portuguese, Dutch and British all joined in. Now, no religion could have forged this unity, no patriotic appeal – nothing but a great drama in which races could act their own share in the epic story of a modern world's making. (Darnley, 1932: 40–1)

The drama metaphor suggests the role of this imagined performance for constituting the new nation. It also highlights the 'fancy [which] sometimes bodies forth possibilities which may never have been realities' because in this event the 'Bushmen', 'Hottentots', 'Basutos', and 'Zulus' were represented in the pageant as 'primitive' and 'pre-historical' people, whose stories were reduced to a single tableau represented as the 'Pacification of the Natives'. Witz describes this scene as representing the supposed period of pacification as 'the vanquishing of savagery in South Africa by civilization and the evolution and development of the Nation's social and commercial conditions' (2003: 44), without engaging with the various peoples' individual historical perspectives or narratives.[9] The one exception to this presentation of the indigenous[10] peoples of South Africa was that of the 'Cape Malays', who were granted one historical episode in the pageant depicting the arrival of their spiritual leader at the Cape in 1694.[11] Apart from these obvious ethnic representations that supported contemporary racial mythologies, the pageant also performed a 'unity' that was misleading, and contingent on strategic forgetting, as Witz notes that there was no representation of the period between 1854 and 1910 in the pageant, 'when the conflicts between the

9 This is clearly illustrated in Merrington's comparison of the representations of the 'Bushman' in the 'Baboon Dance', as 'a host of dark forms with veiled faces fleeing hither and thither in disordered motion, and uttering half-articulate cries of woe. These are the hordes of ignorance, cruelty, savagery, unbelief, war, pestilence, famine and their ilk, the pitiless progenitors of all the misery of man, the inwohners [sic] of black night' who are driven off by the 'silver-clad children' that follow (1999: 253).

10 I use the term 'indigenous' to mean people who were in South Africa when the Europeans arrived, with an awareness of the political implications of the term, particularly as related to post-colonial allocation of rights, justice, and entitlement (cf. Mamdani, 2001).

11 Merrington argues that this was because Dr Abdullah Abdurahman was a city councillor and founder of the African People's Organisation. It may also be because the Cape Muslims enjoyed a privileged degree of integration into many aspects of Cape society at this time relative to other coloured and Black South Africans. I shall return to explore some of the complexities of Cape coloured identity in Chapter 5. See Goldin (1987: 156–81) for analysis of Cape coloured identity formation.

settler communities were at their sharpest and most brutal' (*ibid.*). This highlights the process of selective remembering and forgetting in this staging of the nation's history. The pageant presented the European (Portuguese, Dutch and British) 'discovery' of South Africa as a narrative of Hegelian 'Progress' over 'hordes of ignorance, cruelty, savagery, unbelief, war, pestilence, famine and their ilk' (*Historical Sketch*, 1910), and thus emphasised the need for unity among the settlers.

The form itself was important insofar as Merrington argues that the term 'pageant'

> derives from the Latin *pagus* (field) and *pagina* (page), with a common root of the verb *pangere* (to plant, beget, establish, record, pledge or covenant). Thus we observe that the moments focused on in the pageant are constitutive activities: occupying and marking the land, settling and building, covenanting with God and treating with the 'natives,' and the dedicating of the individual or the community to a special 'calling.' In this sense imperial pageantry is history and imperial history is a pageant; and they are both illusory or subjunctive in their modes of recreation of the past and of dedication to the future. (1997: 4)

The pageant is important for establishing 'constitutive activities' that are seen in metaphysically elevating terms. Thus images of Europeans covenanting with God as they embark on a hazardous journey are foregrounded: examples from the pageant include a scene depicting Vasco da Gama preparing himself spiritually for the voyage of discovery around the Cape in 1497 (*Souvenir and Programme of the Pageant of South Africa,* 1910: 10), or the scene where the English-speaking citizens of Grahamstown in the Eastern Cape present a Bible to Jacobus and Piet Uys before their departure into the interior in 1835. This scene is repeated in the 1938 Voortrekker Centenary celebrations, as is a scene depicting the massacre of Retief and his comrades by Zulu leader Dingaan, followed by the Battle of Blood River. Both of these moments involved a sacred pledge or oath, the significance of which I shall discuss later in this chapter.

Other iconic moments involve scenes depicting the subjugation or occupation of the land; for example, President Hoffman of the newly constituted Orange Free State Republic visiting Moshesh, chief of the Basutos, in 1854, drinking beer with him and presenting him with a plough and a barrel of gunpowder as an act of goodwill (*ibid.*, 90–1). While this scene suggests the processes of negotiating for land, it does not acknowledge the subsequent protest of Boers, which resulted in President Hoffman's resignation, nor the British annexation of Lesotho and Basotho-held areas of the Free State after the discovery of diamonds in 1867.

Despite these gaps, this pageant demonstrated the potentially important role that performance could have played in publicly rehearsing reconciliation, making concrete and disseminating a unified history and formulating a new 'South African' identity at a transitional moment, which included defining the place of women, and of black, coloured and other people defined as being outside the dominant group. It also created a precedent and format for later public performances of history, like the centenary celebration of the emancipation of slaves in the Cape in 1938, and the Voortrekker Centenary celebration of the same year, which completely overshadowed the emancipation celebrations; and the 1952 tricentenary celebration of Jan van Riebeeck's arrival at the Cape (Witz, 2003). Loren Kruger has analysed how some of these tropes were repeated and extended in other colonial expositions, and also challenged in representations of New Africans in the 1936 Empire Exhibition and the 1940 'Africa – a revel pageant', which revealed the paradoxes inherent in the Union Pageant representations of indigenous Africans in the context of neo-colonial modernity (1997, 1999: 47).

However, this raises questions about how South Africa was both affected by dominant European discourses on racial theory,[12] and why it detached itself from the dominant European thinking on race and moved towards apartheid as a defining political ideology. I begin this analysis by tracing the place of Afrikaner nationalism in South African history, and in particular the role of the Voortrekker Centenary of 1938 in the movement towards defining another sense of the nation in South Africa.

Conceptualising apartheid – Afrikaner identity, memory and the 1938 Voortrekker Centenary celebrations

According to van Jaarsveld, the various ways of celebrating the Battle of Blood River (now also known as Ncome) serve as a reliable barometer of the historical, national and political thinking of the Afrikaner (1979: 65–7). Here he draws on Moodie's analysis of the various Afrikaner

---

12 Here I refer to segregation ideology, with its language of scientific racism and eugenics that dominated discourse in Britain and the United States; see Dubow (1995) for a discussion of segregationist ideology in twentieth-century South Africa.

beliefs and commemorations such as the Day of the Vow, as an example of a civil religion, where religion and history are united (Moodie, 1975: 295–300).

The Vow was made on 9 December 1838 and the Battle against the Zulus took place on 16 December 1938. However, although a few Trekkers did keep the vow annually, it was only in 1881 when Paul Kruger, president of the Transvaal Republic, declared that the leaders of the people had been used by God to gain independence from the British in their victory to regain the Transvaal, as he had at Blood River and Majuba, that this commemoration, then known as Dingaan's day, was established more widely. In 1891 Kruger shifted this commemoration from an historic to a religious focus, and warned of divine punishment if their sacred Vow was not kept (Ehlers, 2003: 5). This idea was further propagated by Gustav Preller, a popular journalist and historian, and staunch champion of Afrikaans, which was then an unofficial language, in his biographies *Piet Retief* (written 1906) and *Andries Pretorius* (written 1937), and his screenplay entitled *De Voortrekkers* (1916, known in English as *Winning a Continent*), the first major epic to be produced in South Africa.[13] It is clear that from the nineteenth century this historic moment became the central, constitutive myth for defining and uniting Afrikaners as a people. Key aspects included their being guided and supported by God, which justified their struggle against the various indigenous peoples and the British for control of the interior of South Africa and their quest for independence.

However, Saul Dubow warns against tracing the development of Afrikaner nationalism as 'an unchanging, timeless tradition' defined primarily in terms of 'a socially undifferentiated entity, pursuing its own primordial ethnic agenda' (1992: 209). Deborah Posel also rejects the liberal critical position that apartheid was a 'seamless "grand design"' (1995: 206), and the Marxist interpretation of it as the response to competing capitalist interests.[14] Rather, both these historians insist on reading the development of Afrikaner nationalism in terms of various imperatives.

Dubow proposes that Afrikaner identity 'was forged from the late nineteenth century and the means by which Afrikaner ethnicity was mobilized in order to capture state power in the twentieth century' (1992:

---

13 See Hees's (1996, 2003) analysis of the role Preller's biographies played in defining Afrikaner nationalism, and the role this film played in generating and sustaining the Great Trek as the 'central, constitutive myth of Afrikaans nationalism' (2003: 49).

14 Posel (1995) demonstrates complex tensions and ambiguities within the Afrikaner Nationalist alliance through the 1940s, and as late as the Sauer Commission Report of 1947.

209). He pinpoints the Anglo-Boer War as the particular stimulus for the development of Afrikaner nationalism as a mass movement, although one could argue that the Voortrekker movement of the nineteenth century, and particularly the growing Afrikaans language movement from the 1970s, certainly embodied the key concepts of the movement: a strong desire for self-determination, beyond the interference of the British; a strong claim to the land; and the belief that their actions were ordained by God. Nevertheless, the Anglo-Boer War had been a harsh experience for the Afrikaner, as the British pursued a 'scorched earth' policy, depriving Boers of food, water and access to support on homesteads, and confined their wives and children to concentration camps, where more than 20,000 died. Although by the end of the war the Afrikaners were economically and psychologically devastated, the war had renewed the ties of kinship between Cape Afrikaners and those in the north of the country, and shifted general perceptions regarding the status of Afrikaans as a language. Before the war Afrikaans had been regarded as 'inappropriate for educated discourse . . . the cultured Afrikaner had to choose between two foreign languages, English or Dutch'; but after the war a new generation of lyric poets emerged and expressed the grief of a people, and formulated a sense of dignity and purpose (Moodie, 1975: 40–1), so that the seeds of the language movement that flourished from the late nineteenth century bloomed, and language continued to play a central role in the Afrikaner nationalist movement.[15]

At the Union of South Africa in 1910, Dingaan's Day was proclaimed a public holiday for the whole country, and thus Afrikaner memory became part of the history of the new nation. However, the coalition governments were always perceived as an uneasy compromise, as evidenced by the conflicts that arose over which side South Africa should support in the two world wars (Thompson, 1985: 27–8). Dubow argues that during the Second World War Afrikaners were isolated from the centre of political power, and thus were open to more radical ideas, particularly given the return of many Afrikaner intellectuals from study in Germany, where they had encountered National Socialist ideas (1992: 210). These men included Nico Diedericks, Piet Meyer, Geoff Cronjé and H.F. Verwoerd, who returned from Germany and Holland to formulate complex cultural and theological arguments that supported the idea that Africans were racially inferior to Europeans, and in fact comprise a different 'nation', which God ordained a different place and

15 Afrikaans became an official national language in 1925, and the first official translation of the entire Bible into Afrikaans was completed in 1933; see Moodie (1975: 39–51).

purpose.[16] Although biological racism was evident, this rationale quickly gave way to arguments based more on tradition and experience, particularly because of their suspicion of Social Darwinism and the centrality of neo-Calvinist formulations of the Afrikaner people as a 'Chosen people', with a God-given destiny (Thompson, 1985: 29, Dubow, 1992).[17]

Of particular concern were the ongoing economic and political protests by urbanised black South Africans, the result largely of the rapid industrialisation and expansion of secondary industries in urban areas.[18] After the First World War there had been a massive influx of African men seeking work in the cities, which challenged largely Afrikaans-speaking unskilled and semi-skilled labour (Dubow, 1992: 211). During the economic depression of the early 1930s the growing nationalist movement coalesced around the issue of 'poor whites', estimated at 300,000 by the 1932 Carnegie Commission (Wilcocks, 1932). Dubow argues that this issue 'provided a means by which Afrikaner ideologues could link criticism of the power of English/Jewish capital with popular anti-black sentiment' (1992: 215). The Federation of Afrikaans Cultural Associations (FAK), founded by the Broederbond in 1929,[19] 'focused attention upon the plight of poor whites, the economic dominance of English-speakers and the centrality of Christian-Nationalism as an organising creed' (ibid.), and in the face of a weak coalition government, Hertzog's Native Bills were passed in 1936. Thus the combination of a weak coalition government in a time of socioeconomic crisis together with the emergence of articulate intellectuals who formulated

16 The writings of these men were central to the formulation of apartheid policy; see N.J. Diedericks's pamphlet on nationalism as a philosophy of life and its relation to internationalism, 'Nasionalisme as Lewensbeskouing en sy Verhouding tot Internasionalisme' (Bloemfontein, 1936); Geoff Cronjé's 'n Tuiste vir die Nageslag (A home for the next generation), Stellenbosch, 1945), in which he argues that the racial inferiority of Africans is based as much on tradition and experience as on scientific evidence (1945: 9, 22); see also his later publications, 'n Tuiste vir die Nageslag: Afrika sonder die Asiaat (Africa without Asians, Johannesburg, 1946), Regverdige Rasse-Apartheid (Justified racial apartheid, Stellenbosch, 1947), Voogdyskap en Apartheid (Guardianship and apartheid, Pretoria, 1948), which were widely read and commented on.
17 See Thompson's extended reference to the formulation of this idea by J.C. Rooy, the chairman of the Afrikaner Broederbond, in 1944 (1985: 29).
18 The trade unions were very strong and there had been significant strikes by miners and riots on the Witwatersrand since 1913.
19 This exclusively male, Calvinist organisation [Afrikaans: band of brothers] was founded in 1918 in Johannesburg to promote Afrikaans culture and economic empowerment throughout South Africa in a coordinated way; later it focused on securing and maintaining Afrikaner control over important areas of government. Almost all Afrikaner cultural associations eventually affiliated with the FAK. In 1929 the Broederbond became a secret organisation; see Vatcher (1965: 76–88) and Giliomee (1995: 197–9).

compelling philosophical and theological ideas facilitated the formulation of a policy that would give economic security to a minority group threatened by an indigenous population of vastly superior numbers. Thus at the time of the 1938 centenary of the Great Trek, the Battle of Blood River with the Vow at its heart once again became a central reference point in the formulation of Afrikaner nationalism. Bloomberg says that the 1938 Voortrekker Centenary celebrations

> released an upsurge of nationalist feeling, a sense of solidarity, a yearning for unity, pride in a heroic Afrikaner past and hope for the future, based on a renewed belief in the volk's [nation's] divinely-willed destiny. (1990: 122)

Although this event preceded the National Party's coming to power, and the subsequent implementation of its apartheid policies, it can be argued that this event visually performed ideologies and desires that would define South Africa for more than 50 years.

The plan was to erect two monuments to the Voortrekkers, one on a hill outside Pretoria, the capital of the Union, and the other on the site of the historic 1838 battle in Natal. Both foundation stones were laid on 16 December 1938, the centenary day of the battle. This commemoration was particularly poignant as it evoked memories of the heroic overcoming of overwhelming odds at a time of profound economic depression and social unrest.

Performance played a central role in this national commemoration of what was a controversial and pivotal historic moment in South African history. The ATKV, the cultural association of the South African Railways,[20] conceived of the idea of a small-scale re-enactment of the Great Trek as a folk festival. Exact replicas of the original covered wagons would leave from the statue of Jan van Riebeeck in Cape Town and follow the routes of the Trekkers, finally arriving in Pretoria on the Day of the Vow some four months later.[21]

Roos recalls that 'The trek of 1938 was planned on a very modest scale, and no one could foresee the tremendous surge of enthusiasm which would sweep the country and turn this unostentatious, symbolic journey into the triumphal pilgrimage of a whole nation' (1950: 37), which is illustrated by the response of some 20,000 Afrikaners who gathered at

---

20 Afrikaanse Taal en Kultuur Vereeniging (Afrikaans language and Cultural Association). See Grundlingh and Sapire's analysis of the significance of this recently urbanised group being at the centre of this commemoration (1989: 21–7), while tracing how this festival changed in meaning between 1938 and 1988.

21 I have based my comments on the responses to the Trek from Cape Town to Natal or Pretoria on Roos (1950), Moodie (1975: 175–96) and Grundlingh and Sapire (1989).

the first stop in Goodwood (Grundlingh and Sapire, 1989: 20). Roos's use of the term 'pilgrimage' suggests how this festival had shifted in meaning from being a spectacle to something more symbolic.

He noted that every night each town provided a concert party of 'community singing, games and folk dances' and 'the reenactment of little-known or almost forgotten incidents of local history, so that the Trek itself assumed the character of a kaleidoscopic review of the country's history in vivid form' (Roos, 1950: 40). People responded to this festival by drawing on a long-established embodied repertoire of Afrikaner folk songs, dances, stories and images, and then aligned these with this specific moment of history to define a communal culture. Grundlingh and Sapire suggest that 'drawing on romantic versions of the Great Trek, a vibrant Voortrekker culture, personalized yet participatory and instantly recognizable, evolved; men wore Voortrekker beards, women wore Voortrekker dresses and "Voortrekkerkappies" [bonnets], and infants were given Voortrekker names' (1989: 25). By re-enacting the historic period, and so physically embodying it, the participants internalised the narratives and memories being invoked and performed themselves as an 'imagined community', a 'volk'. This phenomenon of local repertoire meeting a particular national historic narrative was expanded to encompass the whole country as nightly radio broadcasts covered the local enactments and newspapers devoted a thousand words daily to cover the Trek and local responses to it. The Post Office responded to the unexpected public response and issued a series of commemorative stamps, thus creating a literal material marker of this event as a souvenir.[22] This national engagement with these local performances of memory created a broader sense of a 'shared' experience, memories and repertoire, which in turn form the basis for an imagined community.

These enactments and memories were based on a nostalgic version of a heroic, spiritual and mystical past; this is ironic, given the fact that most participants were engaging with these memories within industrialised urban contexts in which these very things were being challenged, which perhaps explains the strength of response to this event.

Although not conceived of as a pageant, this celebration is similar in its staging and performance of particular aspects of history. Ironically, the local enactments may have both enlarged and undermined the overall narrative, as local histories interacted with the more formal

---

22 Stewart articulates how miniaturisation may be an expression of longing and an attempt to contain and relativise a large object or event in relation to oneself (1993: 37–65). She explores how stamps facilitate 'the replacement of the narrative of history with the narrative of the individual subject – the collector' (1993: 156).

narrative in unexpected ways, as Leslie Witz charts in his extended
analysis of the later but comparable 1952 Jan van Riebeeck Tercentenary
Festival Fair (2003).

The commemorative journey culminated in the wagons arriving at
the Hill of the Monument, where 'an enthusiastic crowd of a hundred
and fifty thousand people in Voortrekker costume' (Roos, 1950: 40) welcomed the other half of the Trek and participated in the festivities which
began on Tuesday 13 December and culminated on Friday 16 December
with the laying of the foundation stone by the granddaughters of three
of the leaders of the Great Trek in 1838, witnessed by some 200,000
people (Grundlingh and Sapire, 1989: 20). The Youth Movement completed the dramatic staging of this event as they formed 'a river of fire',
created by Voortrekker scouts holding torches that were lit in relay from
Cape Town to Monument Hill in Pretoria, described as 'symbolic of the
spread of civilization from the Cape to the far north' (Board of Control
of the Voortrekker Monument, 1954: 68). Images of the fire brand as a
symbol of enlightenment and civilisation persisted in the iconography,
particularly in the Ossewabrandwag (Brigade of Ox-wagon Sentinels,
Bloomberg, 1990: 161), formed in response to this festival in 1939,[23]
whose name highlights the import of these signifiers in the Afrikaner
nationalist movement.

This event was important because it brought together various local
cultural performance repertoires, including popular songs and dances,
with a focused historical narrative and specific symbols that clearly
represented the foundational myth of the Afrikaner nation. I now turn
to analyse the role of various aspects of this commemorative festival in
embodying a particular formulation of Afrikaner nationalism.[24]

I begin with actress Anna Neethling-Pohl,[25] who was central to this
event: as an actress of renown she participated as a key figure in the

23 The OB was 'a para-military, ultra-Nationalist mass movement formed in 1939'
    (Bloomberg, 1990: 161-7). 'In 1941 the Christian-Nationalists split into two camps:
    the Nazi-style Ossewa Brandwag (OB) and the NP' (*ibid.*, xxv), but 'reintegrated
    into the NP following the election victory of the NP in 1948 (*ibid.*, 181-2). The
    OB reinterpreted 'the sacred saga' of Slagtersnek, the Great Trek and Blood River
    as acts of rebellion rather than acts of redemptive suffering, with Majuba as the
    central episode of 'the People's history' (Moodie, 1975: 223-4), and were profoundly
    involved in defining apartheid policy from the 1950s. See also Vatcher (1965).
24 For this analysis I draw on material sourced at the Voortrtekker Monument and
    Heritage Foundation in March 2011: photos, programmes and play-scripts, in
    particular the *Sentrale Voortrekker Eeufees 1838-1938* programme, as well as
    Neethling-Pohl's notes of the period (1974).
25 In 1952 she was the co-organiser of the van Riebeeck celebrations in Cape Town, and
    the 1988 Commemorative festival of the Great Trek in Pretoria. She was instrumental
    in the formation of the Cape Afrikaans Theatrical Society, the Volksteater (Peoples'
    Theatre) in Pretoria and the National Theatre Organisation.

historic re-enactments of the key moments of history selected for the event; she was also a central figure in the staging of N.P. van Wyk Louw's play *Die Dieper Reg* at the festival. It has been argued that the Nazi rallies became prototypes for the many historically inspired folk festivals in South Africa, such as the Voortrekker Centenary of 1938 (McClintock, 1993: 69; van Wyk, 1996), and this is not an extreme view given the number of influential South Africans who had travelled and studied in Germany at this time, many of whom were positively influenced by the emerging National-Socialist ideas.[26] Indeed, Neethling-Pohl had travelled to Europe in 1938, where she had witnessed at least one Nazi festival in Berlin, although she allows only one paragraph for its description in her memoir *Dankbaar die Uwe* (1974), where she expresses her fascination with the effect of 'the wave upon wave of burning torches marching by' (1974: 109), these torches are used to similar effect in the Voortrekker Centenary celebrations. It is thus worth considering the dramaturgies that characterised these events, while keeping in mind the influences of the 1910 Pageant of Union, and traditions of folk festivals and carnival.[27]

An important aspect of staging a public event is defining the space: the Nazis designed buildings and stadiums that could accommodate hundreds of thousands of people, and thus evoked a sense of permanence and security, while inspiring awe (Sinclair, 1938: 571). Albert Speer's 'cathedral of light' created the sense of endless walls of light at the Nuremberg rally.[28] As these rallies occurred at a time of economic and social insecurity, the Reich quickly established traditions that suggested stability and predictability. These included a predictable order of events and symbols, including an 'elaborate use of flags, manuals of arms, a sham battle, marching and rousing short speeches, singing and impressive ritual' (Mayo, 1978: 575),[29] with the swastika, an ancient mystical symbol, omnipresent. Each rally had a specific theme, which was highlighted in the congressional oratory (*ibid.*, 571–4). All of this

---

26 On influences, and significant divergences between Afrikaner and Nazi conceptualisations of the volk/nation, see Vatcher (1965: 58–73), Bloomberg (1990: 149–50), Moodie, (1975: 161, 164), Loubser (1987: 47–50).

27 It is worth noting that in South African history the term 'festival' occurs more often than pageant (www.sahistory.org.za/origins-language-culture-and-identity), despite the clear influence of the pageant; this may be due to the occasion's cultural links with Britain. See Witz (2003: 106) on the debate regarding the conceptualisation of the 1952 van Riebeeck Festival in a pageant format, given the dominant carnival atmosphere, which evoked different kinds of public engagement.

28 Speer (1970: 59–61).

29 See Sinclair on the significance of the invocation of the 'blood flag', so named because it was said to bear the blood of its bearer, who fell in the unsuccessful *putsch* of 9 November 1923 (1938: 572).

dramaturgy was designed to evoke a strong sense of the might of the party and the nation.

The role of the audience in such rallies is important. Mayo argues that political rallies ideally keep the role of the audience to a minimum, relying on 'appropriate stimulation from selected charismatic actors' to 'guide the rally play', until it 'develops into the practice of civil religion, i.e. state worship' (1978: 26). For example, at the 1936 Nuremberg rally the mass of people were uniformly dressed and arranged in regimented rank and file, to suggest the ideal 'community', where each individual knew their place, while 'a mystical sense of the greatness of the Third Reich was created in the minds of the participants', via the stagecraft and Hitler's orations (*ibid.*, 25). This is vividly illustrated in Leni Riefenstahl's film *Triumph of the Will* (1935). The dramatic power of 'sacred symbols and semi-religious ceremonies' is evidenced in Hitler's claim that the thousands of people assembled 'did not feel themselves participating in a political demonstration but rather "under the spell of a deep prayer"' (cited in Sinclair, 1938: 583).

There are obvious points of comparison with the 1938 Voortrekker festival, insofar as it was also held during a period of economic and social instability, it established traditions and produced clear symbols and a shared historical narrative for the imagined Afrikaner 'volk'. It is important to note, though, that this festival was not part of the state apparatus, as at this time the organisers were drawn from cultural bodies and they avoided any overt references to politics. It is also important to remember that the narrative and central images were drawn from the late nineteenth century and not created for this event.

As noted, the festival began with the meeting of the ox-wagons in Pretoria. However, between this symbolic event and the climax of the festival with the re-enactment of the Vow and the laying of the corner-stone, various cultural events took place that attached a predetermined historical narrative, with specific symbols, to the cultural repertoire to define the narrative of the emergent nation.

The first of these was the screening of the film *Die bou van 'n nasie* (They built a nation) for children before evening worship on Tuesday, Wednesday and Thursday evenings. It repeated the stories told through the tableaux and performed on the Trek through South Africa, and which were re-enacted at the festival on Thursday morning. The scenes included 'Uys receiving the Bible from the English in Grahamstown', 'Retief being sworn in as governor of the Voortrekkers', 'The trek over the Drakensberg', 'the view over the Blyde', 'the signing of the tract [with Dingaan]', 'the heroic deed of Marthinus Oosthuizen' and 'the crowning of Panda' (Sentrale Voortrekker Eufees, 1938: 17). These

definitive moments that represented Voortrekker history were enacted
for the nation en route, re-enacted at the festival, and communicated to
the next generation through film. Some of these images are specific to
Voortrekker history, particularly those related to the struggle with the
terrain, and others reiterate images from the Union pageant, particularly
Uys receiving the Bible and the dramatisation of divine backing, and the
struggle for and subjection of 'a wild and empty land'. This particular
foundational myth is both significant and highly contested. For decades
South African history books asserted that reconnaissance expeditions in
1834 and 1835 reported that Natal south of the Thukela and the central
highveld on either side of the Vaal River were fertile and largely unin-
habited, much of the interior having been unsettled by the ravages of the
Mfecane[30] (or *Difaqane* in SeSotho). The truth of these reports – many
of them from missionaries – has long been a source of debate among
historians, but recent research indicates that the so-called 'depopula-
tion theory' is unreliable (SAHO, Great Trek, 4; see also Richner, 2005;
Shillington, 2011).[31]

Through these tableaux key moments of history that embodied
central images of the foundational definitions of the Afrikaner nation
were formulated and communicated in accessible ways; they were
made continuous with the present through the cultural activities performed alongside the public addresses and performances – the choirs
and orchestras, various military displays by the army, air force, special
service battalions and the Military College – as well as at weddings and
christenings.

Apart from the Ceremony of the Vow on 16 December, one of the
most significant performance events was the staging of N.P. van Wyk
Louw's 30–minute play *Die Dieper Reg* (Deeper Right), which was
commissioned and written for this event (Neethling-Pohl, 1974: 112),
published by Nasionale Pers in July, preceding the festival in an effort to
evoke interest and engagement with the issues (*ibid.*, 114). The play was
staged on Thursday evening, before the main events of the festival on the
16th. It was also staged in the Pretoria city hall, where Neethling-Pohl
states they performed it five times in one evening to full houses (*ibid.*,
117).

30 *Mfecane* is IsiZulu for 'the crushing', *Difaqane* is Sesotho for 'forced scattering or
   migration', in the 1820s as a result of the political and military upheaval caused by
   the migration of the Nguni people in the eastern region that marked the rise of the
   rule of Shaka over the AmaZulu.
31 This myth was propagated beyond Afrikaner history to all white South Africans; see
   Meena Khorana's analysis of how this idea continued to be disseminated through
   children's fiction during apartheid (1988: 53).

It is described as a play 'about the ordeals of a nation',[32] and is set in the Hall of Eternal Justice, where everyone finally comes to stand trial for their deeds. The Accuser is described as being not a devil-figure, but as a powerful and arrogant Spirit who claims his own right and denies the worth of the Voortrekkers' deeds, demanding that the Trekkers be handed over to him for destruction. The Trekkers express their sufferings, but also demand justice, both because of their suffering, and their faith in and awareness of the value of their blood ('hul bloedsbesef se waarde'), especially given that they were enacting the perceived will of God. In the end the Voice of Justice assures everyone that the powerful and simple deeds of the Trekkers, including their establishing themselves as a nation and subduing the land, is God's will and thus they will prevail. He explains that righteousness is complicated and deeds are simple, but that righteousness is not something perpetually above people or this world, but that it is forever renewed by motivation, deeds and the will of people. Finally the Trekkers acknowledge the worthlessness of their rights in comparison to the completeness of God's righteousness, and two choirs end by singing praise to God, who is above and beyond all, and yet is also evident in the works of men. This play drew on the oral, choral and liturgical repertoires that dominated Afrikaner culture and were thus familiar to the audience. The form also reinforced the way in which the play links the struggles of the Afrikaner people, and their overcoming of these challenges, to the divine ordination of the nation.

This play repeats many of the symbols and rhetoric of Dr D.F. Malan's speech at the Blood River/Ncome site in December 1938. Malan pinpointed the battleground of Blood River as the 'sacred soil' where 'the future of South Africa as a civilized Christian country and the continued existence of the responsible authority of the white race was decided' (in van Jaarsveld, 1979: 71). He then drew a parallel between this battleground and the contemporary labour dispensation – 'if there is no salvation', he declared, 'the downfall of South Africa as a white man's country' would be sealed.

This and other speeches outline the key narratives of Afrikaner nationalism that form part of the performance repertoires that defined the nation. These speeches were read at stops along the road, at the festival and published in the *Gedenkboek van die Ossewaens op die Pad van Suid-Afrika, Eeufees: 1938–1939* (The Commemorative Book of the Ox-Wagon Route in South Africa, Centenary: 1938–1939). The

---

32 The references, translations and summary are my own, taken from the second printed edition of 1942; the first was published in 1938.

meanings of the key symbols are not left ambiguous or unclear. For example, Dr J.D. Kestel's foreword explains that the ox-wagons symbolised 'freedom' for the Voortrekkers and everything they sacrificed for it: their work, struggle and suffering; they also symbolised God's accompanying the Trekkers (ATKV, 1938: 1–2). Mrs Steyn, speaking as the 'spiritual mother of her nation . . . to the mothers of our nation', insisted that this symbolic trek was a gift from God to reveal to the nation the suffering and struggle that is the road to South Africa; to 'recall the nation from wandering in darkness back to the light' so that 'the forces that threaten to overwhelm us may be overcome through faith and unity' (ibid., 4). The poem by the national poet J.D. du Toit (Totius), 'Die trek van die Boerewaens', compares the caravans of North and Central Africa, carrying gold, ivory and precious jewels, to the wagon trains of the Trekkers, who carried the 'Holy Book as their leader and the word as their redeemer, and the qualities of the people as the treasure into greater Africa' (ibid., 6). The book is illustrated with images of beacons of light, and a vast open land, unoccupied, ready to be 'civilised'. The rhetoric and iconography are clear. Similar images and narrations of history are used in the substantial Gedenkboek: Voortrekker-Eeufees 1838–1938 (Commemorative Book), which highlights the place of Blood River as the 'birth-place of Afrikanerdom' (1939: 54–6), the place of 'ons Moedertaal' (our mother tongue, 63–7), and the place of Calvinism in the definition of Afrikaner ideology and identity construction (68–72). Thus both visually and verbally the iconography of a God-ordained struggle for freedom is clearly established in and through this event.

The Festival began and ended with 'Huisgodsdiens' (home worship) every day, thus emphasising the idea that the nation was ordained by God, and placing Christian-Nationalism at its centre. This is most evident in the Day of the Vow programme, where the morning religious service was followed by a Memorial service and the formal laying of the foundation stone, with the Vow at the very heart of this event. Thompson describes this event as an 'outpouring of nostalgia' (Thompson, 1985: 184–6), because of the degree to which it harks back to all that is feared to have been lost: the rural life, freedom, self-determination. These services were preceded by a dawn procession of women and children to the site of the Monument, where they sang hymns. This solemn procession was an enactment of their place in this community – present, active participants, but subject to patriarchal direction. The programme highlights the centrality of religion, particularly the role God is perceived to have played in the ordination of the nation, as evidenced by their victory at the Battle of Blood River. The commemoration also physically illustrated how men, women and children from all classes and backgrounds should take their place and perform their roles in the nation.

The various aspects of this festival bear out Grundlingh and Sapire's argument that this staging of Afrikaner mythology bears all the hallmarks of 'populist movements': it constructed a rhetoric of 'struggle', 'survival' and 'salvation'; it is moralistic rather than programmatic in content and deliberately deconstructed class. It also suggested that everyone could be involved in shaping the future from an idealised past, insofar as it was overtly separate from the centres of political and economic power (1989: 27). It suggests the place of nostalgia in this event, as the average Afrikaner did not feel represented in official political discourses at this time, and was increasingly faced with new economic and social challenges, including increased urbanisation. It is easy to see the appeal of this retreat into the myth of a glorious past, represented in epic terms while myopically concentrating on details of everyday life. These representations suggest nostalgic longing and desire rather than any attempt to realistically or critically represent this historical event. Ironically then, nostalgia was a defining aspect of Afrikaner nationalism which within a decade would become the dominant political ideology for the whole South African nation.

This festival was part of a wider cultural movement, as can be seen in Uys Krige's *Magdalena Retief* winning first prize of £50 from the Krugersdorp Municipal Association for Drama and Opera for the best drama written about the Great Trek in the same year. Plays focusing on this historical period were being actively solicited in South Africa; for example, Gerryts's *Na Vyftig Jaar* (After fifty years, 1937); in Krige's foreword he also acknowledges his indebtedness to Gustav Preller's *Piet Retief* and other works.[33]

Thus rhetoric and performance create an interaction between history, myth and memory to make the past continuous with the present. As the participants enacted this historic moment and their place in the nation in the present, so particular Afrikaner nationalist values were formulated and embodied in and through performance. This in turn created new embodied memories and a sense of belonging for those involved in this festival.

---

33 For an analysis of Preller's role in formulating a romantic vision of the Afrikaner nation through language and literature, see van Jaarsveld (1964: 78–87) and Hofmeyr (1987).

Inauguration of the Monument: 16 December 1949

The actual building and inauguration of the Monument in Pretoria were delayed by the Second World War, and it was finally opened in 1949. In the interim, the more explicit formulation of Afrikaner nationalism progressed, albeit not coherently, in the period leading up to the 1948 election victory (Posel, 1995).

There was much debate about South Africa's allegiances during the Second World War: Hertzog's motion for neutrality was lost to Smuts, who wanted to support the Allies (Moodie, 1975: 192–3). However, after the war, Afrikaner leaders shifted their focus from international to more internal issues. Their concerns are most clearly seen in a continuation of the various *volskongresse* organised by the FAK. In 1934 the focus had been the poor white question; in 1939 it was economic policy and Christian-National education, and mother-tongue education in 1943. In 1944 the focus was on racial policy. Dubow argues that this conference played a vital part in introducing the concept and term 'apartheid' to the Afrikaner nationalist movement as a whole (1992: 216). It passed resolutions that recommended specific economic, social and political policies regarding African, coloured and Indian South Africans that went beyond mere physical segregation, citing Holy Scripture and scientific knowledge to support these policies.[34] Later there was much debate on the justifications for apartheid, ranging from the religious[35] to the scientific. However, it is noteworthy that owing to the strong neo-Calvinist focus of Afrikaner nationalism, it tended to draw on tradition and experience more than on the scientific discourses that had dominated European thought until after 1945. These 'experiences' are part of the early Afrikaner Romantic conceptualisation of themselves as God's 'Chosen people', with 'the Great Trek, the triumph over the Zulu

34 Dubow argues that 'Christian-Nationalism was never a static doctrinal creed providing a convenient blue-print for apartheid. Rather, it acted as a self-referential discourse . . . which could be, and was constantly reinterpreted in the light of political realities' (1992: 217, ff). See also Bloomberg on the role of the journal *Koers in die Krisis* in these debates (1990: 105–7), and Loubser, on the evolution of the theological thought in the context of various European ideological debates (Calvinism, Kuyper, Nazism) (1987: 35–50).

35 See Dubow's (1992: 217–24) analysis of the roles of Afrikaner theologian and poet J.D. du Toit, Dutch theologian and statesman Abraham Kuyper (1837–1920), German Romantic J.G Herder (1744–1803) and political philosopher J.G. Fichte (1762–1814), although aspects of the way these men defined nationalism sat uneasily with the neo-Calvinist insistence on God as the ultimate sovereign ruler.

army at Blood River and the heroic resistance to British imperialism in the first and second Boer wars' (*ibid.*, 224) as the core symbols of this history.[36]

Thompson traces similarities between the events surrounding the 1949 inauguration of the Voortrekker Monument and the earlier 1938 festival: in 1949 15 riders on horseback followed the routes of the ox-wagons of 1938 from 15 starting points, and celebrations were held in more than 400 places (1985: 187). The same mobilisation of a specific Afrikaans cultural repertoire was evident: with boys and girls in Voortrekker movement uniforms and adults in Voortrekker costumes, doing traditional dances while singing Afrikaner folk songs, performing the repertoire of culturally embodied memory.

The programme is very similar to that of 1938, running from Tuesday 13 to Friday 16 December, with similar performance and cultural events.[37] Again it included films, various military demonstrations and choirs, and morning and evening services. Additions included exhibitions of Voortrekker and Kruger memorabilia, and a flag-raising ceremony every morning, which visually exemplified the radical change that had occurred in the position of Afrikaner nationalists since 1938, when they were a minority splinter group to the right of the ruling United Party. The Nationalists won the general election of May 1948 with a bare majority of five seats and gained political power in South Africa. This was celebrated each day of the festival in the flag-raising ceremony, which symbolised the position of power now occupied by Afrikaner nationalists. The historical presentations broadened from focusing solely on moments from the Voortrekker history to a history which encompassed events related to the nation as a whole: they began with 'Retief's journey to Dingaan', and then moved to 'The 1880s', 'The rough period, 1901' (during the Anglo-Boer War, but significantly not overtly referring to it as such), 'Union, 1910' and 'The heroes, 1949'. These titles are taken from Adéle Jooste's *Deur Stryd tot Oorwinning* (From struggle to victory), and the pieces were performed by the Volksteater in Pretoria on the eve of the inauguration of the Monument. This performance presented a clear linear narrative of what was to become the official version of South African history in a way not dissimilar to the way that the key

36 Giliomee (1995: 197–8) challenges this historical formulation of Afrikanerdom, particularly the claim to be God's chosen people, in the second half of the twentieth century.

37 For an account of these I draw on the Inauguration Committee's Official Programme and Commemorative Book (1949) and the *Historical Record of the Opening of the Monument* (1949), as well as the collection of Cecile de Ridder's photos and recollections of the 1949 and 1952 commemorations collated by Richard Searle (ca. 1998).

historic moments were identified by the TRC posters, which also identified key moments in South Africa's post-apartheid history.

Once again, on the Day of the Vow in 1949 there was a dawn procession, but this time with a military brass band, preceded by a cannon
salute and followed by the ceremonial raising of the flag. The memorial
service and inaugural ceremony were also preceded by a pilgrimage
to Monument Hill at noon, where 'in the presence of a quarter of a
million people assembled at the foot of the monument' the Prime
Minister signalled the six boys and six girls dressed in Voortrekker
costume to open the massive bronze doors of the Monument, which
Roos describes as 'a temple' (1950: 40), an apt description given both
its design and the quasi-religious rituals performed on this day. Hymns
were sung and speeches made by Judge Newton Thompson, and
political leaders Dr. D.F. Malan and General J.C. Smuts. These and
other speeches given during the festival were published in Afrikaans
and English in the *Historical Record of the Opening of the Voortrekker
Monument* (1949).

At this moment the focus shifts from performance to archive, as the
symbolic historic narrative of the nation is literally concretised in granite
in the Monument itself. This is clear when one compares the 1938 programme to that of 1949 – the earlier festival was very focused on cultural
activities and demonstrated aspects of Kuyper's romantic understanding of Calvinist history. Kuyper's views allowed Afrikaners to articulate
an heroic mythology of themselves as God's 'chosen people',[38] with a
volksnationalisme that resonates with German Romantic views of the
organic link between culture and nationhood, that the individual is best
expressed through the collective and that nations are subject to divine
historical destiny (Dubow, 1992: 199–220). This form of nationalism
overtly defined the key symbols of the nation: the ox-wagon, culture as
a brand of enlightenment, and the place of each individual in it. History
was used to justify the Afrikaner's racial superiority, authority and claim
to the land. The 1949 festival was political, officially sanctioned, as evidenced by the degree to which government officials involved themselves
in the proceedings (Governor-General E.G. Jansen was chairman as
of the organising committee) and in the flag-raising ceremonies and
singing of the national anthem. This festival demonstrated that the

---

38 Kuyper's views were complex and contradictory, and can be used to argue opposing
     views; Bloomberg (1990: 9) describes his work as 'equivocal' and concludes that 'his
     teaching was an intricate balance of paradoxes'. Nevertheless, his work was central
     to the *Gereformeerde Kerk* in the Transvaal and in debates around the formulation
     of apartheid ideology. For extended analysis of Kuyper, see Moodie, 1975, Loubser,
     1987 and Bloomberg, 1990.

ideologies formulated in 1938 had been realised and that the Afrikaner nation was now a politically functional reality.

The Monument itself is an art deco-style square granite building with a length and width of 40.5 m and height of 41 m.[39] It stands in a commanding position on top of a hill just outside Pretoria and visible from the Parliament buildings. It is surrounded by a stone wall upon which is carved a 64–wagon laager (wagon fort). In front of the entrance is a sculpture of a Voortrekker mother and child, which references the centrality of family to Afrikaner ideology, while foregrounding the qualities of endurance, moral strength and idealised motherhood, while acknowledging the strength and suffering of all Afrikaners in the struggle for South Africa. Large sculptures of Voortrekker leaders stand on three of the Monument's external corners,[40] and on the fourth is an 'unknown' leader, perhaps a nod to those who would follow. All of these suggest power, permanence and dependability.

Inside there is an upper and lower hall which are open to the domed roof, which is designed so that at exactly noon on 16 December a beam of sunlight penetrates a small aperture in the dome and illuminates a marble cenotaph in the lower hall, inscribed with the final words of the national anthem: 'Ons vir jou Suid-Afrika' (We for thee South Africa). Along the walls of the lower hall are tapestries that illustrate key moments of history or aspects of Voortrekker life, which emphasise unity and the overcoming of obstacles. In the basement there is now an exhibition of migration routes of various Southern African people and a museum depicting aspects of Voortrekker life.

The Hall of Heroes, in the upper hall, is lined with 27 panels of marble bas-relief friezes depicting key moments of Voortrekker history from 1835 to 1854.[41] They are striking and have a clear didactic purpose, as can be seen from their inclusion in the inaugural essays and South African history textbooks up to the 1970s and 1980s.[42]

Some 24 speeches were made, and were later published in the inauguration programme. In his speech D.F. Malan, then Prime Minister of

---

39 See Crampton (2001) on the Voortrekkers as 'pioneers of civilization' and of a Christian nation. The architecture was contentious, as Moerdijk's original designs provoked controversy because of the significant influence of Egyptian architecture and symbolism. Moerdijk wanted to refer to Africa's greatness through referencing ancient Egyptian constructions in the inauguration of the Voortrekker Monument, *Official Opening Programme*, 1949. See Irma Vermeulen (1999). See also Sabine Marschall (2001). Masonic iconography is also evidenced in the friezes; see Merrington (1999: 261, footnote 10).

40 Piet Retief, Andries Pretorius and Hendrik Potgieter.

41 For a virtual tour, see www.visitpretoria.co.za/History/voortrekker-monument.

42 Thompson (1985: 276, footnote 119) lists some examples.

South Africa reiterated the connection between the historical narrative, which he traces in profoundly religious terms, and the present generation of South Africans (*Historical Record*, 1949: 13–25). The Official Programme[43] included text of the hymns that would be sung and articles on the meaning of key aspects of the Monument. For example, Gerard Moerdijk explained the architecture (43–55), Dirk Mostert reiterated the significance of the ox-wagons and torches of 1938 (56–64), and both 1938 and 1949 commemorative stamps are on sale and explicated (65–71). The Great Trek (106–15) and the beliefs of the Trekkers (116–24) were again outlined.

Dr Muller's argument on why the Trek was the Afrikaner's only option (86–98) is significant insofar as it is foregrounds the discourse of struggle and survival, while recasting the Afrikaner relationship with the British more positively, which suggests how strongly whites needed to unite, given the growing pressure from black, coloured and Indian South Africans for political representation in Parliament.[44] These ideas are reinforced in the photographs from the Monument friezes that accompany the article, including Mayor Thompson of Grahamstown giving Uys the Bible on behalf of the 1820 settlers to wish them well on their journey, and the arrival of Andries Pretorius in the Cape Colony, where he is greeted respectfully. This speech ends by reiterating the Afrikaners' basis for their faith in nationhood.

Maria Hugo's speech on the role of women in the Great Trek and the building of a nation is substantially longer than any other article and offers an insight into the clearly defined role for women in the conception of the nation.[45] Like the preceding published speeches, this one is accompanied by two illustrations from the panels. One depicts women crossing the Drakensberg saying, 'Better bare-foot than back to slavery' (74), and the other is entitled 'Keeping the laager in order while the men fought' (75), which suggests clearly the roles and narratives ascribed to women both during the Trek and in 1949. Hugo expands to outline the role of women in marriage, as wives and mothers, and she emphasises the need to uphold 'blankedom' (the white race) (72–85). These same ideas are reiterated in the processions and tableaux performed during

---

43 Here, and in future reference citing only pages in this chapter, I refer to the
    Inwyding van die Voortrekkermonument - Amptelike program en gedenkboek,
    1949.
44 See Lovell (1956: 325–7) on this period in the development of Afrikaner nationalism
    and apartheid.
45 For an analysis of how this concept of domesticity developed see Marijke du Toit
    (2003), McClintock (1993) and van der Watt (1996). Elsie Cloete (1992) explores
    how these ideas were promoted through the apartheid era to the present.

the festival, which illustrates how this event demonstrated nationalist ideology in accessible ways for the target audience.

Eloff and Ziervogel's speech on 'The Bantu tribes north of the Orange' (99–105) is an early attempt at writing black South African history. It suggests that the various peoples of South Africa originated from only one or two larger nations, which is important in justifying the imminent legislation on separate development. It emphasised that the Boers always tried to negotiate fairly for land, rather than seizing it (105). Once again accompanying photos of friezes exemplify these ideas: the Boers negotiating with Moroko (100) and Retief sitting at a table with Dingaan signing a grant (102). This historic version of Retief's meeting with Dingaan is contested, particularly regarding the grant, which many historians believe never existed. They also suggest that perhaps the Trekkers' entry onto the land being requested before it was granted was perceived as disrespectful of Zulu authority and a sign of the nature of their future relationship (see Maphalala, cited in Golan, 1991: 116). Nevertheless, both this speech and the use of the friezes illustrate how memories and histories are created and performed to justify contemporary hegemonies.

Grundlingh and Sapire remind us that 'the Great Trek was never to enjoy the same lustre nor serve as inspirational a symbol as it did in 1938' but that 'it continued, albeit in modified terms to justify Afrikaner predominance' (1989: 29), as is evident in the *1952 Jan van Riebeeck Tercentenary Festival Fair*. In 1952 the National Party renamed it the Day of the Vow, which shifted the focus from Dingaan to the Vow, and elevated it to a 'sabbath' in law by legally imposing sabbath restrictions on the activities of the day (organised sport was forbidden and places of public entertainment were closed, etc.) (Ehlers, 2003: 11). This could be seen as an attempt to fix Afrikaner nationalism more centrally into the broader outlines of South African history (van Jaarsveld, 1979: 48–9), but as Ciraj Rasool and Leslie Witz have suggested, this festival highlighted how this public and national history of South Africa was both constructed and contested (1993; see also Witz, 2003).

Towards a 'new' South Africa

Apartheid mythology and symbolism had been 'desegregated and reinvented in the service of nation building' in South Africa from 1938 to the present (Ehlers, 2003). In response to international boycotts, sanctions and protest action against increasing apartheid legislation in the 1960s and 1970s, the discourse shifted away from the victory of nationalism and the focus on unity to engage with issues of isolation. As the struggle against apartheid gained momentum in the 1970s and 1980s many Afrikaners adjusted their approach to ethnic exclusivity and the dominance of the divine mission in their discourse, to accommodate English and moderate black support to secure a stable future for South Africa (Norval, 1996; Ehlers, 2003: 7–12). Some Afrikaner intellectuals accordingly appealed for the inclusion of non-Afrikaners in the Day of the Covenant celebrations, and van Jaarsveld in particular began to re-examine the history of the Great Trek more critically (Grundlingh and Sapire, 1989: 21; Liebenberg, 1988: 18). However, the significance of the particular formulation of this historical moment is evident in the response to van Jaarsveld when he disseminated his revised reading of Blood River at the 1979 Unisa Conference on 'Problems in the interpretation of history with possible reference to examples from South African history such as the Battle of Blood River', when he was tarred and feathered by the AWB[46] (*Rapport*, 1//4/1979: 5). And so the debate over this history continued to rage through the 1980s, and three options were posited regarding the commemoration of this day: the most conservative was an insistence that this remain an exclusively Christian Afrikaans festival; the moderate position was for more inclusion and the incorporation of English and black South Africans; the third view was expressed by people such as John Mavuzo of Inkatha and David Curry of the Coloured Labour Party, who called for its abolition on the grounds of its exclusivity (van Jaarsveld, 1979: 74–80).

However, the broad public response to the 1988 commemorative festival suggests that by this time the Trek and Blood River were no longer important symbols for mainstream Afrikaners. As Grundlingh and Sapire show, the main festival was marked by 'an extremely tepid interest in participating in rallies and Great Trek celebrations, and a faint sense of embarrassment hung over the singularly lacklustre official ceremonies' (1989: 34). The programme highlights social events over symbolic enactments: a road run, cycle tour, sing-along, skateboard competition, mass tree planting, with religious services in the Monument only on 11 and 16 December (*Groot Trek Herdenkensfees 1838–1988 – Commemorative book and programme*). This official event contrasted strikingly with the 'vigour and enthusiasm of the AV' (Afrikaner-Volkswag) commemorations, which Grundlingh and Sapire

---

46   Afrikaner Weerstandsbeweging (Afrikaner Resistance Movement) is a far right
     separatist political and former paramilitary organisation.

note emphasised 'family, self-reliance, "traditional values" and . . . folksy sentimentalism', along 'with a curious meld of imagery and political styles, ranging from the iconography of national socialism and fascism, the techniques of mass charismatic religious observation, rousing anti-capitalist oratory' (1989: 36). Thus for some the Monument and the historical moment still represented a particular formulation of identity and politico-cultural identity, which was why it was so significant during the period of transition in South Africa.

It was against this background that the new South African govern-ment, headed by Nelson Mandela, had to decide how best to engage with these symbols of Afrikaner nationalism after 1994. In an article in *Die Beeld* Wally Serote, head of the ANC's cultural division, was interviewed about what was envisioned for specifically Afrikaans 'monuments, sculptures, the flag, the national anthem and the Afrikaans language' (de Bruin, 15/3/1994: 11). His response suggests that this moment was less about dismantling Afrikaans culture, than about representing more people in public commemorations, and redressing the imbalances of the past, both in terms of memories and symbols. This interview is important when analysing how the ANC has gone about this process of redressing past injustices to date.

Annie Coombes has traced these debates in relation to the specific symbolic complexities of the Voortrekker Monument and its enduring power to galvanise far-right Afrikaner nationalism, as evidenced in the mobilisations around the Monument in the run-up to the first demo-cratic elections in 1994 and the ongoing struggle over representations of South African history from an Afrikaner perspective (2004: 19–34). However, she argues for the potential of 'translation', where, in Spivak's terms, the '"reader as translator" is capable of performing a reading against the grain and between the lines even in circumstances where the raw material reproduces a set of fairly standard colonial tropes', while acknowledging that 'acts of translation depend on a certain familiarity with the text' (*ibid.*, 25). Debates in the press, academic conferences such as the 'Myths, Monuments, Museums' conference at the University of the Witwatersrand in July 1992, and various publications in and beyond South Africa[47] have demonstrated how contested different approaches to 'translating' or rereading monuments are in South Africa. However, here I focus specifically on the way political figures have engaged with the Monument publicly.

On 16 December 1995 President Mandela declared that the Day of the Vow was to be renamed National Reconciliation Day. He was aware that

---

47 See, for example, Karp *et al.* in *Museum Frictions* (2006).

reconciliation is influenced to a large extent by engaging with the past without being determined by it. He knew that this day could not simply be discarded, as ironically it represented the struggle for liberation for both Afrikaners and those in South Africa who had fought against them: while Afrikaners remember their victory over the Zulus in 1938, the ANC remember it as the day Umkhonto weSizwe, the armed wing of the ANC, was established in 1961. Thus in his address Mandela said:

> The Government of National Unity chose this day precisely because the past had made December 16 a living symbol of bitter division. Valour was measured by the number of enemies killed and the quantity of blood that swelled the rivers and flowed in the streets.
>
> Today we no longer vow our mutual destruction but solemnly acknowledge our inter-dependence as free and equal citizens of our common Motherland. Today we re-affirm our solemn constitutional compact to live together on the basis of equality and mutual respect. Reconciliation, however, does not mean forgetting or trying to bury the pain of conflict. Two terrible defects weakened the foundations of the modern South African state that were laid in the great upheaval at the beginning of the Century. Firstly, it rested on the treacherous swamps of racism and inequality. The second defect was the suppression of truth.
>
> Now, at the end of the Century, South Africans have the real chance to strike out along a glorious path. The democratic foundations of our society have been laid. We must use our collective strengths to carry on building the nation and improving its quality of life. (Mandela, 16/12/95)

In this speech Mandela suggests that only by moving beyond a vision of the past as defined by violent encounters between its peoples can South Africans forge a future that belongs to everyone. This vision of the future is predicated on South Africans seeing their identities and histories not as separate, perpetually in conflict, but as 'inter-dependent', with all 'as free and equal citizens' of a 'common Motherland'. Mandela acknowledges that moving beyond the past cannot be predicated on forgetting; indeed he highlights that 'the suppression of truth' has been one of the 'two terrible defects' that 'weakened the foundation' of South Africa. So, instead of suppressing history, the ANC engaged in a symbolic act of redefining it by renaming the day of commemoration. Mandela implies that opening up the past involves re-reading it, in this case, renaming an historical event that represented violent conflict by evoking the notion of reconciliation. It also entails hearing stories that have been marginalised or ignored, and including these memories in the official narratives of South Africa's history. It is not coincidental, then, that on this same day the TRC held its first meeting at the residence of Archbishop Desmond Tutu in Cape Town.

This was among the first in a number of strategic performative acts by the government set to renegotiate the meaning of South Africa's past in the name of reconciliation so as to facilitate a stable future for South Africa. The next significant symbolic act occurred in 1996, when Tokyo Sexwale, the then charismatic premier of Gauteng province, visited the Voortrekker Monument and performatively reinterpreted its history through a series of photos and an article in the *Sunday Times* entitled 'Tokyo's Groot Trek' (15 December 1996). Andrew Unsworth reports that Sexwale, like most black South Africans, 'had never set foot inside' this Monument 'built to honour the white man', with the implication that he is now free not only to engage with, but also to challenge, the formulation of the South African nation as defined by the Voortrekker Monument.

The *Sunday Times* article suggests that while this structure has been perceived as 'a massive monument to conquest, Sexwale approaches it from the other end of history, with all the grace of the final victor'. This grace is evidenced in his acknowledgement that 'The Afrikaner are the only group of whites on the continent who chose to call themselves by its name'. This compliment allayed any fears that Afrikaners might have had of ongoing ANC government hostility, while simultaneously under-lining the point that now official representatives of the government had the power to 're-read' and interpret history.

Coombes notes that in an article for the *Saturday Star* in 1992 Joe Louw 'had pointed out the absences and distortions of the Monument's representations of the past', here 'Sexwale reads it [the past] against the grain' (2004: 35). For example, the article opens with Sexwale comment-ing on the laager of 64 wagons on the wall surrounding the Monument by saying: 'Now I understand the laager mentality, but I am glad there is a gateway, or the whole Afrikaner nation would have been trapped inside'. Later, when the assegais on the gate are pointed out to him and described as symbolising 'the power of Dingane who sought to block the path of civilisation', Sexwale again retranslates the image and denies this interpretation, saying, 'It was precisely the assegai at its height that turned the tide, Umkonto weSizwe, the Spear of the Nation, opened up the gates of civilization', and he insisted on being photographed opening these gates. In this moment Sexwale brings two memories together and reinterprets them for South Africa, suggesting that the black liberation struggle has freed all South Africans from past myths and the histories that have divided the country. Sexwale continues his reinterpretation of history when faced with the friezes of Retief, the battles of Bloukrans and Blood River (see cover image) by acknowledging the resilience of the Afrikaners, and then highlighting that their mistake was 'trekking off alone . . . They should have taken all the oppressed with them, then our history would have been different'. Through these performative acts Sexwale reclaims the Monument for the wider South African population, saying that 'it belongs to all of us'. The article ends with the statement: 'We don't demolish history. . . . After all, time has a way of sorting out history.' In this media performance Sexwale, on behalf of the ANC, reassures the Afrikaans community that they are not going to be annihilated, but are valued for their commitment to the continent and for their resilience, while subtly insisting on a critical re-evaluation and interpretation of the history outlined in the Monument. Again one sees how the powerful combination of narrative, visual image and symbolic performance is used to communicate the important ANC narrative of reconciliation, while re-reading the past in terms of current cultural and political hegemonies.

Both the Voortrekker Monument and the Ncome River Memorial remain contested sites of memory and history.[48] An example of this is evident in the interpretation of the memories by Mossie van den Berg in *Geloftesterk jou stand* (Stand firmly by your vow), which was broadcast as a series in 1997, rebroadcast in 1998 on Radio Pretoria by public demand, and published in 1999. Hannes van der Merwe translated and adapted the 120-page text into a 19-page version published as *The Blood River Vow by the Voortrekkers of 1838 and what it really means to us in modern times*, which is still available at the Monument in Afrikaans, English, French and German. It draws on scripture to reaffirm the Afrikaners' God-ordained right to be the beacons of light and civilisation in South Africa, fighting both the threat of African Barbarism (van den Berg, 1999: 8) and British Imperialism (*ibid.*, 7). It states that any

> Christian believing Boer-Afrikaners who commit reconciliation with the communistic atheistic overpower are like light which became reconciled with undefeated darkness. You become a darkness joiner. You commit treason against the Vow. Your reconciliation kiss on 16 December unmistakably reflects **Judas Iscariot's** kiss in Gethsemane. You over-**kiss** yourself with your own backbonelessness. Ultimately you choke therein all kissing. (emphasis in original, 1999: 10)

48 See Stephen Coan's (2003: 7) experience of visiting the Blood/Ncome River split-site (the Blood River heritage site represents the Afrikaner memory and the Ncome Museum, situated across the Ncome river, represents Zulu culture and perspective on this event). Golan (1991) and Schönfeldt-Aultman (2006) analyse the way this historic event is being used to define the Zulu past and contemporary identity.

It is thus clear why the Afrikaner Eenheidsbeweging (AEB, Unity Movement) objected to Mandela's involvement in a ceremony at the Voortrekker Monument to honour Anglo-Boer War scout commander Danie Theron, particularly given Mandela's statement that his 'own shaping as a freedom fighter has been deeply influenced by Afrikaner freedom fighters' (Momberg, 2002: 1). To compare the black liberation struggle to that of the Afrikaner is to undo the theological underpinnings of the myths of Afrikaner nationalism. Ironically, the narratives of the two ideologies are most powerfully played out in performative events – of reaffirming the vow, or embracing a former enemy's hero as one's own.

The struggle to control the meaning of the Monument has not been limited to historical narratives, but has extended to challenging the formation of gender identity. Maria Hugo outlined the Calvinist puritan position on the ideal Afrikaner woman defined by her modesty, hospitality, hard-working nature, the degree to which she educates her children in the traditions of her nation, determined in the face of opposition, a loving, loyal and virtuous wife and mother (1949: 72–85). Coombes traces how the 1995 photo-shoot for *Loslyf*, an Afrikaans-language porn magazine, provided a 'critique of the most oppressive version of Afrikaner ethnic absolutism'. Dina, the 'Indigenous Flower of the Month', is photographed semi-naked against the Monument and thus challenges the implicitly sexual content and violence entailed in the Voortekkers' taming of nature, conquering the 'savages' and establishing a state (2004: 39–43).[49] This tension between gender formulation, ideology and the Monument persists: in 2004 a pan-African fashion show was held at the Monument. What emerged from this event was a perceived lack of direction regarding the Monument and its representation of history in relation to the present. Bongani Madonda asks 'Africa? Which Africa? Perhaps the fashion splash will point the way' (*Sunday Times*, 2004: 5). The controversy continued in 2005 when *Egoli*[50] actress Michelle Pienaar was photographed from above, lying on the Monument's cenotaph, for the ATKV magazine *Taalgenoot*. Some Afrikaners were outraged, suggesting that this sacred space had been profaned by a coloured woman. The complexity of remembering and

49 Andrew Worsdale (dir.) does something similar in his film *Shot Down* (1987), see Hees (1996: 15–16). See Cloete (1992) and Marschall (2004) for similar analyses of the National Women's Memorial near Bloemfontein.

50 *Egoli: Place of Gold* was a bilingual (English and Afrikaans) South African soap opera which first aired on MNet on 6 April 1992 and became South African television's first daily soap opera on 3/12/1999; it ended its run on 31/3/2010. Michelle Pienaar played Audrey Gillian (Seasons 10–17).

forgetting is highlighted by the ATKV's managing director, Dr Frits Kok's comment that unfortunately the young team used the cenotaph as a background for the photograph 'without being aware of the symbolic values that some people attach to it' (Williamson, 2005: front page); which suggests that while the Monument remains ideologically significant, for many its meaning is unclear, or has changed. What these examples show is that although the Monument no longer has such an exclusive or narrow cultural and historical function, it is still significant as a site of memory (see Grundlingh, 2001).

The current blurred conceptualisation of this Monument is fitting as the past recedes and public attention shifts to the post-apartheid context. And so I turn to analyse the Freedom Park memorial, which is officially twinned with the Voortrekker Monument,[51] as an important example of how the ANC has attempted to address the 'imbalances' of memory and to redefine national symbolism in the post-apartheid period.

Post-apartheid museums: remembering the struggle?

At the start of this chapter I suggested that the degree to which memories and monuments could be deconstructed and redefined was determined to a large extent by the strength of the original narrative, the degree to which the public are aware of, and willing to engage critically with, its formulation and interact dialogically with alternative memories and identities.

It is clear that from its inception in the nineteenth century the construction of Afrikaner identity was predicated on a foundational narrative, and resultant mythology, of struggle. Sabine Marschall's extensive research on post-apartheid monuments and sites of memory suggest uncomfortable parallels between the Afrikaner foundation myth and the 'Struggle for Liberation' myth upon which the new South Africa is being constructed.[52] Although these two myths developed in marked contrast to one another, the similarities between them are disconcerting, particularly in the associated themes which include 'the struggle for freedom; struggle against oppression; notions of deprivation and suffering; the

---

51 The access road connecting these 'two previously divided South African institutions' is being heralded as symbolic of reconciliation, see www.southafrica.info/about/ history/freedom-voortrekker.htm, accessed 18/1/12.
52 See Marschall (2004, 2006a, 2006b).

humble desire for land and a modest home; the enemy's maltreatment of the innocent; relentless resistance; and heroic, male-dominated leadership', all of which are represented by means of elaborate monuments, memorials and bronze statues on pedestals, which imitate colonial and apartheid-era commemorative practices (Marschall, 2006a: 148–9). This is significant, given Caroline Neale's (1985) analysis of post-colonial African historians' focusing on contesting European colonial assertions on African culture and its apparent lack of history. She argues that the drive to counter these assertions was so great that African historians failed to interrogate sufficiently the assumptions underpinning notions of 'civilisation' and progress in colonial histories; and thus many post-independent African histories mirror old colonial paradigms. I want to explore the extent to which the Freedom Park memorial challenges Neale's assertions.

I also ask to what extent these sites of memory have the potential to act as liminal spaces in which people can actively engage with diverse memories and explore the potential for embracing identities beyond the formalised historical narratives that characterise nation-building.

Freedom Park

Museums and monuments constructed in post-apartheid South Africa are implicitly part of the ANC's reconciliation project. Included in the TRC's final recommendations was the suggestion that the government should provide monuments and memorials as symbolic forms of reparation, alongside financial reparations to victims and their families.

In 1999 Nelson Mandela formulated the dream that was to be realised in Freedom Park: 'The day should not be far off, when we shall have a people's shrine, a freedom park, where we shall honour with all the dignity they deserve, those who endured pain so we should experience the joy of freedom'. The project was proposed in 1998, and then allocated 52 hectares on Salvokop, opposite the Voortrekker Monument, in 2000, and it opened in December 2007. This memorial's significance to the state is evident in its budget, which is in excess of R700 million. Baines suggests that it is 'one of the most ambitious legacy heritage projects championed by the Mbeki presidency. Upon completion, it is likely to eclipse Klapperkop [a South African Defence Force commemorative site] not only as a tourist site but as *the* premier heritage site in Tshwane' (2009: 2).

That the park was created in line with the ANC's policy of reconciliation and nation building is clear from the publicity pamphlet, which states that Freedom Park 'stands as a beacon to guide all South Africans on the route of hope and patriotism to a proudly united nation'. It speaks of a 'shared heritage', which is linked to 'the South African tale in the voice of the South African people'. The CEO, Dr Mongane Wally Serote, says that the park stands 'as a permanent reminder for us, now and for future generations, that South Africans did take a step forward to put closure to the past while not forgetting it'.[53] This statement places memory at the centre of the conceptualisation of the 'new' South Africa, but it is a conceptualisation that suggests active dialogue between past and future.

I begin by reading this site against established modes of commemorating national memories. Marschall has suggested that many new monuments and museums in South Africa have replicated colonial and apartheid forms of memory in their statues, and in the architectural form and content of museums and memorial sites, which she clearly illustrates with reference to the Hector Pieterson[54] Museum (2006). Freedom Park is an exception in design and conception. For the most part this memorial is constructed outdoors and designed so that one must read the stories and heritage through black South African symbolic and historical frames, which may not be familiar to many visitors. I turn to specific areas of the site to analyse the significance of this conceptualisation of memory for contemporary South Africa.

The park is divided into two areas: Isivivane and S'kumbuto (see maps, Figures 3.1 and 3.2). The concept of Isivivane is derived from the word 'viva', which means 'to come together in a group'.This 'coming together' involves bringing the past, as represented by the spirits of the dead, and the present together. So the first function of this part of the park is defined as being a symbolic 'resting place for the spirits of those who died in the struggles for humanity and freedom'. This burial area, called the Lesaka, consists of 11 boulders which have been placed in a circle: nine from a place of historical significance from each of the provinces of South Africa,[55] a boulder representing the national government and a boulder representing the international community.

53 www.freedompark.co.za, The Park, Overview, accessed 23/11/11, see also Serote, 2006.
54 The spelling is sometimes rendered 'Petersen', the original family name was apparently 'Pitso' before they attempted to pass for 'coloured.' See www.southafrica. info/ess_info/sa_glance/history/ hector-pieterson.htm, accessed 23/11/11.
55 www.freedompark.co.za, go to The Park, Overview of elements, Isivivane, Boulders for further details.

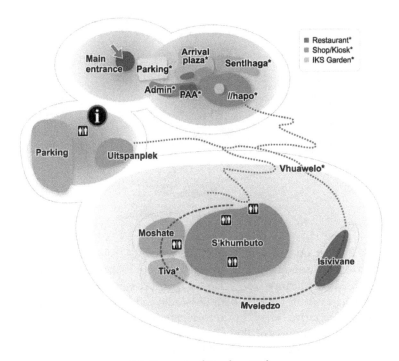

3.1 Elements of Freedom Park.

The boulders themselves are large and suggest permanence, endurance and an implicit claim to the land. This latter claim is important given the Trekkers' claim that they took 'an empty land'. It is significant in another way too; Duncan Brown suggests that the question many first world peoples ask is: 'If this is your land, where are your stories?' (2006: 12). This implies that 'belonging' is intimately tied up with how the 'land' is experienced, represented and narrated by those living on it. This approach to 'belonging', with all the debates around 'indigeneity', has serious implications for claims to land, citizenship and other rights discourses (see Mamdani, 2001).

Each boulder represents a specific story of conflict and struggle in a significant place in the relevant province. For example, the boulder from KwaZulu–Natal, which came from emaKhosini, also known as the 'Valley of Kings', is linked to the history of the Zulus with the Voortrekkers, British settlers and surrounding peoples. King Dingane clashed with the Voortrekkers in this area and the final battle of the Anglo-Zulu War (1879) was fought at Ulundi, south of emaKhosini. This is also where King Shaka defeated clans, such as the Ndwandwes.

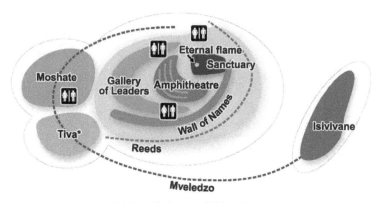

3.2 Detailed map of S'khumbuto.

This boulder thus represents the Zulu people as 'belonging' to South Africa, while simultaneously inviting others to broaden their sense of South African history. This symbolic spatial commemoration uses the boulders to claim the land both physically and through the liberation struggle narrative, which in turn validates the claim to the land. One potential implication of this formulation of memory is that it places those who do not know or share these stories of 'struggle' as 'not belonging', as outsiders.

The alignment of this memorial site with specific black South African cultures and narratives is evident in the various symbols and performances central to it. For example, the burial ground is shrouded in mist, and there is a body of water at both entrances for washing one's hands, for baptism and for drinking, which emphasises cleansing and purity. We are told that 'religious leaders from various faiths imbued Isivivane with a deep sense of spirituality by performing a number of sacred ceremonies and rituals that lay to rest the spirits of our fallen heroes and heroines' (www.freedompark.co.za).[56] These ceremonies and rituals highlight a worldview in which the living and the ancestors are coterminous, which implies a complex relationship between the past and present. People who do not belong to this culture and do not understand the rituals or symbolic meanings are invited to learn, and in so doing take their place alongside the African majority that define the nation.

---

56 Motsei criticises the 'spiritual and physical architects of Freedom Park' for not heeding advice to have women, who are traditionally viewed as the ones who serve as 'a bridge between the unborn, the living and the dead', lead the cleansing ceremony held on 27 April 2004 (2007: 76–7).

Another important symbolic signifier of Isivivane is the semi-circular seating area of the Lekgotla, a space where important matters are discussed in many black cultures of Southern Africa in the presence of ancestors. The area has been constructed around one of the nine Umlahlankosi trees (Buffalo thorn, Eng.), which were also donated by the nine provinces. In many Southern African communities this tree is used in burial rites; the name itself means 'that which buries the chief'. A twig from the tree is still used to attract and carry the spirit of the deceased from the place of death to the new resting place. The Freedom Park website suggests that

> at Isivivane, the individual, group and community pain stemming from past conflicts is transferred into a shared national strength and gives credence to the call for symbolic reparations from the Truth and Reconciliation Commission. This monument further expresses the interconnectedness of all South Africans, irrespective of age or background, and reminds us of the strong ties that bind us together as a nation.[57]

The Isivivane overtly engages with the TRC's symbolic reparations programme insofar as it creates a symbolic space and cultural ritual whereby the spirits of disappeared loved ones are perceived to have been laid to rest. It also offers a space in which survivors and those who were complicit in their disappearance can mourn. This is an example of Sanders's 'mournful commemoration': an 'official and public acknowledgement' of the loss of individuals and of what apartheid withheld from them, including mourning the dead of others' (2007: 49).

S'kumbuto is the park's memorial space and includes the Wall of Names, an amphitheatre 'used for national events and celebrations', a flame which 'burns continuously to remind us of the names we will never know', a gallery of leaders, and a sanctuary where one is invited to think about the history of the country, or on those who have passed on. The concept of S'khumbuto is drawn from siSwati nomenclature and signifies a place of remembrance for those who have died and also a place for invoking their assistance in current and future affairs. Other spaces include Moshate, which functions as an exhibition space; Mveledzo is a spiral path on which visitors are invited to take a contemplative journey; and Uitspanplek is a space with a view at which to rest. Future plans for the site include Tiva, the creation of a large body of water symbolising peace, and the construction of the Pan African

---

57 www.freedompark.co.za/cms/index.php?option=com_content&view=article&id=24 &Itemid=30, accessed 23/11/11.

archives. Once again the narrative is clearly inscribed into the space in terms of symbolic resonance rather than overt narrative.

Paradoxically, while the park invites all South Africans to seek their inter-connectedness, the very particular symbolic and spiritual references used throughout this park insist that all do so from a specifically black South African perspective. There is no reference, for example, to other peoples like the Koisan, Cape coloured or Indian struggles for political representation in the exhibitions, although there was some acknowledgement of the history of slavery at the Cape in a speech given by a representative of the Freedom Park Trust in Cape Town in 2004. However, even this was formulated in broad terms with wider reference to the African slave trade and the Voortrekkers, rather than acknowledging the place of this people-specific experience in South African history (Freedom Park Trust, 2004: 7).[58]

The long and somewhat bitter debate over whether or not SADF soldiers would be included in the Wall of Names, given that names of Cubans who supported the struggle would be included, underlines how rocky the road to reconciliation has been in practice. After names were submitted, and summarily rejected, Afriforum, a watchdog for the protection of minority group rights, together with its sister organisation, the trade union Solidarity, took up the issue on behalf of some of the SADF veterans and an emotional debate ensued. Some veterans erected an alternative memorial at the access road to Salvokop on 16 January 2007 (Baines, 2009: 4–5). In February 2007 Freedom Park hosted a workshop 'to discuss the role, mandate and history of the SADF during the Apartheid era'. The CEO said that 'The Truth and Reconciliation Commission guiding principles are central to this engagement to raising consciousness about the past and understand our responsibility to the present' (Freedom Park Trust, 2007). According to TRC representative Advocate D. Ntsebeza, the prerequisite of 'full disclosure' was not met by the SADF during the proceedings and thus had not met the terms for reconciliation. The particular interpretations of TRC terms and history have defined this debate: as the workshop's chairperson acknowledged, 'both sides have been stated and [. . .] the view of our own history differs significantly'. Dr Serote added that 'What stands out from today's workshop is the matter of perception. Wrong perceptions stem from miscommunication' (press release, 8/2/07), and he called for all to dialogue as widely as possible for reconciliation and further nation

58 See my final chapter for an analysis of the particular significance of the slave narrative for the current renegotiation of coloured identity in the Western Cape.

building. As far back as his Reconciliation Day speech of 2005, Serote has insisted that

> reconciliation can only truly take place when people lay down their arms, join hands and work towards a brighter future as one. . . . both black and white have been hurt beyond repair. It is a sad truth that no amount of words can heal those atrocities; but we can alleviate the impact on future generations. . . . If the past isn't recognised no reconciliation will happen and our children will live the same fate of their forefathers. It will be a case of history repeating itself. (Serote, 2005: 4)

This statement implies that full disclosure regarding the past is the only basis for reconciliation. It does not entertain the possibility that disclosure may not facilitate healing, nor does it acknowledge the terms in which history, reconciliation, or indeed this memorial site are being defined in contemporary South Africa (see Baines, 2009: 7).

The public's response, as evidenced in Baines's poll (24 November 2010–1 January 2010)[59] suggest how contested this issue was as 50% believed that the SADF should be included on the Freedom Park S'khumbuto Wall; 22.22% responded that they should be excluded from the wall, and 22.22% thought that they should be remembered through the End Conscription Campaign (ECC); 5.56% believed that they should be given a separate section on the S'khumbuto Wall. The announcement that a privately funded memorial wall of remembrance for fallen SADF soldiers would be erected at the Voortrekker Monument further increased the tension between these two sites of memory. These debates and the memorial sites themselves foreground particular memories of struggle, while setting specific terms for 'belonging' in the post-apartheid context.

Freedom Park is a fascinating and provocative memorial site insofar as it does not rewrite South Africa's history by directly countering colonial formulations of black South Africa as 'backward', 'barbaric' and lacking in progress, or by appropriating colonial forms. Rather it is constructed against these discourses, consciously mobilising oral history, as opposed to texts, and adopting black South African symbolic references to embody the key concepts of the park, including the terms for reconciliation, as defined by the TRC. However, the symbolism is paradoxical because it invokes a particular formulation of pre-colonial Africa that evokes an idyllic rural landscape and particular formulations of the 'traditional'.[60] The potential paradox of this formulation lies in

---

59 www.archivalplatform.org/polls/entry/december_poll/ accessed 23/09/11.
60 Dr Serote explores these complexities and paradoxes in his novel *Revelations* (2010).

how these idyllic rural and spiritual formulations sit alongside urban
modernity and a very layered, 'rhizomatic' sense of identity in contemporary South Africa (Krueger, 2010); and the same idylls embodied in
the Voortrekker Monument.

The need for 'mournful commemoration' in South Africa, whereby
healing and reconciliation are defined by the interaction of former
opponents, is clear. However, the real challenge lies in finding a safe
space in which to facilitate such encounters. Memorials and museums
need to include spaces where visitors can meet, share experiences and
narratives, as Ciraj Rassool has argued in the context of analysing how
'intangible methodologies' may be deployed in the reinterpretation of
memory in South Africa in community museums such as the District
Six Museum in Cape Town and Freedom Park (2007, 2008; Bharucha,
2007). One of the limitations of more traditional monuments and
museums is their apparent formality, and our sense that we must be
hushed, as if in a sacred space. It is here that one must consider the
specific role of theatre to facilitate the opening up of spaces, both formal
and civic, and to provoke engagement with controversial memories and
identities. A good example of this kind of facilitation is Cape Town's
annual *Infecting the City Festival*.[61]

If memory, with its attendant narrations and symbols, is central to
the construction of individual, communal and national identity, then
exploring alternative and plural memories is crucial for the creation of
an inclusive society. Memories, histories, memorials and monuments
are not fixed, but flexible and open to interpretation and translation. It is
important that we engage with what is included and what is disavowed,
and that we remain aware of the narratives, symbols and how they are
being performed, and thus how they encode and communicate embodied cultural repertoires that will be passed on to the next generation.

---

61 See Moyo (2011).

4

Performing the African Renaissance and the 'rainbow nation'

'Gloria est consequenda'. (Mbeki, 1996)

Thus far I have explored how South Africa has renegotiated its geopolitical spaces, defined in its social relations, political imperatives, value systems and the way it has constituted its authority via the TRC. I have also examined how it has negotiated its psychosocial construction of nation by foregrounding particular memories through the TRC and physicalised these narratives in commemorative spaces, specifically in Freedom Park. I now turn to explore Thabo Mbeki's South African Renaissance project, which is significant insofar as it shifted South African engagement with local memories and histories to situating the country within the context and discourses of the African continent. It also exemplifies how Mbeki sought to engage critically with particular colonial constructions of Africans to redefine the post-apartheid 'rainbow nation' in positive terms. I analyse to what extent this project includes nostalgic longing in its re-envisioning of the nation, and how this compares with how other African countries have approached rewriting their history in the post-colonial context (Neale, 1985).

This project takes its starting point from Desmond Tutu's formulation of post-apartheid South Africa as the 'rainbow nation', a formulation that was elaborated on by Mandela (1995) in his first month of office. It was adopted by the ANC as the political symbol of unity for a country of diverse and divided people. This chapter explores how Mbeki used the South Africa–Mali project, within the context of the New Partnership for Africa's Development (NEPAD), to extend the imagined boundaries of the nation and thus communicate a more positive identity for contemporary South Africans. I focus particularly on how this was achieved through the *Timbuktu Script and Scholarship* exhibition that toured South Africa between August and December 2008. I then compare this cultural exhibition with how South Africa was conceptualised and performed in the opening ceremony of the 2010 World Football Cup. Throughout, I will be evaluating the degree to which these formulations of South African identity and history have been adopted generally and consider to what effect.

The chapter ends by looking at a parallel South Africa-Mali collaboration in the theatrical production of the *Tall Horse*, analysing how this theatrical production compares with the African Renaissance project, as it also deconstructs racial stereotypes.

South Africa as a 'rainbow nation'

The TRC began the process of South Africa's renegotiating of the significance of its past by listening to formerly silenced voices and formulating the terms for reconciliation, forgiveness and national unity. As already discussed, symbolic reparations in the form of new cultural commemorations were intrinsic to this process, insofar as they translated specific aspects of the oral histories into concrete embodiments of the redefined narrative of South African history, while also addressing ongoing issues of loss and the need for mourning.

From the election of the transitional Government of National Unity, multiculturalism was advocated in South Africa, which was celebrated as being 'one nation, many cultures'. 'Unity in diversity' formed the basis for building the 'rainbow nation' for the new South Africa (African National Congress Information Services, 22 April 1996), and it continues to be central to the ANC, as evidenced by its preparations for the centenary celebrations on 8 January 2012: the centenary document is entitled 'Unity in diversity'.[1]

---

1 It traces the legacy of this concept back to Pixley Isaka Seme's call for the 'native' peoples of South Africa to leave behind their differences and unite with the Congress in 1911 ('Native Union', *Imvo Zabantsundu*, 24 October 1911, quoted in ANC, Centenary document, 2011).

However, in his 1996 speech to the Constitutional assembly, in which he formulated his sense of his own South African identity, Mbeki began with the statement, 'I am an African', and then continued thus:

> I owe my being to the Khoi and San whose desolated souls haunt the great expanses of the beautiful Cape . . . I am formed of the migrants who left Europe to find a new home on [sic] our native land. . . . In my veins courses the blood of the Cape Malay slaves who came from the East. . . . I am the grandchild of the warrior men and women that Hintsa and Sekhukune led, the patriots that Cetshwayo and Mphephu took to battle, the soldiers Moshoeshoe and Ngungunyane taught never to dishonour the cause of freedom . . . My mind and my knowledge of myself is [sic] formed by the victories we earned from Isandhlwana to Khartoum, as Ethiopians and as the Ashanti of Ghana, as the Berbers of the desert. . . . I am the grandchild who lays fresh flowers on the Boer graves at St. Helena . . . I come of those who were transported from India and China (Thabo Mbeki, 2001).[2]

In this definition Mbeki acknowledges the diverse peoples who have a history in this contested land: he begins with the Khoi and San, arguably people who have the greatest claim to be 'indigenous' to South Africa. He then refers to the 'migrants', who may have been from Europe or from other parts of the continent, and the 'Cape Malay slaves who came from the East', brought to South Africa by the 'migrants'. This formulation allows them a place in South Africa, while signalling that they are not 'indigenous' to the country. He then speaks of the Zulu, Xhosa and Sesotho people as 'warrior men and women', and compares them to peoples across Africa who 'earned . . . victories' or built empires, like the Ethiopians and the Ashanti of Ghana, suggesting that they have a strong claim to the land and a pan-African identity. However, these comparisons are made without any contextualisation or problematising of very diverse histories of empires, slavery and different kinds of subjugation.

It is worth noting that of all the historical memories of the Afrikaners, Mbeki chooses to reference the 'Boer's' in terms of their struggle with the British, and their being sent to the island of St Helena as prisoners

---

2 This speech echoes Langston Hughes, particularly his poem 'The Negro Speaks of Rivers' (1920, in *The Weary Blues*, 1926). In the conclusion of his statement as Deputy President at the opening of the debate in the National Assembly, on 'Reconciliation and Nation Building', National Assembly Cape Town, 29 May 1998, Thabo Mbeki referred to the 'rage among millions of people' who were frustrated by events that seemed to be moving the country away from its goals of unity and reconciliation. He then referenced an earlier quote he had made to 'the African-American poet, Langston Hughes, who asked, "what happens to a dream deferred?"' and Mbeki notes that 'his conclusion was that it explodes.' This reference suggests the importance of Hughes to Mbeki's conceptualisation of the African Renaissance.

during the South African War,[3] which offers an indirect comparison to the soldiers sent to Robben Island during their struggle for liberation. However, the image of grandchildren 'laying flowers on the graves' may also suggest that South Africans can now sympathise with the Boer past, but need no longer fear it. Their inclusion in this list suggests that all people can find a place in post-apartheid South Africa.

Alongside this litany of peoples, presented in an oral mode evocative of Nguni praise poetry, Mbeki associates the various peoples with particular landscapes. This association is significant when one understands that for many first world nations any claim to belonging in a land is profoundly linked with narrative and story-telling, encapsulated in the question, 'If this is your land, where are your stories?' (Brown, 2006: 1) With just a few mnemonic references Mbeki signals many stories, of peoples and their connection with this land, while reminding his audience of the narratives of loss, communicating a sense of compassion and potential greatness in general terms, without being particular, or contextualising these references and histories in any way. This illustrates how the government has approached reconciliation as an intrinsic aspect of its nation-building project, and how particular memories have been foregrounded to effect national unity. However, there is an uncomfortable sense that this inclusiveness is superficial, as there seems to be an implied hierarchy of 'Africanness' in this speech, with the suggestion that immigrants, particularly those from Europe, but also including those from India, Malaysia and China have the least claim to a place in South Africa, and 'can never quite become authentically African' (Chipkin, 2007: 101). Mtshali argues that this speech suggests 'that the limit of belonging to the democratic nation is not just a function of territorial and historic formation, but is fundamentally rooted in a transcendent notion of humanity contextualised by its struggle against colonialism' (2009: 12). Thus, while the speech may appear inclusive, the subtext may be suggesting that 'belonging' in South Africa is predicated by one's position relative to the struggle narrative in particular.

Any attempt to review the terms in which the nation is being defined is further complicated by the legacies of apartheid, which used ethnicity and culture to create a theoretical racial taxonomy whereby the human species was perceived as a series of separate stable, delimited entities, each with distinctive cultural and physical characteristics that were God-ordained. These characteristics were then ordered hierarchically on the basis of ethnic and cultural differences (Moodie, 1975: 265–6; Thompson, 1985). Legislation enforced and justified these cultural and

3 See Nathan (1999).

ethnically based separations, which were further supported through the construction of discrete histories, national monuments and museums, and popular tales. Jeppson argues that this in turn affected South Africa's approach to anthropology, whereby the Afrikaans tradition of 'Volkekunde' as a discipline 'was a deliberate development of the intellectual underpinnings of apartheid', and as such the term 'ethnos' underpinned the mythology of the 'volk' (nation) and its practice (1997: 68). Many social anthropologists consequently sought to distance themselves from the 'ethnos' theoretical approach to anthropology. This resulted in the concepts of 'ethnicity and 'culture' becoming tainted with racist associations, resulting in the avoidance of 'culture' as a term and concept. Jeppson argues that this resistance to engaging with this concept 'was reinforced and supported by black consciousness politics, by the mass democratic processes striving for national unity, and by a black nationalist position within South African anthropology that promoted the judging of research efforts on the basis of their 'contribution to a national identity' (ibid., 69,). This positioning has affected the way history, sociology, anthropology and archaeology have developed as subject areas, and has complicated attempts to recover and disentangle the terms 'ethnicity' and 'culture' from race discourse in South Africa. Perhaps this explains why the post-apartheid South African government has chosen to foreground 'national unity' rather than attempting to redefine the terms and implications of 'diversity'.

Nevertheless, as became evident in the earlier analysis of the aims of the TRC, the concept of *ubuntu*, translated as 'humanness', 'humaneness', with the sense of having basic respect and compassion for others,[4] has been central to redefining South Africa as a nation. This conception of common humanity allows for inclusion on the basis of behaviour rather than culture or race, and thus offers a strong model for redefining terms of inclusion in this historically divided country.

From his inauguration as President of South Africa on 14 June 1999 until after his second term of office ended on 24 September 2008 Mbeki worked to redefine South Africa in terms that countered negative colonial and apartheid formulations of black South Africans, while offering South Africa a sense of a 'past glory' and reconnecting the country with the African continent. Mbeki's desire to shift South Africa from focusing on its internal issues of struggle and reconciliation to reconnecting with a pan-African vision is embodied in his African Renaissance project.

4 See Ramose (2002) and Louw (2001).

The African Renaissance project

The idea of the African Renaissance has been mooted in South Africa since 1996, with Thabo Mbeki as a leading champion of the idea. Okumu (2002) traces the history, significance and strategies of this movement for the continent and notes that the definition of it cannot be reduced to a paragraph or a page. It is a complex notion, involving more than the kind of economic growth associated with the so-called Asian Renaissance. The African Renaissance includes in its definition 'the process of a country moving towards greater inclusion, health, opportunity, justice, freedom, fairness, forgiveness, and cultural expression', in other words 'jobs, justice and the elimination of poverty' (Okumu, 2002: 10–11, 13, 16).

The African Renaissance Institute (ARI) was founded at an inaugural meeting in Pretoria on 11 October 1999 and acts as the centre from which programmes and ideas related to the African Renaissance are formulated and implemented throughout Africa, although the ARI is situated in Gaborone, Botswana. If royal courts were the centres of study and cultural rebirth in the European context, Africa plans to utilise universities, churches and professional organisations such as legal societies, trade unions, youth and women's organisations to network and disseminate its ideas (*ibid.*, 18).

Although there is a continent-wide engagement with the idea of an African Renaissance, I focus here on Mbeki's particular approach to it in relation to South Africa. As Mbeki and others have argued, restructuring post-apartheid South Africa is a complex process, particularly because the post-1994 peace was the result of negotiations, rather than a military victory, and many would argue that the settlement was achieved through making significant compromises. Thus it was important that South Africa framed its transitional discourse in terms of looking positively to the future, while carefully negotiating and redefining its complex and bloody past. Two strategies were adopted, therefore, both of which I argue were performative in nature.

The first was the establishment of the TRC, to hear and engage with human rights abuses and establish the 'truth' about the past, a process which I have discussed in a previous chapter. However, parallel to this aim was the imperative to establish reconciliation between various historical antagonists (Asmal, 2000) and move the country forward socially, politically and, importantly, economically.

This is where Mbeki's particular approach to the African Renaissance is significant. It meant moving the focus from the problems and conflicts of the immediate past to conceptualising a more positive sense of history and identity for South Africans. In his speech to the Constitutional Assembly, analysed in part at the beginning of this chapter, Mbeki highlighted some of the darker aspects of South Africa's history, 'the beggars, the prostitutes, the street children, those who seek solace in substance abuse, those who steal to assuage hunger' as well as the taxi wars, the political violence of KwaZulu-Natal, rapists, and those whose behaviour 'results in the description of our country and people as barbaric' (2001).

Mbeki then shifted his focus to insist that [South Africans] 'refuse to accept that our Africanness shall be defined by our race, colour, gender or historical origins', rather, as a country there is a need 'to create for ourselves a glorious future, to remind ourselves of the Latin saying: *Gloria est consequenda* – Glory must be sought after!' (Mbeki, 2001: 12) This call defines the aim of this project, which was the means by which Mbeki hoped to revise South Africa's histories, archives and identity formulations. To this end, the Renaissance project went beyond redressing what is perceived as traditional issues of social, economic and judicial development in order to challenge and rewrite the ubiquitous colonial myths of Africans as savage barbarians, who lack a history.[5]

The centrality of these issues in Mbeki's thinking was evidenced in his speech to the United Nations University two years later, on 9 April 1998, in which he challenged 'the long-held dogma of African exceptionalism, according to which the colour black becomes a symbol of fear, evil and death', and he suggested that he wishes Africans would refocus on

> a glorious past of the re-emergence of homo sapiens on the continent. I speak of the African works of art in South Africa that are a thousand years old. I speak of the continuum of the fine arts that encompasses the varied artistic creations of the Nubians and the Egyptians, the Benin bronzes of Nigeria and the intricate sculptures of the Makonde of Tanzania and Mozambique. I speak of the centuries-old contributions of the evolution of religious thought made by the Christians of Ethiopia and the Muslims of Nigeria. (1998: 2)

This formulation has the same breadth of scope as Mbeki's earlier formulation of his identity as an African: all inclusive and contextually unspecific. I argue that restorative nostalgia is central to this project

---

5 Other African leaders who have preceded Mbeki in adopting this approach to history include Dr Namdi Azikwe, first president of Nigeria, who wrote of 'Renascent Africa', and Dr Kwame Nkrumah, first president of Ghana (see Okumu, 2002: 53–60). These appeals to a 'Myth of a Glorious Africa' have been strongly challenged by writers like Soyinka; see, for example, his play *Dance of the Forests* (1960).

insofar as it references a return to unspecified origins of various notable peoples and places in Africa in an attempt to create a transhistorical reconstruction of the lost home, drawing on oral culture, collective pictorial symbols while blurring time frames (Boym, 2001: 49). This blurring requires a conflation of memory, myth and history, and is possible because, as Pierre Nora has argued 'places of memory do not have referents in reality . . . they are their own referent: pure, self-referential signs' (cited in Greene, 1996: 118).

Mbeki's aims are clear: he wanted to challenge colonial and apartheid constructions of Africans as 'barbaric', while reconnecting South Africa with the conception of a glorious African past from which the country had been cut off culturally, politically and economically during the apartheid decades. This challenge may also indicate a political shift, as Mbeki turned from addressing internal matters to focus on South Africa's place on the continent as a whole. However, these initial references were too broad to provide a basis for an Afrocentric rewriting of South Africa, Mbeki needed a more specific focus for his historic revision.

This focus came later in 1998 when Mbeki specified Timbuktu[6] as the focus for his vision of a 'glorious past'. Thus the royal court of Timbuktu of the fifteenth and sixteenth centuries provided the narrative and symbols Mbeki sought insofar as it 'was as learned as its European counterparts'. He cites the Spanish traveller Leo Africanus, who reached the city in 1510, as having written:

> The rich king of Timbuktu . . . keeps a magnificent and well-furnished court . . . here are a great store of Doctors, judges, priests, and other learned men, that are bountifully maintained at the king's cost and charges. And hither are brought diverse manuscripts or written books out of Barbarie, which are sold for more money than any other merchandise. (Reader, 1997, cited in Mbeki 1998: 1)

These references to the sciences, arts and even contributions to religious thought by the Christians of Ethiopia and the Muslims of Nigeria are not arbitrary, but were chosen to challenge long-standing European formulations of black Africans as barbaric animals, such as, for example, Pliny's Dog King of Ethiopia.

Mbeki carefully insisted that the purpose of this project was 'to ensure the restoration not of empires but the other conditions in the 16th century described by Leo Africanus: of peace, stability, prosperity, and

---

6 Various spellings are used for Timbuktu; I have used this one throughout, unless quoting a source.

intellectual creativity' (1998: 3). This suggests Mbeki's care in the way that he proposed to use this history, and an awareness of the criticism levelled at other newly independent African leaders for the way they mobilised the histories of former African empires: 'the centralised, hierarchical polities of the past served as a useful form of indoctrination in obedience to present regimes' (Neale, 1985: 46). It is in Kasfir's sense that Mbeki mobilises this history: 'The most important political heritage of ancient empires is the unifying role of the myths they left behind' (1968: 18). Mbeki is very careful to assure his audience that he is not mobilising empire to structure political hierarchy, but rather he is trying to invoke a unifying myth to create a renewed pride in Africa's pre-colonial past in order to build a more positive sense of African identity, while increasing general confidence in South Africa's ability to manage its post-apartheid present and future.

Mbeki's reasons for investing in this project remained unchanged from the project's inception in 1998 to the launch of the Timbuktu Manuscript exhibition in 2006, as exemplified from a speech he made at a fundraising dinner in Tshwane on 1 October 2005, where he said:

> These manuscripts debunk the myth that the tradition in Africa was always and only an oral tradition. The manuscripts point to the significance of the written tradition – a tradition that long predates the arrival of European colonizers on the soil of Africa.
>
> Timbuktu represents very important dimensions of Africa's greatness and its contribution to the history of humanity. It is world renowned as a centre of trade and a centre of research and scholarship in the fields of science, mathematics, religion. Timbuktu produced and attracted artists, academics, politicians, religious scholars and poets. (Mbeki, 2006: 64)

Here the appeal to Africa's past as a 'civilised' one is argued in terms of the evidence of an advanced written culture, which challenges the predominant notion of Africa as having no written history, or culture, and thus no reliable or verifiable past. He also highlights the quantity and calibre of intellectual scholarship in this empire, as evidence in this exhibition, and the research generated by it.[7] Ironically, in some ways this counter-narrative reinforces the binaries between written and oral cultures rather than nuancing the relationship between these different ways of expressing culture. It also elevates the archive above the embodied repertoire.

---

7 See, for example, the documentary on UCT research, *The Ancient Astronomy of Timbuktu* (2009).

Timbuktu's colonial and post-colonial significance

The choice of Timbuktu as the focus of this project is important. Timbuktu has long been emblematic of a place so remote as to be almost mythical, and indeed many believe that it is not a real place. Joan Baxter, reporting for the BBC world news service, commented that 'The fabled city of Timbuktu is not a myth – it does indeed exist – in northern Mali, on the edge of the Sahara desert. These days, it pretty much lives up to its reputation as "'the end of the world" but once upon a time, it was the centre of important trade routes' (Baxter, 2002: 1).

Even in the twenty-first century Timbuktu is physically difficult to reach.[8] Apart from coffee-table books, with exotic portraits of people and images of the desert, information about it is not widely or easily available. The city's inaccessibility is important for its use in mythologising empire insofar as distance does not allow for easy verification of representation. Consider, for example, the place of Timbuktu in the European psyche of the nineteenth century: Tennyson's epic poetic fantasy *Timbuctoo*, for which he won the Chancellor's Medal at Cambridge University in 1829, echoes the sentiments that surrounded the 'discovery', conquest and remodelling of Timbuktu by Europeans in the modern period, including a profound sense of longing for a glorious past of adventure and wonder.[9] The poem itself refers to Timbuktu as a 'mystery of loveliness', but with a sense that

> . . . the time is well-nigh come
> When I must render up this glorious home
> To keen *Discovery*: soon yon brilliant towers
> Shall darken with the waving of her wand:
> Darken, and shrink and shiver into huts,
> Black specks amid a waste of dreary sand,

8 Kryza notes that while 'there is a sporadic air service to Timbuktu, visitors to the town at the dawn of the twenty-first century can reach it reliably only by camel, Land Rover, shallow draft riverboat or on foot' (2006: xiii).

9 Tennyson hated the poem, which he'd written under duress, and refused to read it at commencement. He also forbade its being published during his lifetime. He had no personal experience of Timbuktu and seems to have been influenced by A.G. Laing's last letters. The poem is available in full at http://pathguy.com/timbuc.htm, accessed 20/8/10. This excerpt is from Thomas Cooper Library, University of South Carolina Rare Books and Special Collections, www.sc.edu/library/spcoll/sccoll/africa/tenn. html, accessed 27/8/10

Low-built, mud-wall'd, barbarian settlements.
How chang'd this fair City! (Tennyson, *Timbuctoo*, lines 238–45)

It is worth pausing to trace both the construction of this 'mystery of loveliness' that was Timbuktu, and the effects of its 'keen Discovery' by colonials. I thus turn briefly to consider nineteenth-century European engagement with this city, following centuries of Islamic influence, before comparing Mbeki's engagement with Timbuktu in the context of late twentieth-century South Africa.

Timbuktu was possibly founded around 1100 by seasonal Tuareg nomads. Within a century it became a significant commercial nexus for the desert traders and peoples from sub-Saharan regions that were difficult to negotiate. By the thirteenth century word had reached the Mediterranean of Timbuktu's wealth, which was evidenced when the great Mandingo emperor of ancient Mali, Mansa Musa, crossed the Sahara on a pilgrimage to Mecca, stopping in Cairo en route in 1324 with a vast caravan of 60,000 men, including a retinue of 12,000 slaves dressed in brocade and silk. The European awareness of Timbuktu is evident in Abraham Cresques's[10] inclusion of the city 'Tenbuch' as the capital of the huge Malian empire in his famous Catalan Atlas for Charles V. Muslim travellers, most notably Ibn Battuta and Hasan al-Wazan, also called Leo Africanus, visited Timbuktu: Ibn Batuttah towards the end of his 29 years of travelling in 1353 (Mackintosh-Smith, 2002: 292–3), and Hasan al-Wazan or Leo Africanus in 1546, as a representative of Fez. Leo Africanus later published *The History and Description of Africa and the Notable Things Contained Therein* for the Renaissance Pope Leo X (Kryza, 2006: xiii–xvi). It is to this description of Timbuktu as a land of immense wealth, which prevailed for 300 years, to which Mbeki returns in the twenty-first century.

However, much occurred in Timbuktu between the time of its glory as an empire and the eighteenth century, when Europeans reached Timbuktu. From the late eighteenth century to the second half of the nineteenth century Europe was engaged in intense industrial and terri-torial expansion, which coincided with equally intense scientific inquiry. These developments and the rivalry between France and Britain for control of key areas in Africa sparked a race between explorers about who would reach and claim Timbuktu first.

In 1788 a group of titled Englishmen formed the African Association with the aim of finding Timbuktu and charting the Niger River. Mungo Park was the first of their sponsored explorers. He made two trips in

10 A cartographer based in Majorca.

search of the Niger River and Timbuktu (departing first in 1795 and then in 1805) and he is believed to have reached the port of Timbuktu on the Niger in 1806, but was forced to continue on down the river, where he is believed to have been murdered. In 1826 the Scotsman A.G. Laing became the first European to reach and enter Timbuktu, but he was disappointed by what he found (Kryza, 2006: 231–238). Facing local political unrest and suspected of spying, he discontinued his quest up the Niger and planned his return to Tripoli. However, Laing disappeared and in 1828 René-Auguste Caillié became the first French explorer to reach Timbuktu; he suggested that there was evidence that Laing had been murdered there.

On his return to France Caillié published his *Journal d'un voyage à Timbouctou et à Jenné dans l'Afrique Centrale* in three volumes (1829), reporting in detail on the city 'of whose population, civilization and trade with the Soudan such exaggerated notions have prevailed.' In 1895 Felix Dubois visited Timbuktu, exploring its history and environs, and wrote *Tombouctou la mytérieuse* (1897). Despite Caillié and Dubois's disappointment at what they found in Timbuktu, both the French and English governments desperately sought to sustain the general sense of Timbuktu as a compelling, exotic 'jewel in the crown' of colonial holdings, and thus worthy of their ongoing colonial endeavours in West Africa.[11]

When the French entered Timbuktu in 1893 they intended to make it the administrative centre for their new French West African territories. Its significance lay in its position between French-controlled Senegal and Algeria, which France intended to connect through a trade network. However, the Yukulor Empire, based in Segou, lay between the two territories, and opposed the connection. The French military retaliated by occupying Bamako in 1883, and the rest of Mali by 1886, thus making Mali the transitional region between Senegal and Algeria. Ironically after this, owing to this annexation and the shift of the French depots south and west of the city, Timbuktu was isolated from the major

---

11 The University of South Carolina's Africana book catalogue notes that the 'English translation of Caillie's account appeared with the imprint of two publishers better known for issuing fashionable novels' (www.sc.edu/library/spcoll/sccoll/africa/africa4.html), suggesting the significant influence of the wider media for the formation and dissemination of the conception of Timbuktu to the wider public. This is supported by the role Jules Verne's *Cinq semaines en ballon* (1863) played in the conceptions of western Africa and how these entered the imagination of a wide European public. Verne drew heavily on the writings and drawings of the explorers Barth and Caillié (see Prussin, 1986: 12-16). For a general survey of West Africa in French literature, see Roland Lebel's *L'Afrique Occidentale dans la Littérature Française depuis 1870* (1925).

trade routes, particularly after they changed from the traditional caravan routes to riverine and railroad routes.

Despite these shifts, Timbuktu's history and construction in the consciousness of the wider world was symbolically important to the French colonial endeavour, as a place of mystery, the 'African Eldorado'. However, its place in the colonial discourse was not simple because within the colonial construction of epistemological boundaries with regards to race and culture, Timbuktu embodied a particularly strong paradox. The French had systematically separated North Africa from sub-Saharan Africa, because of the former's perceived achievements that were used to differentiate race and culture hierarchically. However, here was a city that was presented as Islamic, but was clearly part of sub-Saharan, 'black' Africa.[12] Paul Rabinow maintains that the concept of the 'Islamic city' in North Africa was a by-product of the French ideas of the 'Cité Industrielle', first presented by Tony Garnier to the Ecole des Beaux-Arts in 1899 (Rabinow, 1989: 221). Garnier's particular innovation lay in his juxtaposing of architectures, 'relating older and modern sites', conceptions which Prost drew upon as chief city planner in Morocco (ibid., 224–5). This redesigning of cities of North and West Africa by the French had two functions: to maintain social Darwinist segregation, which justified labour policies, while simultaneously promoting tourism via the 'museumification of Moroccan culture', which was then applied to other parts of French Africa (ibid., 300), and publicised in France via the colonial expositions (Morton, 2000: 77–9).

Timbuktu had never been a coherently designed city, but was rather divided into 'quarters', which Miner suggests took their names from the mosques located in them (1965: 39), but such designations were inaccurate because not all the people were Muslim, and the areas were not inhabited according to ethnicity particularly. Nevertheless, the French began to restructure the city in terms of their conceptualisation of the 'Cite Industrielle', which was segregated on the basis of labour, while allowing the middle classes to mingle for economic reasons. It is possible that the French used Ibn Khaldûn's concepts of a 'proper city' to facilitate this restructuring, as it supported segregation and the illusion

---

12 Labelle Prussin's *Hatumere: Islamic Design of West Africa* (1986) reads Timbuktu as a fascinatingly complex place insofar as worldview is encoded in design. It contrasts Western European, Islamic and African approaches to architecture, their approaches to space and time in ways that are conceptually important both to underscore the complexity of understanding and interpreting architecture and culture in reports by travellers or scholars. This is particularly true of Timbuktu, which was layered in many ways by diverse cultures.

of self-determination.[13] Miner traces how Timbuktu was redesigned to conform to French ideas of an ideal urban centre (*ibid.*, 32–48).

Apart from this physical restructuring of the city in the late nineteenth century, another important aspect of the colonial construction of Timbuktu lies in how it was presented in and through the various exhibitions in France, most notably the West African section of the 1931 Exposition Coloniale in Paris. Here the architectural styles of Timbuktu and Djenné presented a discourse of ambiguity: the great Mosque of Djenné and the Djinguéré-bar in Timbuktu provided the inspiration for the main pavilion's structure, although the styles were attributed to Berber origin. This pavilion was juxtaposed to 'an indigenous village, a mosque from the Sudan, a "fetish" village of straw huts, a restaurant, and huts housing natives' (Morton, 2000: 256). These provided a backdrop for the anthropological displays, where 200 people 'performed' everyday life, as defined by earlier travel writings, in what Leprun describes as

> une subtile organisation visuelle et commerciale qui unit le quotidien et le singulier, tout ceci réclamant une sorte d'harmonie, quels que soient les détours empruntés par l'exposition pour créer une manière d'ethnologie-vérité, dont les artisans sont les otages. (1986: 167)

> [a subtle visual and commercial organisation that unites the everyday and the remarkable/particular, all requiring an arrangement of harmony, whatever the twists and turns borrowed by the exposition may have been, to create an ethnological-truth, of which the artisans/artists are the hostages.][14]

However, this architectural and performative vision of a homogenous west Africa was an ambiguous construction that attempted to present a clear racial hierarchy: with 'the savanna or Saharan *sahel*, associated with Islam and civilisation, and that of the rain forest, associated with paganism and savagery' (Morton, 2000: 264). Morton goes on to suggest that the 'mixture of colonial exteriors with metropolitan

13 Ibn Khaldûn (May 27, 1332 AD/732 AH – March 19, 1406 AD/808 AH) was an Arab Tunisian historiographer and historian who is often viewed as one of the forerunners of modern historiography, sociology and economics (Boulakia, 1971). He argued for 'an original nobility through group feeling and personal qualities', with which people grouped or associated themselves, as opposed to only familial ties (Ibn Khaldûn 1987: 101–2). He thus uses the architectural term 'house' in a metaphorical sense. Thus Ibn Khaldûn's argument on social groupings may have been interpreted to justify segregation as something already indigenous to an 'Islamic city' by the French.
14 For further examples of the presentation of African natives as 'barbarian savages' see Leprun (1986: 108–29, 152–70).

interiors produced an unintended hybridity that subverted the goal of representing the absolute difference between colonised and coloniser' (*ibid.*, 270). One could argue that this complex and sophisticated centuries-old intraculturalism not only blurred the Islamic civilisation/ African savage binary, but undermined it. It challenged simple colonial classifications of culture in terms of ethnicity, culture or religion, and indicated a fluidity and sophistication of culture that pre-dated the colonial presence. Take two examples from the West African region. The first is from the Poro, a men's secret society among the Dan and the Mano people from the Ivory Coast and northern Liberia, where the hornbill mask, believed to embody a spirit, is used in an extensive initiation process. However, the interior surface of the mask is covered in Arabic script and magic squares, both drawn from Islamic culture, to protect the wearer's soul (Prussin, 1986: 80–1). This suggests significant performative interaction between two very different cultures, and indicates new syncretic embodied repertoires that have assimilated the different cultural paradigms. The second example is from Mali, where the Bambara *n'tomo* mask has five horns on it, referencing the efficacy of the number five in the numerical symbolism of Islam. Prussin argues that this 'provides a contrastive use of Islamic symbol in masking tradition. If the face of the mask is intended to reproduce, more or less realistically, the spirit or divinity it embodies, then the five horns appear to communicate publicly the Islamic presence, just as the five earthen pinnacles rising above the facade of a house in Djenné or Tombouctou do' (1986: 82). This cultural artefact evidences how the embodied repertoires of the various peoples living in Mali reflect the degree to which they have adapted and assimilated the diverse conceptual landscapes of the inhabitants.

Such examples of intracultural hybridity and fluidity in the architecture, cultural artefacts and performances of Mali provided fascinating paradoxes that could be used to challenge and expose faultlines in colonial conceptions of Africa; while also suggesting a rich model of cultural exchange and potential layered coexistence for the diverse peoples of contemporary South Africa. The latter potential remained relatively unexplored in the South Africa-Mali project.

However, both these colonial exhibitions, and counter-exhibitions such as the Surrealists' exhibition *La vérité aux colonies*, mounted at the former Soviet Pavilion, which aimed to expose the 'armed robbery at the heart of French colonization' (Morton, 2000: 99), revealed more about French colonial thought and construction of ideology than it did about West Africa. The same can be said of Mbeki's project: the distance from the subject allowed for invention and the embodied performance of specific ideologies that were pertinent to the host organisation, beyond Timbuktu itself.

And once again the 'hidden treasures of Timbuktu' have re-emerged, attracting much attention from scholars and the general public, as is evident by recent books such as John Hunwick and Alida Jay Boyce's *The Hidden Treasures of Timbuktu*, which traces Timbuktu as 'a sanctuary of scholars', where 'scholars and libraries past and present' meet (2008: 80, 126); and the documentaries *The Lost Libraries of Timbuktu* broadcast on 12 February 2009 on BBC4, and *The Ancient Astronomy of Timbuktu* (2009) were produced to foreground research at the University of Cape Town. To a large extent this awareness of Timbuktu has been evoked in South Africa through the *Timbuktu Script and Scholarship* exhibition.

The *Timbuktu Script and Scholarship* exhibition

This project was launched with the Ink Road Symposium, held at the University of Cape Town in August 2005 at which scholars presented papers in Arabic, English and French, with simultaneous translation, that drew attention to the centuries' old legacy of Mali. The proceedings were translated from French and Arabic into English only, despite the original intention to publish in all three languages; the proceedings were then published by the South African government-funded Human Sciences Research Council as *The Meanings of Timbuktu* (Jeppie and Diagne, 2008). This publication traces the history of scholarship in the Sahara and Sahel[15] regions in five parts. It begins by contextualising the Timbuktu project for South Africa, and the meaning of Timbuktu within the context of West African intellectual history. It then explores Arabic-African writings that provide sources for various African histories and invites scholars to revisit these earlier histories. The third section is devoted almost exclusively to the family of Kunti scholars of the late eighteenth and mid-nineteenth centuries, evaluating their contribution to the intellectual life of Timbuktu and the region. Part four considers the many private collections and libraries of Timbuktu, their

---

15 The Sahel is 'that region on the edge of the Sahara stretching from the Atlantic Ocean to the Red Sea, also known as *Bilad al-Sudan* since the medieval period' (Jeppie and Diagne, 2008: vii).

holdings and histories, and provides an overview of the literature available. The last section shifts from West Africa to the eastern half of Africa to consider Arabic literature of Sudan, the Horn countries and Swahili literature written in Arabic script. David Robinson states in his review of this volume that all involved in this project 'have rendered enormous service to the understanding of the intellectual history of African Islam'; though the study is centred on Timbuktu, he argues that it is not limited to Timbuktu, but will stimulate continuing research into that history and 'transform the understanding of the Western Sudan and indeed sub-Saharan African in the coming decades' (2009).

Alongside this academic project, Mbeki raised funds to establish three trusts: to facilitate a conservation programme, including training Malian conservators; to rebuild the Ahmed Baba Centre in Timbuktu; and finally 'to promote academic study and public awareness of the magnificent and ancient African and Islamic heritage in Timbuktu', which he hoped would 'help to erase the denial of the fundamental equality of intellect to Africans' (2005). In his fundraising speech at a dinner at the Cape Town International Convention Centre on 8 April 2005 Mbeki outlined his approach to this project, arguing that 'for the African man to fully understand his present situation, he must trace his roots and the course of his journey to the present; and to make meaningful progress in the future he must not only appreciate but also appropriate his cultural history.' This suggests that more than a retrieval of history is necessary for 'progress'. Mbeki's use of the term 'appropriation' suggests that he is conscious of his use of a history outside of South Africa to illustrate his vision of African 'glory', in some ways drawing on a sense of universal humanism, alongside a pan-African nationalism.

Nostalgia manifests a longing for what has been lost, in this context a sense of cultural pride and dignity denied to black Africans by colonial history; and a refusal to accept present realities, as South African memory and identity remain contested and trapped in a traumatic past characterised by violence. This project illustrates restorative nostalgia as Mbeki attempted to disseminate a positive history that is richer and more challenging than usually admitted, or even allowed by European versions of Africa, while at the same time challenging colonial constructions of Africa as 'backward' and 'barbaric'. By implication this past can challenge similar constructions of contemporary [South] African history and identity.

Through this project, Mbeki also wished to generate closer links with the rest of the continent: both to acknowledge the role many African countries had played in South Africa's struggle for liberation from apartheid and to bridge the gap apartheid had created in separating South

Africa from the rest of the continent as a consequence of cultural and political sanctions. At the same time the project highlighted that South Africa had skills in archival restoration and curation, infrastructure and finance to offer other countries. These ideas had to be communicated to the nation in concrete terms. Thus Mbeki conceived of the physical embodiment of the project in the *Timbuktu Script and Scholarship* exhibition, which travelled thousands of kilometres from the Ahmed Baba Institute in Timbuktu to South Africa, where 40 of the thousands of manuscripts from the various collections toured the country (see Figure 4.1). The exhibition opened on 8 August 2008 at the Iziko Granary in the Castle of Good Hope and then travelled to Grahamstown's Albany Museum (9–15 September), Pretoria/Tshwane's National Library of South Africa (23 September–8 October), Bloemfontein's Oliewenhuis Art Museum (15–29 October), the Durban Art Gallery (5–16 November) and ended in Johannesburg at the Standard Bank Gallery (21 November–1 December).

An official press release was used at all the venues to contextualise the exhibition conceptually.[16] It provided a brief overview of Timbuktu as a flourishing trade centre established in the twelfth century, based on the trade of salt, gold and slaves; it then shifted to its primary focus – the manuscripts themselves. The statement emphasised the manuscripts' age and the intellectual heritage of Timbuktu as 'an important centre of Islamic learning between 1300 and 1600 AD', where 'new knowledge and intellectual debates produced additional works, and religious and private libraries flourished'. It stated that the manuscripts were written 'by scholars and copyists who were part of an African Islamic intellectual tradition centred in Timbuktu'. This tradition included not only Arabic manuscripts but also writings in other African languages, which covered a wide range of subject matter, 'from religion to astronomy and mathematics, as well as history and literary forms'. The press statement highlighted the manuscripts' aesthetic qualities: 'Some of the manuscripts are beautifully decorated with gold illumination and kept in finely tooled leather covers'; and explicitly stated that 'By celebrating these manuscripts as African cultural treasures, the exhibition strives

16 I accessed the media release from the curators of the project in Cape Town. It was issued as a joint statement from the Department of Arts and Culture of SA, Iziko Museum of Cape Town and the Ahmed Baba Institut des hautes Etudes et de Recherches Islamiques, and was changed only slightly at some venues, where an opening paragraph was added to contextualise the particular significance of that venue in the larger tour. This statement was the basis for wider press coverage of the events, e.g. www.ru.ac.za/static/affiliates/am/Timbuktu_Diary_Listing%20-%20 Grahamstown_Final%5B1%5D.doc, accessed 8/3/10.

4.1 TSS 1 Manuscript, from Ahmed Baba Institute, catalogue no. AB, 2/7/07.

to promote the values and objectives of the African Renaissance.' The statement ended as follows:

> The exhibition is an integral part of the South Africa–Mali project which was initiated by President Mbeki in 2002. As a flagship cultural initiative of the New Partnership for Africa's Development (NEPAD), the project aims to conserve the important collection of manuscripts held at the Ahmed Baba Institute of Higher Islamic Studies in Timbuktu through the training of conservation staff and the construction of a building to house the collection of the Ahmed Baba Institute. The exhibition is funded by the National Department of Arts and Culture and supported by Standard Bank.

The Media Report of the Heritage Agency (January 2009: 4) suggested significant media coverage of the exhibition, which was reported on to varying degrees by 25 daily and weekly newspapers, 20 community newspapers, 23 monthly journals and magazines, ranging from *African Business*, *Al Qalam* and *The Property Magazine* to *Woman's Value*. Nine radio stations broadcast interviews with the exhibition spokespeople, and nine national and international television channels covered the events. The agency reported that a Google search on 27 January 2009 on the exhibition yielded 720 entries, including websites of host institutions, provincial and local governments, and wider information networks related to South Africa (Heritage Agency, 2009: 5).

Both the official press statement and other media reports foregrounded the place of this project in the South African Renaissance endeavour, overtly highlighting the rich intellectual heritage, written as well as oral, of Africa that had hitherto been largely unacknowledged in African studies and certainly in apartheid South Africa.

This presentation of an exciting and positive aspect of African heritage and identity was important to South Africa as it emerged from decades of indoctrination of white superiority and black oppression. It is thus not surprising that the press coverage focused on South Africa's positive contribution to this extraordinary African resource and the aesthetic beauty of the manuscripts. However, there was no attempt to analyse the context of the exhibited material itself, particularly its very definite Islamic iconography, content and history. There was also no cultural route into exploring the meaning of these texts beyond their aesthetic beauty for most South Africans, as there was no embodied repertoire through which they could identify aspects of this exhibition.[17]

There is a particular paradox to this exhibition's opening in the Castle in Cape Town, insofar as this venue visually references South Africa's own settler and colonial history, and it thus contains the potential both to celebrate this positive West African history, while highlighting Empire in a very literal way. The issue of Empire is important both in terms of South Africa's history, and Cape Town being a port to which many thousands of slaves were brought from various parts of Africa and south-east Asia, and because the cultural wealth of fifteenth-century Mali was built on its being an Empire, with attendant slavery (Diop, 1987). However, I have found no evidence of engagement with

---

17 With the exception of people with Islamic backgrounds, for example. See Jappie's (2011) report on Cape Malay families revealing Arabic manuscripts following this exhibition.

the contextual frame or implications around the exhibition's various venues, which were very much within the domain of state-sanctioned archives: art galleries, museums and the Castle.[18]

Nevertheless, the Project Media Report concluded that the significant press coverage played 'a critical role in bringing new audiences to the host institutions and in raising awareness of the significance of the manuscripts and the part played by the South African government in their preservation' (Heritage Agency, 2009: 5). This conclusion is important when one considers the social, political and cultural complexity of places such as museums, art galleries and heritage sites such as the Castle in South African history. The 1990s saw a prolific engagement with redefining approaches to museums in South Africa.[19] For example, in 1990 Ronit Ben-Guri, the Education Officer of the new Museum Africa, surveyed attitudes and habits related to the visiting of museums in the Johannesburg area and she discovered that

> only 30 per cent of African respondents to her questionnaire had ever visited a history museum, compared to 87 per cent of white respondents. Many Africans and coloureds refused to visit the Museum because it offended their frame of reference, while others were unaware of the Museum's existence. (Unpublished report of Sept. 1990: 1, 11, cited in van Tonder, 1994: 173)

The positive focus on these venues for the whole of South Africa may have been another attempt to shift attitudes: firstly, to open up spaces that had been perceived as part of the state apparatus to a wider South African audience, who were invited to view positive African history in spaces that previously had been dominated by colonial versions of Africa's culture and history; and secondly to address different ideological and historical approaches to Africa's past.

However, I argue that this project offered a further potential value beyond deconstructing stereotypical colonial representations of Africa's past. To exemplify this I turn to a report in the *Sowetan*, a newspaper focused on a black South African demographic, which engaged with this project beyond its official focus. In his article entitled 'Literacy defeats ignorance' Victor Mecoamere (2008: 17) related South Africa's hosting

18 When I asked one of the curators about this, she replied that pragmatics determined the venues rather than ideological framing of this event (personal communication Cape Town, November 2009).

19 For examples of research undertaken during this period see Davison (1998); Deacon (1998); Hamilton (1994); Hamilton *et al.* (2002); Hutchison (2004); van Tonder (1994); Wright and Mazel (1991).

of the Timbuktu manuscripts to the wider issues of illiteracy and the 2008 South African Literary Awards in Johannesburg. He extended the discourse on the manuscripts beyond highlighting the relationship between illiteracy and disempowerment to trace other alternative histories related to writing as resistance, as evidenced in the Trans-Saharan slave trade. He particularly highlighted newly discovered slave writings by an ancestor of a Muslim family in Cape Town who was brought from Indonesia by the Dutch East India Company, suggesting that slaves more broadly were not illiterate. This further deconstructs simplistic colonial stereotypes and another cornerstone of the colonial endeavour. He also parallels the Timbuktu initiative with South African projects that were formulated to encourage new writing in African languages.[20] This contextualisation of the Timbuktu exhibition illustrates how these manuscripts could have been contextualised in a meaningful way, beyond their aesthetic, for a South African community; by making historical, cultural and political comparisons that justify the cost of the project for South Africa. It offers aspirational yet achievable goals for the broad population who may be struggling with cultural visibility and literacy as a consequence of the legacies of apartheid.

Timbuktu has often provided a useful lens through which a dream could be refracted. In this case, it allowed Mbeki to deconstruct stereotypical conceptions of Africans as 'backward'. However, reaching back to a past uncritically can be dangerous. It is important to acknowledge that Timbuktu was a canvas upon which various medieval empires inscribed themselves,[21] both mythically and in physical terms; and its wealth was predicated on its being an Empire, built on slave trade at some level. In engaging with this history, it is important that South Africa acknowledge what it is contributing to this project, and also what it is ignoring, bearing in mind Bharucha's cautionary insistence on contextualising and historicising both the subject material and one's own relationship to it in any intercultural engagement (1993: 4).

This project had economic significance, beyond its intellectual and

---

20 He specifically refers to the national literary journal *Baobab*, established by the Department of Arts and Culture, and the Xihlovo Xa Vutivi project, established in 2005 as a collaborative effort between the Department of Arts and Culture and Umgangatho Media and Communications to 'put into practice the vision of the Freedom Charter by providing for aspirant writers in all official languages and across all genres' (Mecoamere, 2008: 17).

21 It experienced 'one hundred years of Manding rule, in the fourteenth century; then forty years of Tuareg rule; Songhay rule . . . from the mid-fifteenth to the late sixteenth century; Moroccan rule in the seventeenth century; another brief Tuareg suzerainty; and finally, Fulbe control in the nineteenth century . . . finally the city fell to the French at the turn of the century' (Prussin, 1986: 142).

cultural currency. In the online NEPAD weekly newsletter of 12 September 2008, the South Africa–Mali project was heralded as 'a flagship cultural initiative of NEPAD' (issue 242, section 2). NEPAD was founded at the World Economic Forum's (WEF) annual African summit in Durban in June 2002. In 2008 the organisation stated that

> Nepad is a vision for Africa that aims to tackle issues such as peace and security, good economic, political and corporate governance, and to make the continent an attractive destination for foreign investment.
>
> It is a project of the African Union (AU) and has a steering committee of 15 African countries. Founding countries include South Africa, Nigeria, Egypt, Algeria and Senegal.
>
> A Nepad positioning document says: 'The New Partnership for Africa's Development is a pledge by African leaders, based on a common vision and a firm and shared conviction, that they have a pressing duty to eradicate poverty and to place their countries, both individually and collectively, on a path of sustainable growth and development and, at the same time, to participate actively in the world economy and body politic'. (NEPAD, 2008)

The business and economic sectors in South Africa are very clear that the South Africa–Mali project was important in the way that South Africa was positioning and performing itself in relation to the continent and world. The project created broader awareness of the skills South Africa has to offer, particularly in building collaborative infrastructure. For example, *Business Day* (15/8/08) ran a detailed account of South Africa's contribution to the process of preservation of the manuscripts under the direction of Alexio Motsi, head of the National Archives in Pretoria. In the professional magazine *Built*, Damaria Senne begins her article by suggesting how South Africa's contribution to the rebuilding of the Ahmed Baba Institute in the South Africa–Mali project demonstrated South African construction and engineering industries could engage with emerging markets by means of 'collaboration spanning bilateral agreements between countries; strategic alliances between complementary disciplines; and partnering local players in the same niche' (2008: 10). She specified that although South Africans were 'in strategic positions, such as general manager of the project and foreman' to 'ensure that international quality standards are maintained', that they were aware of intercultural issues like cultural context, and economy, and so they recruited South African artisans 'of the Islamic faith', and used a Malian construction firm, labour and resources in this project (*ibid.*, 12). The article ends by highlighting the South African building industry's potential to expand and 'to generate business in Africa and the Middle East' (*ibid.*, 12–13).

South Africa's 'staging' of itself in and through this project is multifaceted: it focused on reciting 'Africa's glorious past', while simultaneously signalling that South Africa has knowledge, skills, expertise and money to offer the continent.[22] However, this project has not had the impact of the 1938 Festival or the 1949 Voortrekker Monument inauguration, nor of Freedom Park.[23] I contend that this is because the project remained at the level of exhibiting an archive, without allowing the wider South African public a way into the mythology of the glorious past through a shared embodied repertoire, such as the songs, stories and costumes of the Voortrekker commemorations, or the culturally specific symbols of Freedom Park. I think the Timbuktu exhibition has encouraged more people to adjust their sense of Africa's intellectual history, and to grasp its economic potential, but I am not sure it has mobilised a sense of the 'glory' that Mbeki had envisioned. Ironically, this potential glory was perhaps first felt in the 1995 Rugby World Cup series hosted by South Africa when President Nelson Mandela invoked the rainbow nation in his opening speech: 'Your presence in South Africa confirms the unity in diversity and the humanity in healthy contact that our young democracy has come to symbolise. On behalf of our rainbow nation I welcome you all' (in Steenveld and Strelitz, 1998: 620). In their comparative analysis[24] of the extent to which South Africans have adopted the rainbow as a political symbol of unity, Helga Dickow and Valerie Møller's report that 'sport and the populist-supported Reconstruction and Development Programme have increasingly become the main focus for feelings of national pride' (2002: 199). I therefore turn to reassess what the 2010 World Cup revealed about the way that South Africa has staged itself internationally as the 'rainbow nation' and compare this with Mbeki's African Renaissance project.

---

22 The cost of rebuilding the Ahmed Baba library was initially set at R13.5 million, raised primarily through charitable events by Thabo Mbeki, targeted at South African businesses (www.safrica.info, 4/4/05, accessed 14/11/08). It is worth comparing this figure to the cost of the National Library of South Africa, which opened in Pretoria in 2007 and cost R160 million (www.southafrica.info, 13/12/04, accessed 14/11/08).
23 This is further evident in post-Mbeki South Africa's reluctance to intervene in recent conflicts in Timbuktu which have put the library and its contents at risk, see Patel (2012).
24 They surveyed attitudes immediately after the 1994 elections, in 1996, and in 1999 after the second general elections as a basis for this report.

Staging the 2010 World Cup

In the opening ceremony of the World Cup South Africa performed a vision of itself to more than 215 countries and hundreds of millions of viewers worldwide. Although the ceremony opened with women from different ethnic groups forming lines from the centre of the stadium to the various football venues through the country, it carefully resisted any ethnic presentation of South Africa in 'traditional' ways, reminiscent of apartheid South Africa, with the pre-colonial dances often seen at tourist villages or mines. Instead South Africa presented itself as a multicultural, diverse yet unified country very much engaged with modernity and postmodernity. It signalled the value of things of the past, as suggested by the opening praise singer Zolani Mkhiva, and the 'Welcome to Africa' song performed by the nine drummers who represented the nine other venues, while the women represented the people of South Africa who would host this event at its respective venues. Modernity was signalled by the simultaneous projection of images of the venues on the giant screens.

The performances that followed in the opening ceremony created a layered dialogue between a recognised popular South African repertoire and wider contemporary transnational popular cultures. For example, the second sequence began with the well-known 'Click Song' (*Qongqothwane* in Xhosa) accompanying the entrance of people of all ages and races with a gigantic puppet dung beetle. The choice of this African insect surprised some, mainly non-Africans who did not fully understand its symbolic significance. Mark Lawford of the *Daily Mail* suggested that 'the Lion King might have been better' (2010: 2), and the BBC television commentator wondered 'Why this creature?' (11 July 2010). The puppet was both fun and evocative of old African symbols. Instead of staging a traditional cleansing ceremony to prepare the space, the beetle was invoked as an African symbol of creation, and also associated with the removal and recycling of waste to create something useful. In ancient Egyptian iconography the scarab beetle was linked with the rising of the sun, so the beetle was intended to remove all negative energies and prepare for the games, while suggesting the dawning of a new day for South Africa. Ironically, the 'dung' was represented by a wonderfully beaded football, which may be read as an ambiguous play on old associations with this creature and its place in these games. This is an example of how an intercultural invention may be performatively invoked to shift tradition, perhaps suggesting how South Africa is reinventing itself and its place in the world.

Similar comparisons may be made with the calabash, used traditionally as a gourd from which to drink, and with the Baobab tree, which
was used in the ceremony to represent the six competing African
nations. Traditionally the Baobab is a symbol of endurance, conservation, creativity, ingenuity and dialogue. It serves as a meeting place for
many villagers to discuss community matters, relate the news of the
day, tell stories, or teach moral lessons to the young, as the San people
of Southern Africa still do. For some peoples of the African savannahs
the tree is sacred and in South Africa it is a protected tree; it is said to
be one of the 'World Trees', or Tree of Life by many of the cultures on
the African continent.[25] However, international and local audiences
may have experienced this icon differently, dependent on the degree
to which they understood the allusions, or they were merely appreciat-
ing a colourful image of the African states representing the continent.
Nonetheless, this staging of traditional symbols both acknowledges the
allusions and offers plural, creative, even postmodern artistic revision-
ings of them, although still formulated along the lines of nation – with
the flags of the six African countries competing in the games decorating
the baobab tree.

Song is central in representing African history and culture. The music
performed was diverse, supporting a sense of the complex and rich
cultural diversity represented in the games, as well as alluding to South
Africa's place on the continent. This is evident in the range of performances from Timothy Malloy's 'Song of Hope', originally to have been
sung by young tenor Siphiwo Ntshebe in classic operatic style, to TKZ's
rap and WHP's hip hop. The six African countries were represented in
a collage of several popular African songs, presented by Algerian Afro-
pop artist Khaled, South African jazz star Hugh Masekela, Ghana's
Osibisa, Mijam from Cote d'Ivoire and the Ballet Nationale from
Cameroon. Multi-Grammy winner R-Kelly, in a sequinned hoodie,
joined the Soweto Gospel Singers for the song 'Sound of Victory',
which interestingly registers 'seeing the rainbow and sun overhead' and
opening our eyes to global warming, before it addressed the potential
football victories ahead. It was significant that the audience joined in the
chorus, drawing on an African performance expectation of participation to involve audiences emotionally. However, the official song of the
2010 World Cup 'Waka Waka' (This time for Africa) was performed by
the Colombian singer Shakira, 'an icon of world music' (Mackey, 2010),
and the band Freshlyground from South Africa, and was sung in both

25 See http://arted.osu.edu/kplayground/baobabtree.htm, accessed 21/10/10, for more
    details.

English and Spanish.[26] The song is based on a traditional African soldiers' song 'Zangalewa',[27] which makes a pertinent comparison between battle and the football games to follow. Shakira and Freshlyground performed the song at the pre-tournament concert in Soweto on 10 June. It was also sung at the opening ceremony on 11 June and at the closing ceremony on 11 July. This song offered a layered engagement with specific African struggle memories, while inviting all to enjoy the intercultural style and music, as singers from two continents took this song from a specifically West African struggle context and remixed it to produce something new.

The shift to new symbols included the ubiquitous and controversial vuvuzelas, which, despite the complaints about them, allowed everyone to contribute vocally to the event. The official mascot for this World Cup was Zakumi, an anthropomorphised leopard with green hair, first presented on 22 September 2008. His name came from 'ZA' (the international abbreviation for South Africa) and the term *kumi*, which means 'ten' in various African languages.[28] The mascot's colours reflected those of the host nation's playing strip, yellow and green. Even the match ball was designed with this symbolism in mind: it was named the *Jabulani*, which means "bringing joy to everyone" in Zulu (though the truth of this was much debated by international players).[29] It featured 11 colours, representing each player of a team on the pitch and the 11 official languages of South Africa. A special match ball with gold panels, called the *Jo'bulani*, was used in the final match in Johannesburg. These symbols old and new suggested that while South Africa recognises and values its traditions, it is also looking forward to collaborating with and contributing to the wider international community.

Visually the ceremony directly expressed South Africa's call for 'compassion which can create hope' in the screened message from Nelson Mandela, a sentiment that was reiterated in the song that followed. The next scene welcomed the international audience back to Africa, 'the cradle of humankind, where man took his first steps across the face of the earth. We are all children of Africa and now we have returned home.'[30] This was visually presented in the large map of the continent,

26 Shakira.com. 26 April 2010. www.shakira.com/news/title/shakira-records-official-fifa-world-cup-2010-song, accessed 5/6/10.
27 This title comes from a word created by Cameroonian sharpshooters for better communication between them during the Second World War (Mackey, 2010), and was picked up by Nigerians during the Nigerian Civil War.
28 See 'Leopard takes World Cup Spotlight', BBC Sport, 22 September 2008.
29 '2010 World Cup Jabulani Adidas Ball', *Shine* 2010. 4 December 2009.
30 'The Cradle of Humankind' project parallels much of this view in its formulation as a project. It is a fossil site of some 47,000 hectares that is being excavated. It is

and the world, created with quilted squares and large footprint cut-outs across it. The rhetoric of unity in diversity is evidenced in the costumes and dance steps, which were eclectic and innovative rather than authentically referencing any specific cultural group or style. It was open and inclusive, mirroring Mbeki's inclusive definition of all potentially being 'African' in his 1996 constitutional speech. The ceremony suggested the diverse histories of Africa, while foregrounding its talent and potential in the present and future, particularly given the prominence of the 300 children that performed at various stages of the ceremony.

I argue that these very different public performances, the South Africa–Mali manuscript project and the 2010 World Cup ceremonies, suggest the way that South Africa envisions its ideal identity: as inclusive, pan-African and forward-looking socially and economically. However, I would also contend that the way in which these projects were conceptualised and presented as public displays failed to engage the public at large with the complexities involved in negotiating diversity and all its associated challenges. They displayed desire and allowed the general public an experience of a positive collective identity, with only the vague outlines of a repertoire emerging from the World Cup events. A real foundation for the 'rainbow nation' would require evoking embodied repertoires that are recognisable to large groups of South Africans, which would offer a basis for enacting unity in diversity in reality.

Another South Africa–Mali collaboration: *Tall Horse* (2004–05)[31]

I now turn to another engagement with colonial constructions of Africa in the collaborative South African Handspring Puppet Company and the Malian Sogolon Puppet Company's theatrical production of *Tall Horse* (2004–05). This production explores many things, including the relationship between 'darkest Africa' and 'enlightened Europe'; and how a sense of the past impacts on our relationships, both personal and political, and informs our sense of the present. Both thematically and performatively, the production explores the implications of the

described as one of the world's most important archaeological sites. The Furneaux Stewart GAPP (FSG) consortium is responsible for this R163-million development. See www.southafrica.info/travel/cultural/cradle-centre.htm, accessed 14/11/08. See too the SABC series *Shoreline* (2009)

31 This analysis draws on my article in *Theatre Journal* (2010c).

constructed nature of discourses, and how these can both conceal and reveal the ideologies that shaped their formation.

Handspring Puppet Company is a multiracial South African theatre company founded in Cape Town in 1981. It works primarily through collaborative processes of improvising and devising texts, often adaptations of classic European texts, with actors and puppets. Their puppets are generally an eclectic mix of puppets developed from the European marionette tradition, combined with Central- and East-Asian forms, particularly the Japanese *Bunraku* style, where the puppeteers are visible.[32] Handspring has extended the role of the puppeteers by allowing them to interact with the puppets by means of facial expressions and physical gestures. They have also continued to develop the experiments begun with visual artist and filmmaker William Kentridge to create multilayered performances that juxtapose back-projected images with the actors and puppets onstage. In much of their work they explore specific issues related to memory and identity construction in post-colonial Africa.

The Sogolon Puppet Company performs in the Malian Segou puppet masquerade tradition under the direction of Yaya Coulibaly, a leading exponent and custodian of the Sogo bò puppet theatre.[33] The company works in the Malian Bamana[34] tradition, which is a complex one, because the performances range from sacred and ritual performances, through the semi-sacred performance, to traditional and popular theatre, all using masks and puppets. However, the rules attending the making and use of these masks and puppets differ, depending on performance context. The Sogolon Puppet Company's international and collaborative work focuses on popular secular performances. Thus while aspects of tradition and spirituality are inherent in the form, the Sogo bò puppet masquerade extends beyond encoding cultural values and beliefs to enable the various communities to 'assert and renegotiate their [contemporary] identities' (Arnoldi, 1988: 96).

The idea for this collaborative project was first brokered in June 1999 by Alicia Adams, the vice-president for international programming and dance at the John F. Kennedy Center in Washington, DC. Initially, it was

32 Adrian Kohler outlines his approach to puppetry and the development of Handspring's work in 'Thinking through Puppets' (Taylor, 2009: 42–147).

33 For an outline of the intercultural aspects of this collaboration see Hutchison 2010c. This research draws on Mary Jo Arnoldi's work on contextualising the Sogolon Puppet Company, as she has written the seminal study on Sogo bò puppet masquerade (see Arnoldi, 1976, 1988, 1995, 2001).

34 I use the term 'Bamana,' as opposed to 'Bamara,' which was a French ethnological term adopted from Fula, Arab and Berber informants, who used the term 'Bambara' to refer to those 'who refuse to pray'; see Rene A. Bravman (2001: 36).

envisaged as a massive Broadway spectacular, but when the funding for this fell through, the production was reconceptualised more modestly in scale and form. In 2002 AngloGold Ashanti and Business and Arts South Africa agreed to fund the project, and the collaborative project that resulted in *Tall Horse* was initiated in 2005.

The story of the *Tall Horse* is based on a historical account of a giraffe, named Sogo Jan,[35] who is captured in southern Sudan, taken up the Nile River in a felucca and shipped across the Mediterranean to France in 1826 as a gift for the King's menagerie. The giraffe was a bribe from Mehmet Ali, the Ottoman viceroy of Egypt, to dissuade the French from involving themselves in the Greek War of Independence. The animal wintered in Marseilles and in the spring of 1827 took several months to walk to Paris, creating a sensation along the way and, some say, inspired the design of the Eiffel Tower. The story of this journey is narrated by Atir, the giraffe's handler, a freed Sudanese slave who offers an African perspective on France in this multimedia production. The story of Sogo Jan and Atir is framed by the contemporary story of Jean-Michel, a student from Paris who has travelled to Bamako in Mali to research a collection of artefacts from nineteenth-century Egypt in the hope of finding 'anything that might relate to a certain slave belonging to a French consul in Egypt in 1926' (Burns, 2006: 242);[36] this slave is his ancestor.

The play is complex and explores many post-colonial issues, including Africa's relationship with Europe and vice versa; the role of stereotypes in cultural engagement; how context affects events; and how such events are remembered in and through history.

As outlined earlier in this chapter, the scramble for Africa coincided with Europe's industrial and territorial expansion, with intense inquiry into many aspects of science, not the least Social Darwinian hierarchies. It is thus not surprising that the play opens with the Malian researcher asking the French student about the European Enlightenment while *"grinding the noses [from mummies] with a mortar and pestle"* [italics in original]:

> DR KONATE: The Enlightenment. Did they find it? Your scientists were convinced they were finally seeing into the true nature of things. Europeans have ordered much of the world we inhabit and fixed everything in its place: plants, animals, men, predators and prey, 'Enlightened Europe' and

35 *Sogo* in Bamana means 'animal' or 'horse'; it is also the name used for puppets and masks that represent animals. *Jan* means 'tall.'
36 All references to the play come from this published edition of the play and hereafter I will cite only page numbers.

'Darkest Africa'. Those who control the naming of things control our perceptions. And perception is reality, n'est-ce pas? But if you know where to
look from you will be able to see. (241)

This opening statement outlines a number of provocations that lie at
the heart of this play: it establishes the central binaries that plague post-
colonial interaction and, in its irony, implies that the play hopes to challenge and perhaps move beyond these binaries, which are often central
to the way that memories and histories are constructed and mobilised. It
signals a particular interest in the significance of the European scientific
ambition to define the 'true nature of things', to define and fix 'everything in its place' by 'naming' things and thus controlling perception.
This European colonial perception of Africa as a place inhabited by
'savages', without history, is the same formulation which Mbeki wished
to challenge.

The focus of the European scientific inquiry is the giraffe Sogo Jan
in the first instance. She is examined by the scientist St-Hilaire, and a
Fashion Designer, who seek 'the essence of her being' (258). These scientific and cultural explorations exemplify Western patterns of objectify-
ing the exotic 'other', either to control it, or for the purpose of cultural
appropriation, as suggested in the giraffe's later incarnations in French
fashion and the Eiffel Tower (259). However, these processes are not
presented as simple or one-directional, as is seen by the stage-business
in this opening scene: Dr Konate is grinding up mummies to sell either
as anti-aging creams (255), or whole to collectors, who use them to
validate Europe's superior sense of itself. Here, Africans are exploiting
certain European scientific and sociological paradigms for economic
gain and are not mere victims of these paradigms. This visually articulates Said's argument that complex complicities are involved in various
subjugated peoples' engagement with colonial and imperial powers,
often for economic reasons (1991, 1994).

This juxtaposition of cultural perceptions and categories offers an
ironic, and at times paradoxical, frame for Sogo Jan's journey from
south to north that is not simply counter-hegemonic. The paradox is
centrally embodied in Sogo Jan herself, since giraffes do not fit into the
neat binary categorisations of the Enlightenment. Giraffes are neither
prey nor predator (263); they are not generally hunted by any predator
other than man, nor do they hunt. Sogo Jan also moves through both the
African and European contexts, while also being bound by them.

All the interactions in this play are focalised through Atir, a freed
African slave who accompanies the giraffe to Europe, since Sogo Jan
will trust no one else and refuses to take food from anyone else. This

focalisation raises questions of stereotypes in the context of colonial and post-colonial discourse. Homi Bhabha has argued that stereotypes have been a means of regulating authority within a colonial context, because they can simultaneously distance the Other, while suggesting that the Other is something knowable and thus subjectifiable, something that can be studied and finalised (Bhabha, 1983: 202). However, the use of stereotypes does not only reveal hegemonic strategies, but he suggests that when they are used alongside mimicry they can form an important counter-hegemonic device. This is because mimicry is 'constructed around ambivalence; in order to be effective, mimicry must continually produce its slippage, its excess, its difference. . . . the sign of a double articulation' (Bhabha, 1994: 122) This 'slippage,' or doubleness, is important in the context of stereotyping, because it suggests both imitation and mockery. Mimicry reveals both the constructedness of the stereotype and its ambivalence in the colonialist discourse, while revealing that stereotypes are hybridised and historicised constructs rather than simple states of being.

The play stages the first encounter between 'darkest Africa' and 'enlightened Europe' in a provocatively stereotypical way, with an African slave and exotic beast encountering French aristocrats, who consider themselves 'enlightened' in their '*curiosité*' about 'marvels and monstrosities' (Burns, 2006: 253). The French fawn and flatter the exotic slave and wild animal in an atmosphere that is 'erotic and highly charged' (256–7), as evidenced in sexually ambivalent references that point to stereotypes about African virility. They have no real sense of Atir or Sogo Jan as living beings outside of the zoo, natural history museum, or travelling curio exhibits so common in nineteenth-century Europe.[37] This approach to them is important because it reflects in microcosm a wider nineteenth-century European approach to Africa as being both monstrous and marvellous. The French aristocrats discuss Atir and Sogo Jan along with references to the 'young negro playwright Dumas,' the acquisition of exotic mummies, both negroid and pigmy,

---

37 Much has been written about exotic exhibitions of animals and humans, but take, for example, Nancy Henry's comment on the references to lions in George Eliot's *Adam Bede* that suggests that 'animals in captivity became symbols of British exploration and power'; see Nancy Henry (2002) *George Eliot and the British Empire*. Cambridge: Cambridge University Press. See also Robert Bogdan (1988) *Freak Show: Presenting Human Oddities for Amusement and Profit*. Chicago: University of Chicago Press; Guillermo Gómez-Peña, with Elaine Peña (2005). *Ethno-techno: Writings on Performance, Activism, and Pedagogy*. New York: Routledge; and Robert J. Hoage and William A. Deiss (eds) (1996) *New Worlds, New Animals: From Menagerie to Zoological Park in the Nineteenth Century*. Baltimore: Johns Hopkins University Press.

and 'a human foot with seven toes alleged to be of Egyptian origin' (254–5).

However, these references to stereotypes of African barbarity and exoticism are relativised when they are juxtaposed with France's own history. The play alludes to the French Revolution: the Fashion Designer's comment that a 'new longer neck-line is on the cutting edge of French fashion' (259) parodically echoes earlier references to the Crusades and children chopping off the head of a cat with a toy guillotine, a reference that highlights the political unrest in Lyon. These allusions raise questions about our perspective on marvels and monstrosities: who or what is marvellous, and what is monstrous? They also begin to deconstruct the binary of 'darkest Africa' and 'enlightened Europe'.

Not only France is challenged about its stereotypes; Atir initially falls into the stereotypical role of exotic, over-sexualised African male, as 'each day a new lady lay in his arms' (262) Later he becomes the lover of Lady Clothilde, wife to Count Grandeville de Largemont, Prefect of Marseilles. She convinces Atir to adopt the clothes of a French dandy, although he returns to Sudanese dress when he meets King Charles X. This ambiguous attempt to assimilate Atir into France raises the question about how Africa makes sense of itself when encountering a European perspective and values. It also explores whether identity may be refashioned outside of binaries: whether we can escape the notion that '[a]ntelope exist because lions must eat, and Africa exists for the benefit of Europe' (255). The answer, in part, lies in the importance of specific contexts for large questions about relationships and the construction of personal and cultural identity. One cannot speak broadly of 'Africa' or 'Europe', but of more specific times and cultural positioning. This is well illustrated by Petrus du Preez's analysis of how this company addresses both theme and production process to critically explore how 'the African is exoticised by Africans themselves' (2011).

The degree to which personal and broader socio-political issues are interrelated, and are to some extent co-dependent, is suggested by the political debates that occur throughout the play. First, the viceroy's gift is given to ensure that he will maintain control in the Mediterranean and keep France out of the conflict in Greece. Then, the first interaction between the King and Queen of France suggests the relationship between the colonial naming of things, political conflict and hegemony. The Queen begins by challenging Charles's own personal peculiarity of preferring walking to riding, which she insists is against 'the natural order of things' and 'does not become you' (244); she then asks him why he is so focused on his menagerie and hunting instead of 'meeting with

your generals and fabricating reasons to invade other countries. Why
can't you be more pre-emptive, like America?' (265) When Charles
retorts by wanting to know 'why we can't all get along?' she replies:
'Because it is not profitable' (266). These references to the relationship
between political norms and economics which echo present debates
in the context of the nineteenth century, suggests the complexities of
power and identity. These large states and systems are juxtaposed with
the naivety of Atir and Sogo Jan, who can have no sense of the significance of their part in these complex games. The contemporary extension
is signalled by the newspaper reporter's response to the Egyptian viceroy
offering to withdraw from Greece, provided that France agrees to form
an alliance with him against the Turks; he says, 'Who let the dogs out –
woof, woof, woof' (271), which references the Baha song.[38]

These ideas on political interrelatedness and the circulatory nature of
historical processes are extended by the performative and visual aspects
of the play. One of the images reinforcing this idea throughout is that of
a ball of dung which is rolled about the stage at different times during the
play. The discussion between Viceroy Mehmet Ali and the French Consul
Drovetti about how to placate the French contextualises the image:

> MEHMET ALI: Do you know why the ancients of this god-forsaken land
> worshipped the scarab beetle?
> DROVETTI: I believe your Highness, that it symbolised the regeneration of
> life.
> *From Mehmet Ali's massive belly beneath his robes emerges the scarab with
> a ball of dung, which he rolls around the stage.*
> MEHMET ALI: It rolls a ball of dung around, like the sun rolls across the sky.
> And out of the dung comes new life, the little hatchling beetles. Egypt is a
> dung heap, Drovetti. But out of that heap of black slaves and the decay of its
> dead past, we are bringing new life to the present. We are rolling, Drovetti.
> You and I are the dung beetles of Egypt. And that places us in the company
> of the gods. (248)

The dung rolling around the stage reminds the audience of the role Egypt
has played as the gateway between North and South, East and West for
centuries, and how its history has been constructed and contested by
various peoples for their own political ends.[39] It also suggests how diffi-

---

38 Several commentators, including Maureen Dowd, have associated the title of the
    song with Bush's foreign policy, equating 'Let the dogs out' with 'Let slip the dogs of
    war', in Marc Antony's speech in Shakespeare's 'Julius Caesar', www.phrases.org.uk/
    bulletin_board/49/messages/1123.html, accessed 25/1/12.
39 For example, the debates as to whether ancient Egypt was Grecian, African or Arabic,
    and today whether it is part of the Arabic or African world.

cult it is to separate histories and mythologies from local contemporary politics, as we see in the way the Timbuktu project was used in South Africa to suggest a literate, glorious African past, without translating the particular context of the texts and images for the audiences. Similar performative layering is evidenced in the use of back projection and puppets. Projections of digitalised images, which include patterns that are meant to signify various religions and cultures; so the crescent moon represents Islam, the cross Christianity, the Star of David Judaism, other images include an image of the Grand Mosque and the pyramids. At other times we see a map of the Nile, palm trees, birds and boats as Atir and Sogo Jan travel; a shadow-puppet play comments on Atir and Clothilde's love scene; and, finally, a giraffe walks across the Parisian skyline and morphs into the Eiffel Tower. These images juxtapose the local with the global, suggesting broader contexts and influences that reflect on the specific moment; this in turn layers the narrative, offering a contrapuntal, complex response to what at first seems to be Atir and Sogo Jan's linear journey from Africa to Europe.

The puppets provide an important perspective on the debate about perception and representation, breaking the binary of one group speaking about or representing another. Puppets represent all of the characters, except for Atir and Jean-Michel, and scientists Dr Konate and Geoffroy St-Hilaire. Atir and Jean-Michel are both naive men who represent the displaced 'Dark Continent'. They seek a way 'home', but get caught up in wider concerns: Atir by the giraffe and Jean-Michel by his own past. The scientists, Dr Konate and St-Hilaire, are more sophisticated in their approaches both to their own culture and to the one they are encountering. It is important that the two actors each play both a European and an African character, because this creates a balance of perspectives whereby each representation is both constructed and simultaneously critiqued, and we are left with neither an overwhelming sense of naivety nor of sophistication for either culture.

The puppets are important in highlighting that the characters are not real, but rather are representations of particular ideas. There were 60 puppets of 14 different types in the show, ranging from full-body *castelets* to rod puppets.[40] The Malian tradition is non-realistic and uses specific symbolic referents such as colour to suggest status; for example, the Queen Marie-Therese is reminiscent of the Malian divinity Farrow, who is blue, with an exaggerated bust to indicate her fecundity. She is also several meters tall. The King is 'worn' strapped in front of the body

40 For visual images of the range of puppets for the production, see www. handspringpuppet.co.za/html/frameind.html, accessed 14/1/10.

of his operator. These are strange representations of French royalty and thus distance the audience from the figures twice: first, because they are puppets, and second, because of the unfamiliar aesthetic. These non-realistic puppets create a self-reflexive trope, suggesting how representation and interaction may be manipulated, while exploring the place, use and construction of cultural stereotypes and forms of Otherness.

The significance of this for exploring memory, history and identity in a post-colonial context is suggested by Bill Ashcroft's (1994–95) argument that important strategies to resist the constructed colonial stereotype include the control of textual representation, the appropriation of language, and the interpolation of cultural production into dominant systems. It may be argued that the use of puppets here goes beyond resisting constructed stereotypes to challenge the binary that underpins them, thus achieving Ashcroft's concept of interpolation, which, he argues, 'gestures to the capacity to interpose, to intervene, to interject a wide range of counter-discursive tactics into the dominant discourse without asserting a unified anti-imperial intention, or a separate oppositional purity' (*ibid.*, 183).

The *Tall Horse* offers an experiential sense of how histories, peoples and ideologies are constructed and performed relative to politics and power. It deconstructs binary notions of civilised and barbaric peoples or times, and suggests that it is in relationships that we cross borders – literally and socially. If one compares this play to the Timbuktu project, what one notices is that both use material artefacts to present a narrative, but while the Timbuktu project offers a complex deconstruction of an old myth, it ironically reconstructs another that is just as decontextualised as the colonial myth was. The journal of Atir and Sogo Jan is less about constructing or deconstructing specific narratives than exploring the implications of these constructions for their lived realities; for example in how Atir negotiates performing 'exotic blackness'. It is less focused on resolving difference or justifying cultural histories than on asking questions about relationships and the interrelatedness of peoples and histories. It also emphasises the role of perception and interpretation in understanding both the past and the present.

It is in these more complex engagements with the past that this play offers a clear example of how the ideal proposed by Mbeki in his definition of himself as 'an African' may be imagined – not in an all-encompassing, unspecific humanity, but in the image of the giraffe – which Yaya Coulibaly says 'has the height to look' (cited in Millar, 2006: 233). So we are invited to step back, to see ourselves as an/other and thus see difference differently, and the local in relation to the global, self in relation to the other with some degree of ironic distance.

However, it must be acknowledged that theatre is an ephemeral experience which may provoke thought, but not necessarily change. What may be more effective using the manuscript exhibition or this play as provocations for debate, would be creating workshops for community development in a safe, neutral space, much like the *Truth in Translation* project. In this way art, with its aesthetic frame and the distance it creates from everyday life, has the potential to act as a catalyst for individuals to define what the 'rainbow' means for them and thus realise a meaningful renaissance for South Africa.

5

Post-apartheid repertoires of memory

Artists . . . are not agents of power, but campaigners for invisible values no human being can live without. (Brink, 1996: 58)

I turn now from these performances of memory by state or cultural institutions to look at embodied repertoires in the public sphere and in theatres. While the TRC clearly attempted to hear hidden stories and renegotiate the perceptions and values of South Africans, its effect was limited because a state of mind, values, and peoples' views cannot be easily changed. Thus the extent to which the creative arts can facilitate further dialogue on the past and what the 'rainbow nation' means for individual people are important insofar as the arts can reach local communities in spaces outside of everyday reality.

Researchers looking at theatre in South Africa since Mandela's liberation in 1990 note how the new political dispensation has provided the potential for theatre to extend beyond broad narratives of nation building to explore 'social problems arising from displacement, urbanization, and poverty' (Kruger, 1999). Johann van Heerden (2008) traces the consequences of transformation of the state-subsidised Performing Arts Councils both in financial terms and also in the ways creative artists have responded to South Africa's new circumstances and identified new areas of focus and creative stimuli. These have included people redefining themselves not only in terms of race, but also as cultural, gendered, social, religious and economic communities (Rudakoff, 2004; van Heerden, 2008; Krueger, 2010). Mike van Graan argues that this does not mean that South Africans should think that there is no longer a need for 'protest theatre', as South Africa faces high levels of unemployment, poverty, crime, extraordinarily high rape statistics, and ongoing deaths as a result of AIDS. Rather, he calls for 'the rise of theatre that boldly, unequivocally and unashamedly speaks truth to the powers that be' (2006: 283–7). This requires both a sense of the role theatre has had in South Africa's liberation struggle, and developing an awareness of the effect the new context and new audiences' interests and needs have on contemporary theatre practice.

Loren Kruger has noted that there has been some 'confusion in post-apartheid theatre institutions' with the transfer of management of state institutions such as the provincial theatres to former 'outsiders' (like Walter Chakela at PACT and Mbongeni Ngema at Durban's Playhouse), which she argues has led 'not so much to innovation than to variations on the struggle formula', and revivals of South African classics (1999: 195). I shall return to the issue of revivals later in this chapter. Gay Morris (2008) addresses the complex and ongoing tensions that exist between state-subsidised, urban theatres and the so-called 'township' theatre. She suggests that although the latter functions on an ad hoc basis, it is engaged with issues that are pertinent to its constituencies, especially to young people, and as such holds unrecognised potential for making a significant contribution to contemporary South Africa.

University drama departments and the many festivals in South Africa provide important spaces for bringing these different communities together. Festivals in particular provide a significant platform for exploring personal, social and political issues in innovative ways (Hauptfleisch, 2007). Renegotiating spaces and the place of theatre in contemporary society is important, given the imperative for the country to facilitate dialogue between people divided not only historically, but also geographically, socially and economically. Economics is especially important, as the price of theatre tickets often determines the audience for a show. Thus, expanding sites of performances beyond traditional theatre spaces is crucial in facilitating access to more diverse creative artists and audiences. Moving theatre beyond state-subsidised venues also allows for different kinds of relationships with audiences, beyond the tendency for passive consumption encouraged by a proscenium arch design. This is especially evident in festivals such as Cape Town's *Infecting the City* (2008–11),[1] which Awelani Moyo argues 'has

---

1 See interview with Bailey on ITC (2010b).

attempted to make the arts more widely available to the public whilst stimulating debate about current social issues by making use of the embodied energy and creativity of urban public spaces' (2011: 10). Various conferences such as the Dramatic Learning Spaces conferences and special issues of the *South African Theatre Journal* show serious engagements by South African artists and researchers with redefining space, both physical and conceptual, and engaging with the issues that arise from theatre being an embodied art form as opposed to visual or textual forms of representation.

Bhekizizwe Peterson points to the remit facing academics and critics in the new South Africa, suggesting that 'there needs to be a greater interest in marking the specific social relations operative within the sphere of performance'. This includes 'taking cognizance of vertical as well as horizontal divisions amongst theatre groups, their articulation with the institutions that disseminate performance and its public and scholarly reception – control, access and location of performance spaces, means of advertising, sponsorship, patronage relations between practitioners and critics' (Peterson, 1995: 582). He goes on to argue that the relationship between race and class needs to be further nuanced in order to 'unbundle our understanding of creative processes, racism, sexism and ethnocentrism from the analytical impasse inherent in the base/superstructure metaphor and its functionalist explanations' (*ibid.*, 579). Mtshali argues that this is particularly important in analysing what 'blackness' means when referred to as the central trope of the post-liberation imaginary (2009: 18). He argues that this is especially important in theatre, where the body as subject is present in the performance, both with regard to the performers and audiences. Their presence creates the potential to destabilise broad ideological inscriptions of bodies and thus disrupt meaning structures, while at the same time fracturing any singular definition of identity, belonging or master narrative of memory or history.

New artists are emerging and new plays are being published[2] that engage with these ideas while resisting the impulse to bury or forget past myths, stories and identities, while they explore how new ones are being forged. I now turn to look at specific examples of repertoires that are being invoked in the new South Africa; and how old forms are being used to engage with memories both to justify and challenge established relationships in the contemporary context. I consider specific patterns

2 Edited collections include Perkins (1998), Graver (1999), Fourie (2006), Homann (2009b), Coetzee (2009); individual playwrights published by Junketts include Mike van Graan, Robin Malan, Fatima Dike and Rajesh Gopie, and Oberon books has published Lara Foot Newton, Paul Grootboom and Yael Farber.

of innovation and issues that arise from these patterns in contemporary South African theatre.

Post-apartheid repertoires

Diana Taylor suggests that popular songs, dances and stories are part of our 'intangible heritage', ways in which knowledge is both stored and transmitted (2007b: 22–3); I thus turn to look at ways in which particular South African repertoires of memory are being mobilised and consider their effect.

HIV/AIDS has been a highly controversial issue in South Africa, as evidenced in Thabo Mbeki's position on the pandemic during his presidency. Nevertheless, young people are mobilising repertoires that emerged from the apartheid period to engage with this devastating problem now. For example, *isicathamiya* is being used by singer-dancers across generations to engage with the AIDS pandemic in KwaZulu-Natal.[3] Although *isicathamiya* is not a pre-colonial Zulu performance form, it constantly references older African cultural forms such as the wedding song *umbuloko* (Gunner, 2007: 133), and thus weaves together older and more contemporary repertoires. However, the history of *isicathamiya* is itself significant, as it was developed by marginalised urban working class men who incorporated ethnically specific rural songs and dances into new urban styles.[4] These men came as migrant workers from various places on the subcontinent to urban centres in South Africa, and the form emerged as an expression of their negotiated identity and sense of belonging in their new contexts.[5] Liz Gunner's research shows how singers of various ages are now using the rhetoric and the semiotics of this performance form to challenge the status quo, including configurations of generational authority. This has resulted in the voices of youths being heard in the broad public sphere, where behaviour is consensualised. *Isicathamiya* performance usually occurs in the context of a competition, which *de facto* facilitates debate and discussion of highly contested social issues, such as virginity (*ibid.,*

---

3 Gunner's research was part of a larger research project at the University of Natal, Pietermaritzburg (2001–03) which explored issues of 'Orality, Literacy and Colonialism' in KwaZulu-Natal.

4 See Erlmann (1990) on the development of *Isicathamiya* performance in South Africa, 1890-1950.

5 See Clegg (1982).

140). These youths have thus found a form through which they can acknowledge the complexities of AIDS-related questions, while reflecting critically on community values and practices. This is one example of how embodied repertoires are being used to negotiate tensions between customary practice and modernity, generational authority and the place of youths within the broader context of national policy-making.

Cultural activity, poetry, song and dance have always been central to the ANC's strategy of resistance to apartheid. Spontaneous group singing was integral to mass gatherings, funerals and political rallies. Shirli Gilbert (2007) traces how the establishment of the Mayibuye Cultural Ensemble (1975–80)[6] and the Amandla Cultural Ensemble (c.1978–90)[7] affected international perceptions of, and support for, the liberation struggle, and we could add Ladysmith Black Mambazo to the list of groups that raised awareness regarding South Africa's position in the international arena. These groups were clearly 'weapons of the struggle', and as such focused on 'condemning the regime and informing the world about apartheid' (Gilbert, 2007: 436). The centrality of this cultural history raises the question of the place of these songs, dances and poetry in the present.

Amandla! A Revolution in Four Part Harmony (2002) is a visual documentary on the development of the struggle repertoire in South Africa in terms of song, dance and physical gesture. It is an invaluable record of the way this repertoire changed to reflect the growing militancy of resistance in South Africa. The film includes scenes of workshops in which contemporary youths are learning apartheid liberation songs and dances, as important aspects of the embodied repertoire of South African memory. However, given the current context in which reconciliation is still more aspirational than realised, this repertoire needs to be transmitted with an awareness of historical context to avoid provoking contemporary youths to engage actively in racial conflict. It seemed to me that the youths in the documentary performed the songs and dances with energy and excitement, but inevitably they also performed militant anger, because that is what these songs and dances embody. The significance of the stakes involved in the way in which contested repertoires, such as the militant struggle songs and dances, are transmitted and performed in the contemporary context is illustrated in the conflict between Julius Malema and the human rights organisation AfriForum in the South Gauteng High Court over the right to sing the

---

6 Under the direction of by Barry Feinberg and Ronnie Kasrils.
7 Initially directed by musician Jonas Gwangwa, but later under the direction of the ANC.

struggle song 'Dubul'ibhunu', translated as 'Shoot the Boer' (The Right Perspective, 2010; Ndletyana 2010). The South African High Court ruled that it is now illegal to sing this song, 'because it incites hate and violence against a particular ethnic group' (The Right Perspective, 2010), but Malema, and the ANC spokesman Jackson Mthembu argued that it is part of ANC history and that 'the high court did not make an effort to get input from the ANC as owners and experts on the struggle song on its mean [sic], its history and its purpose' (*ibid.*). The defence argued that Mr Malema was nine years old when Mr Mandela was freed and thus he was not singing of his own experience. They also noted that this song had particular implications in the context of recent murders of white farmers. It is thus clear that memory and particular embodied repertoires of the past are powerful, and negotiating their meaning and how they are to be performed and understood in the present context are highly contentious matters.

A second issue emerges from this precedent of using song to publicly express a political position, namely the way songs and dances continue to be mobilised in the context of legal trials in South Africa.[8] I turn to two recent trials during which the struggle song 'Umshini Wami' (My Machine Gun) was sung as commentary on the proceedings.

The first occurrence was when Jacob Zuma, then Deputy President of South Africa, sang 'Umshini Wami' during the trial of businessman and former ANC activist, Shabir Shaik, in Durban in early 2005. Liz Gunner notes that this song references the pre-1994 struggle period, and in particular its role in the 'debate about how to fight the "just war"' (2008: 42). Gunner reiterates Diana Taylor's view on the repertoire as being a form of embodied memory that engages in a dialogue with archives and narratives, and thus contributes to contemporary political debates and constructions of identity. Gunner argues that 'Zuma's sung intervention highlighted the presence of a somatic grammar where the links between body, song, and a wider social meaning assumed a momentary coherence' (2008: 29), as it highlighted the way in which the ANC had 'seized back agency and the power to determine the flow of change in the new era' (*ibid.*, 30). In so doing, the song 'broke into popular public memory by recalling an earlier and more dangerous way of being' (*ibid.*, 37) during the struggle, and thus 'sent a warning to any complacent settling into a negotiated liberal democracy at the very same time that it gave hope to the longing for social and political change. It was utopian but it

8 See Cole (2010: 28–62) on performance in the contest of political trials between 1956 and 1964.

held, too, the possibility of a violent praxis' (*ibid.*, 40, 48). This is clear in the words of the song:

Umshini wami	[My machine gun]
Umshini wami	[My machine gun]
We Baba	[Oh Father]
Awuleth' umshini wami	[Please bring me my machine gun.]

The performance of memory here is layered and significant as it draws attention to the ANC victory, reminding the broad public of the terms of the struggle, while hinting at the potential for future mobilisation, in the spirit of restorative nostalgia, if these terms are not deemed to have been met.

Inevitably, because of the terms of the struggle narrative, this song implicitly defined insiders and outsiders. The masculine terms of this song's definition of 'a seamless masculinity with little place for gendered identities in the new state to come' (*ibid.*, 27) excludes women and any who were not active participants in the struggle for liberation. Although this song frames the repertoire of the dominant male ruling class, the way in which it was adapted to criticise current ANC leadership, and evolved into common parlance very much in the way proverbs often do,[9] suggests how unstable repertoires are, easily shifting from being used supportively to being used to challenge dominant power systems.

This and other liberation struggle songs and dances were performed outside the courthouse in the second example, at Jacob Zuma's rape trial in February 2006.[10] Here Zuma's supporters sang in his defence and praise, while activists against the abuse of women sang critical responses, with the police, the judiciary and the media as their audiences. Songs, T-shirts and placards were used to visually perform ideological positionality on the case. Even the spatial arrangement of the parties was significant, with the supporters of the alleged victim, mainly women, confining themselves to a section of the Supreme Court block (the corner of Pritchard and Von Wielligh Streets), while Zuma's supporters moved over a wider area, even attempting to intimidate the women's rights group at one stage. Groenewald (2010) traces how this performance event outside the Supreme Court in Johannesburg not only revealed the 'splits in post-apartheid democracy', but also demonstrated the ongoing role the liberation repertoire has for legitimising power in contemporary South Africa. Issues were wide-ranging, from Zulu

---

9 See Gunner's detailed analysis of how this happened in this instance (2008: 33–40).
10 I have referenced Motsei's (2007) analysis of the trial in relation to particular issues related to perceptions of gender and the limitations of the TRC in an earlier chapter in my analysis of van Graan's *Green Man Flashing*.

ethnicity and race, to traditional views of gender roles, as opposed to women's rights. This was particularly evident in the physical performances, as 'Zuma supporters burned pictures and an effigy of the victim, and burned G-strings and condoms, and sang songs depicting the victim as a bitch' (*ibid.*, section 6.2; Motsei, 2007: 117–44). The terms in which power was perceived is illustrated in the contrast in foci: 'while Zuma supporters encouraged the spirit of militancy, women's rights groups urged their supporters to exercise their rights, for example to speak out' (Groenewald, 2010: 5, section 6.3). This seems to highlight a gender split that suggests that the men were supporting a hegemony conceived in terms of a particularly masculine formulation of memory, which drew on the liberation struggle history for its validation, whereas the women seemed to be advocating individual rights. This is further borne out in the terms of protest that each group formulated: while the men protested against 'poverty and unemployment as their plight, the women's rights group sang about their suffering as oppressed women, which included the issue of seeing women as mere objects for sexual exploitation. The songs referred to the rape of men as well' (*ibid.*, section 6.6), a topic that is taboo in South Africa. A close analysis of the gestures and lyrics of these songs reveals a real split in perceptions of where memory and tradition ought to stand in relation to contemporary gender issues. Many of these criticisms support those made regarding the terms of the TRC mandate, particularly in relation to violence and the constructions of gender during apartheid.

Thus, debates on these unresolved issues continue in the public domain in and through performance forms, illustrating the power and enduring nature of the diverse embodied repertoires of memory in post-apartheid South Africa. They also highlight how memory can be unstable and beyond control; in contrast to archives which may be better managed in terms of interpretation and access. Repertoires are important as they reveal what issues are uppermost in public consciousness, and they have the potential to challenge dominant hegemonies defined in and through the archives (see Hamilton, 2011).

Restaging South African and European 'modern classics'

Another trend in both large state-sponsored venues and smaller theatres has been the 'revisiting of both local and global "modern classics", iconic South African works from the days of the struggle and European greats of the 20th century' (Thurman, 2010).[11] Thurman reports that after 'the usual glut of new pieces at the National Arts Festival' South Africa returns to theatre that characterised the apartheid period. I want to explore possible reasons for and implications of this trend, exploring how this relates to memory and the place of the theatrical repertoire in contemporary South African theatre.

I have suggested that reflective and restorative nostalgia is often evident in newly independent countries. Both kinds of nostalgia imply a longing for what is lost, or never achieved. It seems to me that despite the TRC's making public diverse experiences of apartheid and expanding a sense of the country's many histories, many South Africans do not necessarily subscribe to the narrative that has emerged, particularly insofar as it is framed through the lens of the dominant black, male ANC struggle narrative.[12] A consequence of this dominant narrative is that many people do not know where they belong in the 'rainbow nation', as their experiences are not reflected in the dominant repertoires, archives or various memorial sites. And so they return to the past, often in ways that express an acute sense of longing and loss for what seems to be lost, or never attained. One manifestation of this is the many revivals of plays created in the 1980s like the Wits Theatre 2010 'SA Season', which included Percy Mtwa, Mbongeni Ngema and Barney Simon's *Woza Albert!* (1980), Mtwa's *Bopha!* (Arrest, 1986),[13] Simon's *Born in the RSA* (1985), Paul Slabolepszy's *Saturday Night at the Palace* (1982), and Gçina Mhlophe's *Have you seen Zandile?* (1986).

Two things strike me about these plays – their canonicity as plays that addressed everyday realities of the turbulent 1980s, and the centrality of dreams and fantasies in the plays: we have only to think about Styles's 'strongroom of dreams' in *Sizwe Bansi is Dead* (Fugard, 2000: 159), or the fantasy scenes in *The Island*, where John and Winston imagine speaking with their families and achieving their freedom; or scenes of resistance and the resurrection of struggle heroes in *Woza Albert!*. In the 1980s these plays staged dreams of change and rehearsed possible ways of achieving it. In the post-apartheid context, though, they have a very different resonance. Immediately following the introduction of the new democracy many of these plays were performed in celebration of what had been achieved. However, almost two decades later there is a different atmosphere at revival performances, a much stronger sense

11 See Larlham (2007) on the revivals at the 2006 Grahamstown Festival.
12 Each of these terms is critically analysed in relation to contemporary definitions of identity in Mangcu (2011).
13 And its remake as a film in 1993, directed by Morgan Freeman.

of nostalgia as audiences contemplate the degree to which these dreams have been realised for the majority of South Africans, for example, in terms of the basic necessities outlined in *Woza Albert!*, where individuals dream of having enough food, education and fair working conditions. The longing continues, and the nostalgia deepens, not for the conditions of apartheid, but for the certainties of the struggle and a sense of belonging.

Have you Seen Zandile? was criticised in the 1980s for being apolitical, nostalgically dwelling on an idealised rural childhood;[14] however, in the post-apartheid context theatres have gone back to this play. This may be because, as Jennifer Delisle suggests, *Zandile* offers an 'experiential nostalgia' (2006: 338), which acts as a counter-discourse to the struggle and trauma narratives that characterised protest theatre and TRC testimonies. In 1994 Ndebele called for a shift in literature from 'spectacle', particularly related to group survival, to the 'rediscovery of the ordinary'[15] in literature. This comment relates to Sachs's (1991) call to rethink the way culture is mobilised in South Africa. Both men insist that artists and writers need to look at 'the way people actually live', peoples' everyday experiences, emotions and memories, mediated by personal reflection, and explore what can be learnt from these reflections (Ndebele, 1994: 50, 57). *Have you Seen Zandile?* is a clear example of how a play can explore the everyday while reflecting on the particular issues related to women's experiences and memories of apartheid, including loss and longing, which inform their position in the post-apartheid context.[16] The power of this approach to memory has not been lost to new playwrights, for example Farber's *Amajuba* (2008c), which traces five people's different experiences of everyday life under apartheid.

David Graver argues that 'South Africa's favourite subject of nostalgia is Sophiatown. The intellectual and cultural vibrancy of this integrated, 1950s Johannesburg suburb has made it an enduring image of urban African culture before the boot of apartheid came down' (1995: 104) As such, Sophiatown provided a context for the dream of a post-racial society where people could negotiate life together, irrespective of race, class or gender. Loren Kruger refers to it as a 'set', 'an actual but thoroughly imagined place that came, despite the violence perpetuated by police as well as tsotsis [gangsters], to symbolize a utopia of racial

14 These criticisms have been countered by Mda (1996), Perkins (1998), Walder (1998).
15 This essay was originally written in 1984.
16 For an analysis of Mhlope's position on feminism versus wider community-building, see Walder (1998).

tolerance and cultural diversity' (1997: 576).[17] Theatre keeps returning
to these dreams, reflecting critically both on the hopes and the extent
to which they have or have not been achieved in revivals of plays such
as *Sophiatown*, or with new plays such as Bloke Modisane's musical
Sophiatown to Bloke (1994), which reminds its audience of the dreams
for which many fought and died.

The second trend is the restaging of European classics, or adaptations
of these in the South African context. It could be argued that these classics are part of South Africa's theatrical repertoire, which has kept South
Africa connected to the wider world. However, these plays also provide
useful frames that facilitate the exploration of complex or taboo issues.
This is clear when one considers the particular Shakespearean or Greek
tragedies that are staged, plays like *Othello*, *Macbeth* and *Medea*; also
specific plays from the European avant-garde.[18]

Since the mid-1990s these engagements with classic European texts
have involved experimenting with performativity and non-realistic
forms. For example, Handspring Puppet Company consciously explored
the effects of working with puppets and multi-media in *Woyzeck on the
Highveld* (1992, unpublished), *Faustus in Africa!* (1994, unpublished)
and *Ubu and the Truth Commission* (Taylor, 1998). An important aspect
of this Company's work is the way they suggest links between colonialism, apartheid and the present, which challenges any impulse to see
these as separate historical periods with different issues. Brett Bailey's
use of ritual in *MacbEth – the opera* (2001), *Medeia* (2003) and *Orfeus*
(2006) draws an audience into the performance, and thereby insists on
their active engagement and response in negotiating issues of collective
responsibility in the context of social upheaval and violence.[19]

Mark Fleishman has also explored contemporary issues through the
lens of classic texts with his company Magnet Theatre. An example of
this is his production of *Medea* (1994). This play was pertinent, given
that it was produced a few months after Mandela was inaugurated as
president in a context of ongoing threats of violence, as it explores the
birth of a new dispensation from the ashes of an old system, marked
by conflict and betrayal. This production dealt both with the history of
colonisation and the complex moral decisions of the liberation struggle,
where the forms of resistance chosen by activists could be compared to

17 Kruger's (2001) analysis of more recent theatrical engagements with the city of
    Johannesburg extends a sense of the symbolic place of the city in formulating
    memory and identity in the post-apartheid urban context.
18 See van Zyl Smit (2008, 2010) on Greek tragedies, and Kruger (2004) and Germann
    (2008) on Brecht in South Africa.
19 See Bailey's (2003) diary entries on his process.

Medea's killing her children; an act which can be interpreted as revenge and/or as a means of protecting herself and her children.[20]

Medea's cast was multiracial; and the script was multilingual, including English, Afrikaans, isiXhosa, isiZulu, tsotsitaal (gangster slang), and Tamil; but instead of simply mirroring the new 'rainbow nation', the play critiqued the complexities involved in forging this nation, as the details of the plot were altered slightly in each language. This meant that the extent to which the audience made sense of the show depended on their linguistic abilities, and the degree to which they were familiar with the framing text. This offered a dramatic illustration of the complexities involved in South Africa's negotiating its multiple and complex contexts, perspectives and memories in the post-apartheid context. It also highlighted the significance of the framing text, which is an exploration of the possible reasons for committing an extreme act of violence, given that the nation was about to engage with these issues in the TRC hearings.[21]

This play also illustrates how a European 'classic' can provide a frame for theatrical innovation, as directors Mark Fleishman and Jennie Reznek experimented with physical embodiment and various South African oral traditions, which facilitated the inclusion of various voices and styles into the performance. This suggested how verbatim theatre continues to be central to South African theatre, as peoples' lived realities are incorporated into the fictional frame to explore communal experience and memories.[22] Fleishman's move away from focusing on a text to focusing on 'core images' resulted in the production moving away from an Aristotelian linear structure or being strongly text-based (Francis, 2006: 109), which required that the audience make sense of the play both visually and linguistically, drawing on different competences.[23] This destabilised the dominance of text and challenged European theatrical hegemonies, while simultaneously highlighting the gaps between a sensory experience and how it is communicated through language, and the multiplicity of possible interpretations of any event – issues that were highly problematic at the TRC. This embodied form facilitates the exploration of current socio-political issues while raising questions related to historiography, particularly regarding how

20 Halligey (2005) explores how Fleishman uses mythology to explore cultural identity in this play.
21 For further analysis of this play see Francis (2006) and Rudakoff (2006: 133–4).
22 See Fleischman (1990) on his developing conception of workshop theatre, and Hutchison (2010b) on verbatim theatre in South Africa.
23 This is one of the reasons why few of Magnet's works have been published as texts; Fleishman holds strong views on the importance of embodied practice (Fleishman and Davids, 2007).

interpretation and subjectivity affect the way in which we read the past and perceive the present. These explorations resist the staging of a single master narrative and suggest how an embodied performance can destabilise dominant hegemonies. Fleishman has argued that his work has been 'about remembering in the postcolony' (2011: 8). I will return to the significance of this in his more recent engagement with 'coloured' history and identity in the Western Cape.

It is clear that these restagings are not symptomatic of simple restorative nostalgia, an uncritical longing for the past, but suggest critical engagements with the gap between changes that were dreamt of and the realities facing contemporary South Africans.

Other contemporary playwrights continue to engage with unrealised dreams of change, indirectly, in new works. For example, Mpumelelo Paul Grootboom[24] offers a very different sense of contemporary urban township life than Sophiatown in his hyperrealist plays Cards (2001), Inter-Racial (2005), Relativity: Township Stories (developed with Presley Chweneyagae, 2005), Telling Stories (2007), Fore-Play (2009) and Welcome to Rocksburg (2009). These plays explore the implications of the rhythms of everyday urban life being determined by crime, rape and intimidation, especially for youths in the context of the HIV/AIDS pandemic. Grootboom has been nicknamed the 'Township Tarantino', because of the way in which he explores extreme violence and explicitly sexual issues by combining drama with dance, music and the film-like directing, which creates a level of distance from which audiences can engage with very dark and taboo subjects. Like Mike van Graan, Grootboom insists on the need to engage with these taboos, despite being criticised for not portraying 'the right image of blacks' (2008).

Reza de Wet is another playwright who has consciously used nostalgic dreams to critically explore post-apartheid issues. Her characters' fantasies often involve pathologies, where physical illness is related to psychic illness. For example, in Diepe Grond (first performed in 1986, translated African Gothic, 2005),[25] the first play in Vrystaat-trilogie (Free-State Trilogy, 1991, translated as Plays Two), the black nursemaid embodies the fantasy of the benevolent black mother who welcomes back the incestuous white children who have murdered their parents. Carli Coetzee (2001) critiques the implications of this fantasy, which omits to imagine the position of the black mother, or the potentially displaced black siblings. Nag, Generaal (Goodnight, General, 1988, translated as

---

24 Grootboom is resident director of the South African State Theatre.
25 This was the first Afrikaans play to be produced by the Market Theatre and has won a number of awards.

Breathing, 2005) explores the psyche of the wife of a Boer leader who returns home from the Anglo-Boer war (1899–1902), wounded and dying. The woman turns to Naas, a young 'brown' man who is a traditional healer, for help. This play proposes psychic healing by turning to an exotic 'alternative' spirituality.

de Wet's second trilogy, *Trits* (1993, published in English as *Plays One*, 2000), offers apparently naive folkloric stories to explore an oppressive, matriarchal order, defined by the myths and manacles of the Afrikaans–Calvinist tradition. Reza de Wet explores the everyday monotony of rural life through the eyes of various young female Afrikaans protagonists who dream of escape. These plays at once challenge Afrikaner nostalgia for a mythic rural wholeness, while exploring female suppression of sexual desire, which is condemned as 'wicked', revealing how many Afrikaner women have been complicit in female oppression. They also suggest that as long as women are afraid to engage with their own sexuality and sexual fantasies, they will remain puppets in a male dominated world. The fantasies and apparent nostalgia in these plays are used to reflect on the need to analyse and revise the terms in which this culture approaches gender, spirituality and its own history.

South Africa is revising paradigms that were either foregrounded or backgrounded during apartheid, including spirituality and the place of pre-colonial African cosmology with its attendant approaches to the place of ancestors[26] and the spirit realm in contemporary South African society. This is evident in Serote's novel *Revelations* (2010), Brett Bailey's plays *iMumbo Jumbo* (1997), *Ipi Zombie?* (1998), *The Prophet* (1999), and Chris Zithulele Mann's play *Thuthula: Heart of the Labyrinth* (2004). These plays provoked considerable controversy, particularly regarding the representation of Xhosa culture (van Heerden, 2008: 148–50, 226–7). Nevertheless, as Mandla Mbotwe, has argued, township popular rituals and spirituality may be crucial to exploring contemporary urban 'village' identity, with its 'many cultures, languages, ideologies and levels of economic status' (2010: 241). His collaborative isiXhosa production *Isivuno Sama Phupha* (Through dreams they speak, 2008) engages with Turner's ideas on social drama, liminality and theatre's potential to transformatively intervene in society. Thus, 11 members of the Khayeltisha community and four students staged a collaborative exploration of the place of dreams in township life at University of Cape Town's Arena theatre.

26 See Benedict Anderson's (2011) analysis of the potential implications of Weber's arguments regarding the relationship between nationhood, the idea of goodness and expectations associated with becoming 'worthy ancestors' for South Africa's new democracy.

It is thus clear that reaching back to past memories and cultural
paradigms is facilitating the renegotiation of how identity is formulated, and critically trying to move South Africans beyond simple racial
classification.

Performing history: methodologies for interrogating historical narratives

Another important way of engaging with the past is by dramatising
specific historic moments. There are many 'historic' plays, some subsi-
dised by central and local government, like much of Mbongeni Ngema's
work since 1994, and others that are independently produced and more
experimental. Ngema's popular 'historical' plays such as *Sarafina II*
(1995), *The Zulu* (1999), *1906 Bhambada* (2006) and *Lion of the East:
Gert Sibande and the Potato Boycott* (2009) are significant because they
have received relatively large subsidies. For example, Ngema received
some R14 million from the ANC-government (Pearson, 1996: 73)
to deal with HIV/AIDS in *Sarafina II*; and *Lion of the East* was commissioned by the Mpumalanga Department of Culture, Sports and
Recreation to commemorate the 50th anniversary of the 1958 Potato
Boycott led by ANC activist Gert Sibande. Ngema, was granted R22
million (Mtshali, 2009: 50–1). Mtshali analyses the significance of these
relatively large budgets, arguing that these plays are less about engaging critically with previously marginalised histories than attempts to
construct and maintain an official idea of local histories that simultaneously uphold the dominant liberation struggle narrative (*ibid.*). As such,
they do not purposefully reframe and reposition history in order to
provoke new ideas and ways of thinking for a community, as a Brechtian
approach to political historical theatre might do (Kruger, 2004); rather
they illustrate how history may be mobilised to reinforce specific state-
sanctioned narratives that support particular new 'official' versions of
South African history.

Andrew Buckland's *Makana – the Missing Lynx* (2001, unpublished)
exemplifies a more critical engagement with history. This play explores
the decisive Battle of Grahamstown between Xhosa leader Makana
and the British in 1819. Rather than present itself as a historical documentary, the play unravels the complexities of the historical figure and
the events that surrounded him. The subtitle is indicative of the play's
approach to the history, referring to the totemic name of Makana, while

punning on the 'missing links' of colonial historiography. Eckhard Breitinger suggests that the non-realistic, non-historical images and movements used in this play are 'farcical and comical, but they induce the spectator to speculate on historical realities and verisimilitudes' (2007: 42). The non-realistic form is important as a methodology for interrogating an historical narrative, as it highlights the potential for multiple readings of the narratives, and thus highlights rather than obfuscates the ambiguities associated with historiography. Fleishman engaged with the same historical figure in *53 Degrees* (2002/3), the first production in a series that engaged with specific moments in history, archives and sites of memory in embodied and performative ways that do not privilege text or the spoken word, but focus on images, sounds, movement to create a sense of reconstructing a fragmented sense of the past in relation to the present. I will return to some of this work later in the chapter.

Of the various experiments with non-realistic explorations of historic subjects, Brett Bailey's plays are among the most controversial. His historic plays include the dramatisation of Chief Nicholas Gcaleka's journey to Scotland in 1996 to retrieve the head of his ancestor, King Hintsa kaPhalo, paramount chief of the amaXhosa who was killed by a colonial posse in 1836 in *iMumbo Jumbo* (1997); *The Prophet* (1999), which relates the story of Nonqawuse, a 15-year-old girl who persuaded the Xhosa people to sacrifice all their livestock to overcome the British in the mid-nineteenth century; and *Big Dada – The Rise and Fall of Idi Amin* (2001), which moves outside of South Africa to explore dictatorship in contemporary Africa. The controversy centres on Bailey's eclectic mix of spiritual forms: trance dance, African *sangomas* (diviners/shamans), consciously structuring the plays in the form of an *intlombe*, a play within a ritual (Bailey, 1998: 193), in combination with overt melodramatic theatricality, 'pantomime caricatures' and exhibitionism which requires audiences to explore how they construct their own realities, particularly in relation to memory and conflict.

Ritual is often mobilised in times of crisis. In a ritual context a liminal space and time is invoked to facilitate a structured engagement with irrational emotion, particularly fear, to facilitate a symbolic rebalancing of a situation or community. Victor Turner argues that out of liminal or liminoid situations such as public ceremonies, performances or carnivals, new symbols and paradigms arise and are fed back into the 'central' socio-political arenas (1982: 28). This would suggest that Bailey is inviting the audience to engage with contested histories or memories, while acknowledging emotions like fear. The layered performance allows an audience to acknowledge their emotional attachment to an idea or memory, while facilitating their stepping back to evaluate this memory, emotion or idea.

The issue in Bailey's work seems to be the extent to which Bailey goes beyond exposing subjective emotion to facilitate critical evaluation. Bailey has been criticised for simply juxtaposing brutal excesses of violence with eclectic popular music, art and performance forms that provoke laughter.[27] For example, in response to *Big Dada,* Breitinger argued that the highly sophisticated combination of freak and peep show formats prevented the play from rising 'above pure spectacle in yellow press style', and that the representation of Amin as 'the bloodthirsty clown' did not explore 'the reasons, motivations, structures supporting that clown that would bring us a little closer to an understanding of the Amin phenomenon' (2001: 184). Krueger reads this play differently, suggesting that Bailey's works share Dionysian aspects of tragedy, refusing anyone 'consolation, exoneration or reprieve' (2010: 153–70). These responses highlight the complexities involved when experimenting with new performance forms in the context of violent histories and memories; given South Africa's diverse cultural frames which are not sufficiently established to allow too much experimentation and intercultural experimentation, perhaps.

Nostalgia as 'melancholia of freedom'

Addressing the issue of belonging is central to dismantling apartheid ideologies. Thus the post-apartheid government took up Tutu's formulation of South Africa as the 'rainbow nation' as the state metaphor for this diverse and divided nation. However, evidence suggests that many South Africans feel increasingly ambivalent about this concept. Helga Dickow and Valerie Møller's trend study on the acceptance of the rainbow as political symbol of unity suggested that

> the number of supporters declined steadily over time; the number of 'non-believers' increased from 11% in 1994 to 28% in 1999. The most dramatic change of perception appears to have occurred among Indians. In 1994 Indians were overwhelmingly 'believers' (75%), in 1996 mainly 'opponents' of the political interpretation of the rainbow (44%); in 1999 the proportion of non-believers (37%) was almost equal to that of supporters. In the

27 For images see www.thirdworldbunfight.co.za/ productions.

second round of research it was observed that the personal interpretation of the rainbow had shifted from the political to the religious sphere among substantial proportions of South Africans. In the third round, the most significant shift was to 'non-belief'. (2002: 184)

This shift is ironic considering that initially the Indian constituency had been 'among the staunchest "supporters" of the rainbow as political symbol in 1994, [and] were most likely to endorse the rainbow's political significance with 67%; whites the least (40%)' (*ibid.*, 188). Dickow and Møller suggest that this change is a result of this group's perception that now this symbol is more divisive than reconciliatory, because of its place in official government rhetoric.

Thomas Blom Hansen has described many Indians' reactions to the changes in their position in South Africa as revealing 'melancholia of freedom' (2005). This melancholia is perhaps better described as a collective nostalgia which looks back to a time during which Indians were seen as being part of those discriminated against by apartheid, and thus part of the resistance movement. However, the changes wrought by the new South Africa have brought multiple losses to many South African Indians:

> Loss of economic security, loss of the township as 'our place'; loss of perceived existential and physical safety; loss of a sense of 'community unity' which was the product of the apartheid regime's racialized deployment of political repression; and finally, a more imperceptible version of what Hegel famously called the 'loss of the loss,' that is, the disappearance of the blockage – unfreedom and apartheid – that prevented true self-realization and thus could explain a range of problems and shortcomings in everyday life. (Hansen, 2005: 298)

The problem is succinctly outlined by Krijay Govender, who compares Indian and black women's negotiation of identity in the post-apartheid context, asserting that

> the South African Indian woman's position of marginality differs from that of the South African black woman's experience. The South African Indian woman is marginalised by race, class, sex and a sense of 'not' belonging to the African continent. It could be argued that this sense of 'not belonging' is a part of a constructed nostalgia: she is referred to as Indian (which is a reminder of India) – as opposed to 'white' or 'black'. (Govender, 2001: 36)

This negotiation of identity in post-apartheid South Africa is complex, as the subject must renegotiate his or her place in society in multiple terms and not simply in relation to race. For the Indian subject this has taken a particular form, insofar as many contemporary Indians refer back to the *charou* culture to reflect critically on their longing for a past that is not retrievable. Ordinary working class Indians in the township were colloquially referred to as *charou*s [literally 'burnt man' in Afrikaans]. The culture includes jokes, puns and everyday mockery and satire that is 'associated with superstition, gullibility, funny accents, ridiculous submission to the white *baas*, and excessive drinking' (Hansen, 2005: 298, 303). Many plays look back at this culture wistfully, while also recognising that it is no longer appropriate for urban, middle-class Indians and that its representation is an 'idealization of a wholesome community life of the past (*ibid.*, 299).[28]

Rajesh Gopie's play *Out of Bounds* (first performed in 2003) explores this nostalgia among successful educated Indians. It touches on Indo-African relations, but also explores political space, filial relations, sexuality, identity and being uprooted. Gopie critiques the Indian political space for becoming 'pretty much the same as the middle-class white political space. It's where we don't want to know anything about apartheid – as if it didn't affect our lives' (Moodley, 1999). This comment highlights Indian amnesia in the face of post-apartheid realities, with a corresponding reversion to explore nostalgic memories of *charou* culture which Hansen argues in this play 'becomes a colourful, even innocent, past that has to die, tragically, to enable modern Indians to evolve and attain true freedom as modern individuals' (2005: 313). Much stand-up comedy in particular 'make[s] the non-contemporary features of the *charou* culture into a farce' (*ibid.*). However, what is evident is that the position of contemporary Indians in South Africa is too insecure for this humour to be celebratory, suggesting an acknowledged departure from this past. There is a strong sense of nostalgic longing for the innocent and perceived coherence of knowing where one belonged and what one was fighting for and against, without a resolved alternative being presented in this play.

It is perhaps significant that contemporary Indian women playwrights are less caught up in this particular nostalgia for *charou* culture than their male counterparts. While male playwrights focus on race and class issues, gender issues remain largely ignored, and women still continue to be represented as stereotypes at best and easy targets of ridicule at worst.[29] Muthal Naidoo has argued that because the South African

---

28 This echoes much of the sentiment of Jacob Dhlamini's *Native Nostalgia*, which is an account of happy reflections of particular experiences of urban black South Africans living in townships like Thandukhanya, near Piet Retief, or Katlehong, near Germiston.

29 Krijay Govender's (2001) analysis includes Ronnie Govender's *The Lahnee's Pleasure*,

Indian community 'is such a tiny community, it is seen from without to be a homogenous group. Meanwhile, it is an extremely diverse group with different religions, languages, customs, class and political affiliations leading to all kinds of internal tensions' (1993: 1), which are dramatised in her protagonist Seetha in *Masks* (1983). Thus, Muthal Naidoo[30] set the pace for the generation of female playwrights whose work was performed in the 1990s: Ismail Mahomed (*Purdah*, 1999), Nadine Naidoo (*Nadia*, unpublished), Krijay Govender (*Women in Brown*, unpublished) and Devi Sarinjei (*Acts of God*, unpublished). These plays explore issues of gender and religion alongside race and class in the new South Africa.

Nostalgia is powerful as it can evoke sympathy, to the extent that memory is something shared. At their best, these plays invite an audience to reflect critically on their own dreams and fantasies, to evaluate the reason for a sense of loss or longing, and then consider how to achieve what they feel has not yet been accomplished. The plays draw attention to the legacies of apartheid and invite an audience to engage with and continue to deconstruct them.

Similar explorations of belonging and disavowed memories are evident in contemporary attempts to renegotiate coloured identity.

Dramatising Cape coloured history and identity

One of the most dogged issues facing post-apartheid South Africa is the issue of terminology, as my framing note on terminology suggests. The apartheid terms of racial classification are complex and the process of dismantling them fraught with conflict, as evidenced in Thobeka Mda's challenge, entitled 'Can Whites Truly be called African?' (*The Star*, 17 June 1999), in response to Max du Preez's claim to be 'an African . . . an Afrikaner' (*The Star*, 24 June 1999).[31] These terms, and the way in which

---

Kriben Pillay's *Looking for Muruga* and Aldrin Naidu's, *Mooidevi's Muti* (Tails of the Bengal Tigers), and the two skits, *Four Weddings and a Plastic Surgeon* and *SAA Steamy Seema* (2001). Ashwin Singh's plays (*To House, Looney Lahnee Show, Spice 'n Stuff, Marital Blitz*) deconstructs class and implies criticism regarding women as objects of desire, but they do not suggest how this could or should be changed.

30 She has written numerous plays, see www.muthalnaidoo.co.za/wip-theatre-plays-othermenu-113, or Naidoo (2008).

31 This polemic raged between journalists John Matshikiza, Max du Preez and Lizeka Mda, and academic Thobeka Mda in *The Star* and *Weekly Mail & Guardian* from 17 June to the end of July 1999. See also van Zyl Slabbert (2011).

they define identities, remain trapped within apartheid paradigms and their attendant values, hierarchies and even memories. Therefore, negotiating identity must begin with unravelling the assumptions and values of the racial classifications of apartheid, and nuancing a sense of identity by acknowledging the complex simultaneity of various aspects which define individual subjectivity, like ethnicity, gender, language, religion, history and memory, which is my focus here. South Africa has long been trapped in a prescriptive approach to identity, so it is worth engaging with Deleuze's alternative, rhizomatic model of approaching identity, where 'any point can be connected to anything else' (1993: 29–30), to challenge the more hierarchical arboreal model. Elizabeth Grosz articulates Deleuze's concept of multiplicity thus:

> A multiplicity as not a pluralized notion of identity (identity multiplied by *n* locations), but is rather an ever-changing, nontotalizable collectivity, an assemblage defined not by its abiding identity of principle of sameness over time, but through its capacity to undergo permutations and transformations, that is, its dimensionality. (1994: 192)

This definition allows the subject to escape from having to prioritise aspects hierarchically, allowing him or her to place language, culture, gender, religion in dialogue with one another.[32] It also suggests the pertinence of theatre, where the simultaneous presentation of various images and ideas is more easily staged than in artistic forms where ideas must be presented more chronologically.

In this process it is important to consider not only memories that are perceived as positive or desirable, but also those that are, or have been, disavowed. As an example I turn to consider how the histories and memories of Cape coloureds are being re-examined, particularly with reference to slave narratives, in the process of their renegotiating their identity and sense of belonging in South Africa.

The term 'coloured' is used to refer to South Africans of mixed racial background, usually from South-east Asian, European or African-European backgrounds. There is much debate about this definition of racial identity: Zimitri Erasmus and Edgar Pieterse (1999) and Erasmus (2001) have traced the evolution of the term and argue that it may serve different purposes, both politically conservative in the apartheid sense of defining racial difference, and also politically radical as a self-descriptor. I am particularly indebted to Erasmus's (2001) later collection of essays on new perspectives on coloured identity, including Reddy's analysis

---

32 Although as Nadia Davids's *At Her Feet* demonstrates, this is more easily proposed than achieved.

of how the classification was used by apartheid governments to 'mop up' 'residue from other classifications' (2001: 71). Pumla Gqola's (2010) analysis of the various issues that inform discourses on coloured identity, particularly the re-engagement with slave narratives, frames my analysis of how performance has contributed to an exploration of history and memory in the Western Cape.

Discussing 'coloured' identity is particularly fraught, because often the term implicitly conjures up colonial historical constructions of degeneracy and shame (Wicomb, 1998). It also implies inbetween-ness, which can suggest both not-belonging and a creative hybridity that allows for self-identification. The latter falls into the sphere of creolisation, which in recent South African studies has moved beyond theorising linguistic creolisations to consider the phenomenon either as 'any mixing of various strands to result in a hybrid formation which constantly draws attention to itself as dynamic and disruptive';[33] or it is theorised 'under the very specific conditions of slavery and its ensuing inequalities' (Gqola 2010: 29). I want to look at how contemporary negotiations of coloured identity in terms of renegotiating memories of slavery highlight the faultlines in the currently dominant discourses of the rainbow nation and the liberation struggle, which do not foreground these aspects of colonialism and apartheid, while simultaneously sug-gesting the potential for a more dynamic and disruptive approach to engaging with identity formation.

Cape coloured identity is most often represented with reference to the New Year Carnival. Until recently the New Year Carnival was one of the few ways in which Cape Town's slave history was acknowledged. Between 1652 and 1808 approximately 63,000 persons were brought to the Cape as slaves, and probably as many were born into slavery. In 1834 there were 36,169 slaves in the Cape: 26.4% were brought from other African countries, such as Mozambique, or the east African islands; 25.9% were from Madagascar; and 22.7% from areas now termed Indonesia (Shell, 1994). Although the Company forbade the enslave-ment of the indigenous Khoisan peoples, many of the Khoi people were forced to leave their own pastoral or hunter-gatherer lifestyles because of illness and colonial intrusion to work as serfs for European farmers, where they lived in close proximity to their European masters and these masters' slaves, and thus a creole society began to evolve in the Cape.[34]

33 See the work of Sarah Nuttall and Cheryl-Ann Michael (2000).
34 Although this was mostly at the level of subcultures, with vast discrepancies between classes, it is worth remembering that between 1665 and 1784 at least 32 official weddings between people of different races were celebrated at the Cape church (Martin, 1999: 55; Schoemann, 2007).

Armstrong and Worden argue that this sub-culture provided the basis for the urban working-class culture of the nineteenth and twentieth centuries in Cape Town (1992: 148).

Martin traces some of the diverse cultural aspects of Cape Town: as Dutch Reformed Christians believed that baptised slaves should be freed, or could not be sold, very few slave children were baptised and slaves were not converted. This resulted in Islam, brought from South-east Asia, spreading among the slave population, which is why the term 'Cape Malay' is used interchangeably for 'Cape coloured', but this is problematic as not all coloured people in the Cape are Muslim (Baderoon, 2004). Martin also traces how Afrikaans developed as Portuguese creole, Malayu and other Asian languages written in Arabic script interacted with Dutch to become Afrikaans (1999: 55–7). This history is important when one considers the place of Afrikaans in South African history, and how it has been perceived as a marker of Afrikaner hegemony. Revisiting the language's history is a way of revising relationships and definitions of belonging in the country.

As the New Year celebration was the most important festival for the colony, it brought together many aspects of this complex culture. As slave owners celebrated the New Year on 1 January, slaves were allowed 2 January off, and so celebrated a 'second new year', which from the beginning of the nineteenth century included street parades with musicians. This context of the New Year is significant in the light of Jo Roach's (1996) arguments on the relationship between memory, performance and substitution. He argues that 'newness enacts a kind of surrogation', which is the process whereby a culture reproduces or re-creates itself by filling the gaps brought about by change. Notably, in the context of the colonial endeavour 'it also conceptually erases indigenous populations' (1996: 4). This is evident in South Africa, where the history of slavery has been all but denied until recently (Gqola, 2010). But Roach continues, suggesting that although forgetting is central to establishing new colonies,

> a great deal of the unspeakable violence instrumental to this creation may have been officially forgotten, circum-Atlantic memory retains its conse-quences, one of which is that the unspeakable cannot be rendered forever inexpressible: the most persistent mode of forgetting is memory imper-fectly deferred. (1996: 4)

This embodied remembering is evident in the New Year Carnival, which was a public performance that expressed the slaves' disaffection with their situation, particularly in terms of their invisibility. This was not recognised by the colonial masters, who described these performances

5.1 Company members of Magnet and Jazzart Theatre in *Cargo* (2007).

as 'frivolous' and 'fantastical'. They did, however, recognise something inherently disturbing in the performances: a description in the *Cape Times* of 4 January 1886 says that 'they seemed like so many uncanny spirits broken loose from – say the adamantine chains of the Nether World' (in Martin, 1999: 90). This reference to the uncanny and 'Nether World' is significant because in many ways the slaves lived like ghosts, between worlds, non-people who were not allowed symbolic markers of being human, like belts, buckles, buttons or shoes, a fact that Fleishman references in his engagement with this history in *Cargo* (see Figure 5.1).

The image of ghosts is also significant because, as discussed in Chapter 2 on dramatic engagements with the TRC, haunting signals unresolved conflict. Roach traces how in the modern European worldview the living are separated from the dead, rather than being omnipresent, as in many other traditions. However, the consequence of this segregation is that the living struggle to 'remember who they are' (Roach, 1996: 47–55). This public performance by the slaves, who in some ways are the living dead, allowed them to remember and celebrate the fact that they were people, while at the same time forcing their colonial masters to engage with them as living ghosts, and the consequence of their subjugation. This event takes place in a liminal time and space, which opens up the possibility both for addressing crisis and suggesting change. Thus, the Emancipation Procession of 1834 may be seen as a symbolic gesture of courage as the now-liberated people visibly performed their freedom, literally filling the streets with their presence and voices, and as they continued to enact this memory, they reminded the European colonisers of a history they would perhaps have preferred to forget.

Various other histories and narratives are embedded in the performances of the New Year Carnival.[35] An important influence was that of the American blackface minstrels, who first visited Cape Town in 1848 and by 1860 had inspired local imitations. The minstrel style placed this slave tradition in dialogue with comparable trans-Atlantic traditions (Meltzer, et al, 2010: 2; Davids, 2007: 134–8; Martin, 1999: 84–8). The carnival literally retained disavowed slave memories as an embodied repertoire. Some of the songs, like the Alabama Song, commemorate a local historic event,[36] other songs such as 'Rule Britannia' overtly criticised colonial rule in its adapted lyrics; one variation reportedly went:

> Come Britannia, the civilizing one,
> Make the nation into slaves . . .
> Your tyranny will soon humble
> Those that call this land their own.
>
> (Christine Winberg's translation, cited in Martin, 1999: 91)

These songs embody the various European influences on this creole community, as they demonstrate the strong influence from American vaudeville or minstrel shows, the various church repertoires; and popular songs from Amsterdam which a retired Dutch sailor and a Capetonian singer taught the local people (*ibid.*, 93). They also suggest a significant degree of interaction between people from various cultural and racial backgrounds in the nineteenth century, and how surrogation occurs between participating cultures (Roach, 1996: 5)

The carnival inevitably articulated cultural contestations, as it provided a space in which 'social codes are reversed and participants act out personas considered unacceptable in "conventional" society' (Meltzer, et al., 2010: 17). This was most evident in the figure of the 'moffie', a term derived from an old Dutch word 'mof', used in the Cape to refer to any stranger; it is now used extensively in South Africa to refer pejoratively

---

35 There are various groups that perform: the Klopse Nagtroepe also called Malay choirs, Hollandse Teams or Sangkore and the Christmas Bands. Each group has a specific uniform, which is also evaluated in the competitions that are central to the New Year Carnival. See Jeppie (1990), Martin (1999) on the New Year Carnival

36 The capture of the Unionist *Sea Bride* by the Confederate raider the *CSS Alabama* in Table Bay at the time of the American Civil War; this inspired the naming of a rigged cutter in Cape Town in 1864, which linked the West Coast to Cape Town before the railway link was built, as well as signalling less salubrious relationships between sailors and local women.

to homosexual men. The 'moffie' has been a central figure in the Klopse (literally, clubs or troupes), and Nagtroepe (literally night troupes) since the 1940s as a male performer who dresses in women's clothing and performs subversive humour, songs and self-parody. It has always engaged with the most controversial figures or aspects of the community and in contemporary society highlights how contested sexual orientation is in the context of defining coloured identity (see Jeppie, 1990: 81). The shift in this figure from representing notions of non-belonging, being a 'stranger' to contemporary associations of this figure with alternative sexual orientations suggests how repertoires morph to reflect contemporary concerns, while retaining traces that reveal the origins of values, here ways of performing belonging or not-belonging. The carnival also provides a forum for engaging with issues of current concern or interest. For example, in 2011 many floats represented aspects of the 2010 Football World Cup and cited HIV/AIDS.

The post-apartheid context has provoked new engagements with old histories and memories in Cape Town. The forced removals of people living in District Six in the late 1960s resulted in the formation of three distinctive communities: people living in Manenberg, Langa and Protea Village, and Kirstenbosch. These people were separated according to apartheid racial classifications, which divided families and communities and led to their having different memories of the removals, and their developing very different social and cultural identities. The District Six Museum has been careful to organise various events, including workshops and conferences to hear different voices, and to avoid representing the history of the area as a single, coherent narrative.[37] The museum has also created diverse creative engagements with the history of the area, including site walks and a sound archive, which includes oral testimonies and recordings of various music traditions that defined the area.

An important aspect of the museum's work has been its collaborative community projects with the Magnet Theatre Company, such as *Vlam* (Flame, 1999) and *Re-imagining Carnival* (2003). *Vlam* involved community groups from various races, classes and ages in creating masks, large sculptural objects, backpack puppets, musical instruments out of PVC plumbing pipes, lanterns, dance and music in modes reminiscent of the West African masquerade tradition, which may or may not have invoked actual memories of the origins of slaves from this area. Then, on 16 December 1999, Reconciliation Day, 500 participants paraded through Cape Town to a large vacant lot in District Six, under the

---

37 See website for previous events, and Bennett *et al.* (2007) on the 2005 *Hands on District Six* Conference.

shadow of Table Mountain, where with the help of Southern Edge Arts (Western Australia), they ritually burnt the giant puppet figures as a symbolic act of cleansing of past losses and anger for the 3000 people present. This event again highlights the importance of ritual as a catalyst that can symbolically bring people from very diverse racial, ethnic, class and religious backgrounds together to address grievances, and then facilitate a symbolical letting go of the memories or grievances that divide them. Although one may argue that the effect was limited, Thompson argues that it 'can *linger*' (2005: 235, emphasis in original) beyond the event, in the embodied memories. One could argue that this community project extended the carnival repertoire to demonstrate the potential for cooperation across wider communities and rehearsed a way of their moving forward together in the future.

The *Re-imagining Carnival* project looked at the so-called Cape Coloured Coon Carnival, now renamed the New Year Carnival, and how it impacts on contemporary Cape coloured identity.[38] In 2002 the museum again collaborated with Fleishman as he researched and workshopped *Onnest'bo* (colloquial Afrikaans for 'upside-down', 2002) which revisited forced removals, slavery and the fragmented memories of people who had been resident in the District Six area. Fleishman and Davids (2007) reflect on the place of these two theatrical pieces in engaging with local people's memories in the context of performance repertoires such as the New Year Carnival that are culturally central to the area, but also contested and layered. Davids suggests that as a dominant cultural practice the carnival suggests the possibility of a collective identity, while reclaiming disavowed memories and ownership of the street, as participants verbally remember and recite the names of streets and landmarks that are no longer there (2007: 130–1, 140). Fleishman and Davids point out an important difference between a theatrical engagement with memory, and history:

> Theatre as an embodied practice is capable of stimulating, through a combination of affect, intellect and various sensory modalities, an empathetic bond between audience and stage. And it is this empathetic and emotional telling that is prioritised when theatre participates in historiography and memorialisation, not a factual telling. (2007: 161)

38 In 2011 Iziko Museums curated a number of related exhibitions: 'Ghoema & Glitter: New Year Carnival in Cape Town' at the Castle of Good Hope; 'Slaves at the Cape: Oppression, Life and Legacy' at the Slave Lodge; 'Made in Translation: Images from and of the Landscape', which looked at issues of translation of Leo Frobenius's collection of large-scale copies of rock art, 1928–30; and 'Mapping Bo-Kaap: Histories, Memories and Spaces', at the Bo-Kaap Museum.

This suggests that repertoires engage with more than factual narrative, they acknowledge emotional memory, and facilitate understanding and empathy, even for those who do not share the memory or history at hand.

Carnival is an example of how critical nostalgia may be used to renegotiate contemporary identities by addressing shameful or disavowed aspects of memory. There are obviously other ways to critically engage with heritage, memory and specific cultural constructions of identity. For example, Nadia Davids's play *At her Feet* (2002) suggests the complexities of Cape Muslim women negotiating South African identity in terms of race, ethnicity, local gender hegemonies and stereotypes, particularly surrounding food[39] and religion. It also asks where they stand in relation to the Muslim world on issues such as *purdah* and honour killings.

Fleishman's *Cargo* (2007) offers a more focused 'performative engagement with the archive of slavery at the Cape' (Magnet Theatre website), which extends beyond exploring slavery at the Cape to addressing the related issues of archaeology, heritage, memory and ownership of the past. Fleishman (2011) recounts how the production was triggered by the discovery of the remains of some 3000 persons on a multimillion-rand real estate development site on Prestwich Street, Cape Town in 2003. Fierce debate between archaeologists, business and cultural activists ensued about how best to engage with the bodies of marginalised and disenfranchised persons of the nineteenth century (Weeder, 2008). Many of the issues raised echoed the fierce debates triggered by the return of the remains Sara Baartman, the Hottentot Venus, to South Africa, explored in Myer Taub's play *Sara Baartman: the Hottentot Venus and the Wonders of things Unknown* at the Little Theatre, Cape Town in 2002.

In conceptualising his approach to this production, Fleishman draws on Pierre Nora and de Certeau to explore how a performance can engage with archives and 'get at what has been left out, the voices and their bodies'.[40] In this process Fleishman engages with material that has been translated and is missing, alongside issues of absent subjects, which he seeks ways to 'make present', and re-member, by 'put[ting] the body back together again'. This is not a simple process both because there are always holes in the archive and because 'the forms that emerge often tend towards disruption, discontinuity, irony and endless repetition,

39 See Gabeda Baderoon (2002, 2007) on Muslim food and identity.
40 All these references without citation are from the Magnet Theatre website notes on *Cargo*.

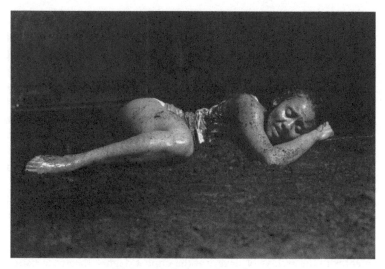

5.2 Leverne Botha in *Cargo* (2007).

denying the potential for recuperation and easy reconstruction.' In other words, the process of reconstructing the past resists coherent narration. This production addresses these issues by using core images to evoke the fragments, the voices and bodies that have been lost, and thus 'make the archive speak in unspeakable ways' (Fleishman, 2011: 15, see Figure 5.2). Using inventory lists the cast improvised with associations to find ways to embody their subjective responses to the objects and records of various slaves' experiences, including images of violence. This resulted in 'a collection of compound images', consisting of physical, vocal and musical gestures that referred to fleeting glimpses of the past (*ibid.*, 17). Fleishman insists that these are 'not re-enactments, but recreations of what remains of the past' (*ibid.*, 18), which allow for those involved, performers and audience alike, to 'play at assemblage' and thus, Fleishman argues, 'we generate possibilities through the adventure of experimenting and improvising with fragments of the past and what we make of them in the present' (*ibid.*, 19). This particular way of engaging with memory and archives suggests an awareness of the complex layers of interference, of time, place and translation. It emphasises the role of imagination and the centrality of current agendas in any engagement with the past.

The importance of slave narratives is increasingly being acknowledged in South Africa by historians and those working in the fields of memory and culture, as evidenced by the South African Cultural Museum being renamed the Slave Lodge in 1998. This awareness has involved individuals engaging with previously disavowed slave histories in their personal lives, as can be seen in the South African iblog 'Cape-Slavery-Heritage' which is a public forum for debate on historical events, figures and terminology.[41] For example, the suggestion that a street in Cape Town be named after Kratoa Eva van Meerhof, a woman regarded by many as a highly significant Khoe figure of the seventeenth century, has sparked a heated debate over terminology and reference. She had family in important positions among more than one Khoe clan. She lived in a Dutch household in her youth and served as an interpreter in the 1658 war between the Dutch and the Khoe. In 1659 she married a Dutch man, Pieter van Meerhof, becoming the first Khoe woman formally to marry a colonial. The Cape-Slavery-Heritage iblog traces the debate between her family, represented by Patric Tariq Mellet, and the city council regarding the name by which she should be remembered (Mellet, 2011).

Exhibitions like 'Slaves at the Cape: Oppression, Life and Legacy' (Slave Lodge, 2011) offer a strange mix of 'facts' about life as a slave in the Cape colony and opportunities for imaginative engagements with the slave experiences. This exemplifies how embodied memory can be mobilised to encourage a broad public to engage with more subjective aspects of this historical period, and thus enable empathetic response with material that may not be part of a visitor's own history. The imaginative installations included a set-like recreation of a slave ship, the *Meermin*, which was sent by the Cape VOC authorities in the eighteenth century to Madagascar to trade with local rulers and return with enslaved men, women and children. The Column of Memory consisted of wooden segments that could be rotated independently of one another. The exhibition description suggested that

> turning the rings in the column, each inscribed with names of slave inmates of the Slave Lodge, becomes a means of triggering memory, even a metaphorical release. The rings in turn are associated with tree rings, the passing of time, and the story handed down over generations that slaves brought to the Cape were auctioned, as commodities, under trees.

Opposite the column, written on the wall in gold paint against a dark brown background the words of Maika Ndlovu's poem 'Slave Dream' were inscribed: 'In the light of memory and remembering * Through the streams of our senses * Reconnecting * Recollecting * We find our way home' (2005). This poem suggests a clear link between recovering slave memory and renegotiating coloured identity and belonging

41 See http://cape-slavery-heritage.iblog.co.za/ on this debate.

in contemporary South Africa. It also suggests that nostalgia is central to the process, insofar as this past is reconstructed rather than remembered, in ways that support present narratives of belonging. The slave narratives highlight how the slaves literally and economically built Cape Town, and thus imply that coloureds have a legitimate claim to belonging in Cape Town and its surrounding areas.

This exhibition was directly linked to the exhibition 'Mandela: Leader, Comrade, Negotiator, Prisoner, Statesman', which traced Mandela's long walk to freedom, by a corridor. The latter exhibition drew direct parallels between the slave narratives and Mandela's experiences, suggesting that he was also 'not born free', which suggests an attempt to parallel the slave and struggle narratives and thus to dismantle Cape coloured mistrust of the ANC. It acknowledged the Mandela administration's failure to develop an effective strategy to address the effects of HIV and AIDS, and then listed his success stories, including the TRC, his projects for development, housing, building democracy and the Constitution. Under the heading 'Uniting a Nation', it highlighted how Mandela used the 1995 Rugby World Cup to unite South Africa.[42] In highlighting Mandela, the least controversial ANC figure, this exhibition clearly attempted to suggest parallels between the nation's struggle narratives and the slave narrative, and thus close the gap between the national narratives and the coloured people in the Cape. Again, ideological ideas are connected to particular and emotive memories in and through a specific embodied persona.

These theatrical performances, exhibitions and cyber engagements suggest that memory and history are fundamental to how South Africans are negotiating what is remembered and forgotten, and thereby 'writing' and performing themselves in the present.

Conclusion

It is clear that the attempt to get South Africans to engage with their various memories of the past and thus revise ways in which people engage with one another in the present through the TRC, symbolic reparations, including various memorial projects, and the African

---

42 See Maingard (1997) for an analysis of the way this event represented identity and re-imagined the nation; also the film *Invictus* (2009), dir. Clint Eastwood, Warner Bros.

Renaissance, has been only partially successful. This may be because the state has attempted to create a coherent, overarching master narrative of reconciliation for a 'rainbow nation' under the rubric 'unity in diversity'. Although there is a declaration of equality and diversity, it is clear from the archives that have emerged from the TRC, the conceptualisation of the African Renaissance Project in South Africa, and the public discussions concerning identity in post-apartheid South Africa (Mangcu, 2011) that this is not the perceived reality for all South Africans. In part, this is due to the diversity of people's experiences of apartheid, and also because of the particular ways in which the 'Struggle for Liberation' narrative has been foregrounded. Also, some of the foundational aspects of apartheid, including its systemic socioeconomic inequities, institutional violence and the ways in which gender roles have been defined in relation to these struggle narratives have not been deconstructed, but remain contested issues in post-apartheid South Africa.

Looking at how the nation has been conceptualised and performed at various moments of transition: the state of Union in 1910, the 1938 Centenary of the Great Trek, and the latest interregnum as the country moved from apartheid to democracy in the early 1990s, suggests the significance of performance in communicating particular conceptions of the nation to the wider public. Embodied repertoires, including popular songs and dances, stories and the citation of specific memories and histories, are central to creating a sense of a shared community. The extent to which individuals identify with these repertoires and historic narratives determines the extent to which they feel that they 'belong' in the nation.

The importance of shared narratives has been demonstrated in the way the embodied TRC testimonies have facilitated a greater awareness of the harsh realities of apartheid and created a wider acknowledgement that South Africa's history is more diverse than formerly understood, despite various objections to the terms of the TRC. However, Mbeki's failure to link his Renaissance project to an embodied repertoire familiar to South Africans has resulted in the Timbuktu Manuscript project remaining an intellectual concept rather than really engaging people with a more positive sense of African history and achievements. It could have highlighted South Africa's potential for offering comparable research, scholarship and art to the world, while at the same time critiquing the place of slavery in the history of Empire, both in Africa and Europe. This failure suggests the limitations of restorative nostalgia, which lacks critical reflection on what underpins the sense of longing or lack, in this case for a positive sense of African achievement, and responding to this need in the present. In some ways the performances of South Africa's aspirations and potential were more successfully communicated in the 2010 World Cup public events than in Mbeki's Timbuktu Script and Scholarship exhibition. The opening and closing ceremonies and the television presentations of South Africa acknowledged various traditions, while offering new interpretations of old symbols and repertoires, and creating new symbols, which situated South Africa as a progressive modern country, engaged with other contexts. This was achieved primarily through eclectic music, dance and new media.[43] This, and other examples discussed in this chapter, show how old repertoires can be mobilised and transformed into new repertoires and traditions that can address contemporary issues, negotiate new identities and perceptions of a nation.

It has been inspiring to see how theatre is engaging with these issues, both reflecting back critically through revivals of apartheid classics, and in new work which is exploring innovative ways of engaging with diverse, complex and at times unspeakable stories. Of particular note is how many artists are engaging in different ways with issues related to gender, sexuality, violence, ghosts and fragmented identities and memories. In both official and theatrical performance it is important that artists keep engaging critically with various manifestations of nostalgia, while considering the ethical and affective consequences of innovative performance forms, particularly when engaging marginalised or vulnerable people. The shift away from text-based theatre emphasises the importance of the embodied subject and the multiple ways in which we make meaning collectively and individually, translating sensory experience into words and images in specific spaces and times. This emphasis on performance presents particular challenges for the archive, which at best will keep the embodied repertoire and archive in dialogue.

The issues facing South Africa in the post-conflict situation and the way these are dealt with in critically evaluating archives and repertoires of embodied memories are not unique to the country, but are paralleled in other countries facing similar issues, like Northern Ireland (Coulter and Murray, 2008), Bosnia, Rwanda or Kenya. There is much value in scholars working on various aspects of post-conflict restructuring sharing both the questions and best practices they encounter in their work. Thus we keep archives and repertoires open for reinvestigation and reinterpretation, in dialogue, and so continue to be 'campaigners for invisible values no human being can live without'.

---

43 See examples in Kerr (2011) of how performance and new media are interacting to challenge contemporary issues, including constructions of nationhood in various parts of Africa.

SELECT BIBLIOGRAPHY

Al Sayyad, Nezar. 1991. *Cities and Caliphs – on the Genesis of Arab Muslim Urbanism*. New York and London: Greenwood Press.

Alexander, Karin, Diana Batchelor, Alexis Durand and Tyrone Savage. 2004–2005. Truth Commissions and Transitional Justice: Update on Select Bibliography on the South African Truth and Reconciliation Commission Debate. *Journal of Law and Religion* 20: 2, 525–65.

Ally, Russell. 1999. *The Truth and Reconciliation Commission: Legislation, Process and Evaluation of Impact*. University of Pretoria: Centre for Rights, Occasional paper No. 12.

Althusser, Louis. 1993. 'Ideology and Ideological State Apparatuses (Notes towards an Investigation)', in *Essays on Ideology*. London and New York: Verso, 1–60.

Amadiume, Ifi and Abdullahi An-Na'im (ed.) 2000. *The Politics of Memory: Truth, Healing and Social Justice*. London: Zed Books.

ANC (African National Congress). 1996. *Statement to the TRC*, August 1996. Marshalltown [Johannesburg]: ANC, Department of Information and Publicity.

ANC. 2011. Centenary document, *Unity in Diversity*, www.anc.org.za/show.php?id=8803, accessed 5/12/11.

Anderson, Benedict. 1991. *Imagined Communities: Reflections on the Origin and Spread of Nationalism*. London and New York: Verso.

Anderson, Benedict. 2006. *Imagined Communities*. London: Verso.

Anderson, Benedict. 2011. 'The Goodness of Nations', in Xolela Mangcu (ed.) *Becoming Worthy Ancestors: Archive, Public Deliberation and Identity in South Africa*. Johannesburg: Witwatersrand University Press, 109–18.

Anderson, Michelle J. 1999–2000. Rape in South Africa. Heinonline, *1 Geo. J. Gender & L.* 789–822.

Armstrong J.C. and N.A. Worden. 1992. 'The Slaves', 1652–1834, in R. Elphick and H. Giliomee (eds) *The Shaping of South African Society, 1652–1840*. Cape Town: Maskew Miller Longman.

Arnoldi, Mary Jo. c.1976. Bamana and Bozo Puppetry of the Segou Region Youth

Societies, in the collection of Joan and Charles Bird, Department of Creative Arts, Purdue University.

Arnoldi, Mary Jo. 1988. Performance, Style, and the Assertion of identity in Malian Puppet Drama. *Journal of Folklore Research* 25: 1–2, 87–100.

Arnoldi, Mary Jo. 1995. *Playing with Time*. Bloomington: Indiana University Press.

Arnoldi, Mary Jo. 2001. 'The Sogow – Imagining a Moral Universe through Sogo bò masquerade', in Jean-Paul Colleyn (ed.) *Bamana: The Art of Existence*. New York: Museum for African Art, 77–93.

Ashcroft, Bill. 1994–95. Interpolation and Post-colonial Agency. *New Literatures Review* nos. 28–9, 176–89.

Ashforth, Adam. 1990. *The Politics of Official Discourse in Twentieth-Century South Africa*. Oxford: Clarendon Press.

Asmal, Kader, Louise Asmal and Ronald Suresh Roberts. 1997 (1996) *Reconciliation Through Truth: A Reckoning of Apartheid's Criminal Governance*. Cape Town: David Philip, Oxford: James Currey Publishers, New York: St. Martin's Press.

Asmal, Kader. 2000. Truth, Reconciliation and Justice: The South African Experience in Perspective. *Modern Law Review* 63: 1, 1–24.

Auslander, Philip. 1999. *Liveness: Performance as Mediatised Culture*. New York: Routledge.

Austin, John L. 1962. *How To Do Things with Words*. Cambridge: Harvard University Press.

Baderoon, Gabeda. 2002. Everybody's Mother was a Good Cook: Meanings of Food in Muslim Cooking. *Agenda* 51, 4–15.

Baderoon, Gabeda. 2004. Oblique Figures: Representations of Islam in South African Media and Culture, unpublished PhD thesis, University of Cape Town.

Baderoon, Gabeda. 2007. 'Catch with the Eye: Change and Continuity in Muslim Cooking in Cape Town', in Sean Field, Felicity Field and Renata Meyer (eds) *Imagining the City: Memory, Space and Culture in Cape Town*. Cape Town: HSRC Press, 115–32.

Bailey, Brett. 1998. Performing so the Spirit may speak. *South African Theatre Journal* 12: 1/2 (Sept.), 191–207.

Bailey, Brett. 2010a. *On The Sea of Longing*, statement on thirdworldbunfight website.

Bailey, Brett. 2010b. *Mail and Guardian* interviews Brett on Public Art and Infecting the City, Dec., www.thirdworldbunfight.co.za/files/MAIL_&_GUARDIAN_INTER VIEW_WITH_BRETT_BAILEY_ON_PUBLIC_ART.pdf, accessed 21/12/11.

Baines, Gary. 2007. The Master Narrative of South Africa's Liberation Struggle: Remembering and Forgetting June 16, 1976. *International Journal of African Historical Studies* 40: 2, 283–302.

Baines, Gary. 2008. Blame, Shame, or Reaffirmation? White Conscripts Reassess the Meaning of the "Border War" in Post- Apartheid South Africa. *InterCulture* October, 214–27.

Baines, Gary. 2009. Two Hills and Three Walls of Remembrance, posted 24/11/11, www.archivalplatform.org/images/resources/Baines_2009.pdf, accessed via December newsletter.

Balcomb, Anthony. 2000. 'The Power of Narrative: Constituting Reality through Storytelling', in Philippe Denis (ed.), *Orality, Memory & the Past*. Pietermaritzburg: Cluster Publications, 49–62.

Baxter, Joan. 2002. Timbuktu – City of Legends', BBC World News, 15/04/02, 5 pages. http://news.bbc.co.uk/1/hi/world/africa/1911321.stm, accessed 18/10/10.

Benjamin, Walter. 1969. 'Theses on the Philosophy of History', in Harry Zohn (trans.) *Illuminations*. New York: Schocken Books.

Bennett, Bonita, Christchené Julius and Crain Soudien (eds). 2007. *Reflections on the Conference Hands on District Six – Landscapes of Post-colonial Memorialisation*. Cape Town: District Six Museum.

Bennett, Jill and Rosanne Kennedy (eds) 2003. *World Memory: Personal Trajectories in Global Time*. Basingstoke: Palgrave Macmillan.

Bezuidenhout, Aletta. 2005. 'Aletta Bezuidenhout', in Irene Stephanou and Leila Henriques (eds), *The World is an Orange: Creating Theatre with Barney Simon*. Johannesburg: Jacana Media.

Bhabha, Homi K. 1983. 'Difference, Discrimination and the Discourse of Colonialism', in Francis Barker *et al.* (eds) *The Politics of Theory*. Colchester, UK: University of Essex Press, 194–211.

Bhabha, Homi K. 1986. 'Signs taken for Wonders: Questions of Ambivalence and Authority under a Tree Outside Delhi, May 1817', in Henry Louis Gates, Jr. (ed.), *'Race', Writing and Difference*. Chicago: Chicago University Press, 163–84.

Bhabha, Homi K. 1990. 'DissemiNation: Time Narrative, and the Margins of the Modern Nation', in Bhabha, H.K. (ed.), *Nation and Narration*. London and New York: Routledge.

Bhabha, Homi K. 1994. *The Location of Culture*. London and New York: Routledge.

Bharucha, Rustom. 1993. *Theatre and the World: Performance and the Politics of Culture*. London: Routledge.

Bharucha, Rustom. 2000a. *The Politics of Cultural Practice: Thinking through Theatre in an Age of Globalization*. London: Athlone.

Bharucha, Rustom. 2000b. Beyond the Box: Problematising the "New Asian Museum", *Third Text* 14: 52 (Autumn), 11–19.

Bharucha, Rustom. 2007. The Limits of the Beyond – Contemporary Art Practice, Intervention and Collaboration in Public Spaces. *Third Text* 21: 4 (July), 397–416.

Biggar, Nigel (ed.) 2003. *Burying the Past: Making Peace and doing Justice after Civil Conflict*. Washington, DC: Georgetown University Press.

Billington, Michael. 2007. *State of the Nation: British Theatre since 1945*. London: Faber and Faber.

Bloomberg, C. 1990. *Christian-Nationalism and the Rise of the Afrikaner Broederbond in South Africa 1918-48*. London: Macmillan.

Bogues, Anthony. 2007. South Africa: On becoming an Ordinary Country. *Boundary* 34: 2, 171–86.

Boraine, Alex and J. Levy (eds) 1995. *The Healing of a Nation?* Cape Town: Justice in Transition.

Boraine, Alex. 2000. *A Country Unmasked*. Cape Town: Oxford University Press.

Botha, C. Graham. 1938. *Our South Africa – Past and Present*. Cape Town: United Tobacco Cos (South) Ltd.

Boulakia, Jean David C. 1971. Ibn Khaldûn: A Fourteenth-Century Economist. *Journal of Political Economy* 79: 5, 1105–18.

Boym, Svetlana. 2001. *The Future of Nostalgia*. New York: Basic Books.

Bozzoli, Belinda. 2004. *Theatres of Struggle and the End of Apartheid*. Edinburgh: Edinburgh University Press.

Bravman, Rene A. 2001. 'Islamic Ritual and Practice in Bamana Ségou—the 19th Century "Citadel of Paganism"', in Jean-Paul Colleyn (ed.) *Bamana: The Art of Existence*. New York: Museum for African Art, 35–44.

Breitinger, Eckhard. 2001. Farewell to the old Standard Bank National Arts Festival in Grahamstown? *South African Theatre Journal* 15, 178–91.

Breitinger, Eckhard. 2007. 'The Winds of Change and the Spirit of the Place', in Susan Arndt, E. Breitinger and Marek Spitczok von Brisinski (eds) *Theatre, Performance and New Media in Africa*. Bayreuth: Bayreuth African Studies, 82, 39–50.

Brink, Andre. 1996. *Reinventing a Continent: Writing in South Africa 1982-1995*. London: Secker & Warburg.

Brown, Duncan. 1998. *Voicing the Text*. Oxford: Oxford University Press.

Brown, Duncan. 2006. *To Speak of this Land: Identity and Belonging in South Africa and Beyond*. Durban: University of KwaZulu-Natal Press.

Brown, Wendy. 2000. 'Futures', in *Politics Out of History*. Princeton, NJ: Princeton University Press, 139–45.

Bryant, Chad. 2000. Whose Nation?: Czech Dissidents and History Writing from a Post-1989 Perspective. *History & Memory* 12: 1 (Spring/Summer), 30–64.

Burr, Lars. 2002. 'Monumental Historical Memory: Managing Truth in the Everyday Work of the South African Truth and Reconciliation Commission', in Posel, D. and G. Simpson (eds) *Commissioning the Past: Understanding South Africa's Truth and Reconciliation* Johannesburg: Witwatersrand University Press.

Buthelezi, Mbongiseni. 2011. Reckoning and Disavowal: Where is Army Conscription in our Collective Memory? *Archival Platform* Thought Piece: Heritage Day 2011.

Butler, Judith. 1988. Performative Acts and Gender Constitution. *Theatre Journal* 40: 4, 519–31.

Butler, Judith. 1990. *Gender Trouble: Feminism and the Subversion of Identity*. London and New York: Routledge.

Butler, Judith. 1993. *Bodies that Matter – On the Discursive limits of 'Sex'*. London and New York: Routledge.

Butler, Judith.1997. *Excitable Speech: a Politics of the Performative*. London and New York: Routledge.

Caillié, René-Auguste. 1829. *Journal d'un voyage à Timbouctou et à Jenné dans l'Afrique Centrale*, 3 vols., Paris: Editions Anthropos. Trans. *Travels through Central Africa to Timbuctoo; and across the Great Desert, to Morocco, performed in the years 1824–1828*. (2 vols). London: Henry Colburn & Richard Bentley, 1830.

Calland, Richard. 2009. 'Illuminating the Politics and the Practice of Access to Information in South Africa', in Kate Allan (ed.). 2009. *Paper Wars: Access to Information in South Africa*. Johannesburg: Wits University,Press, 1–16.

Carlin, John. 2008. *Playing the Enemy: Nelson Mandela and the Game that made a Nation*. London: Atlantic Books.

Caruth, Cathy (ed.). 1995. Introduction: *Trauma: Explorations in Memory*. Baltimore, Md.; London: Johns Hopkins University Press, 3–12.

Chapman, Audrey, and Bernard Spong (eds) 2003. *Religion and Reconciliation in South Africa*. Philadelphia: Templeton Foundation Press.

Chipkin, Ivor. 2007. *Do South Africans Exist?* Johannesburg: Witwatersrand University Press.

Clegg, Johnny, 1982. 'Towards an Understanding of African Dance: the Zulu *isishameni* Style', in Andrew Tracey (ed.) *Papers Presented at the Second Symposium on Ethnomusicology*. Rhodes University, Grahamstown: ILAM, 8–14.

Cloete, Elsie. 1992. Afrikaner Identity: Culture, Tradition and Gender. *Agenda*, 13 (Culture and Tradition), 42–56.

Coan, Stephen. 2003. A Tale of Two Museums. *Natal Witness*, 22/07/2003.

Coetzee, Carli. 2001. 'They Never Wept, the Men of My Race': Antjie Krog's *Country of My Skull* and the White South African. *Journal of Southern African Studies* 27: 4 (Dec.), 685–96.

Coetzee, Yvette. 1998. Visibly Invisible: How Shifting the Conventions of the traditionally invisible puppeteer allows for more dimensions in both the Puppeteer-puppet Relationship and the Creation of Theatrical meaning in *Ubu and the Truth Commission*. *South African Theatre Journal* 12.1–2: 35–51.

Coetzee, Yvette. 2006. Invisible Angels. *Oprah* magazine (April),102–5.

Cole, Catherine M. 2010. *Performing South Africa's Truth Commission*. Bloomington and Indianapolis: Indiana University Press.

Collins English Dictionary. 1994. Aylesbury: HarperCollins, www.harpercollins.co.uk.

Connell, R.W. 2005a. Hegemonic Masculinity – Rethinking the Concept. *Gender & Society* (Dec.), 19: 6, 829–59.

Connell, R.W. 2005b. *Masculinities*. Cambridge: Polity Press.

Coombes, Annie E. 2004. *History after Apartheid: Visual Culture and Public Memory in a Democratic South Africa*. Durham: Duke University Press/Johannesburg: Witwatersrand University Press.

Conquergood, Dwight. 2002. Performance Studies: Interventions and Radical Research. *TDR*, 46: 2 (Summer), 145–56.

Coplan, David. 2000. Popular History: Cultural Memory. *Critical Arts* 14: 2, 122–44.

Coulter, Colin and Michael Murray (eds) 2008. *Northern Ireland after the Troubles*. Manchester and New York: Manchester University Press.

Crampton, Andrew. 2001. The Voortrekker Monument, the Birth of Apartheid, and beyond. *Political Geography* 20: 2 (Feb.), 221–46.

Currin, Brian. 1995. Epigraph to 'Uniting a Nation', in A. Boraine and J. Levy (eds) *The Healing of a Nation?* Cape Town: Justice in Transition.

Darnley, the Earl of (ed.) 1932. *Frank Lascelles: Our Modem Orpheus*. Oxford: Oxford University Press.

Das, Veena. 1987. The Anthropology of Violence and the Speech of Victims. *Anthropology Today* 3: 4, 11–13.

Das, Veena. 1996. Language and the Body: Transactions in the Construction of Pain. *Daedelus* 125: 1, 67–92.

Das, Veena. 2000. 'Introduction', and 'The Act of Witnessing: Violence, Poisonous Knowledge, and Subjectivity', in Veena Das, Arthus Kleinman, Mamphela Ramphele and Pamela Reynolds (eds) *Violence and Subjectivity*. Berkeley: University of California Press, 205–25.

Davids, Nadia. 2007. Inherited Memories: Performing the Archive. Unpublished PhD, Drama Department, University of Cape Town.

Davison, Patricia. 1998. 'Museums and the Reshaping of Memory, in S. Nuttall and C. Coetzee (eds). *Negotiating the Past – The Making of Memory in South Africa*. Cape Town: Oxford University Press, 143–60.

de Brito, Alexandra Barahona, Carmen Gonzaléz-Enríquez ad Pamolma Aguilar. 2001. *The Politics of Memory – Transitional Justice in Democratizing Societies*. Oxford: Oxford University Press.

de Bruin, Philip. 1994. Regering moet culture byeenbring, *Beeld* 15/03/94, 11.

de Certeau, Michel. 1984. *The Practice of Everyday Life* (trans.) Steven F. Rendall. London and Berkeley: University of California Press.

de Certeau, Michel. 1988. [1972] *The Writing of History*. Tom Conley (trans.). New York: Columbia University Press.

Deacon, Harriet. 1998. 'Remembering Tragedy, Constructing Modernity: Robben Island as a National Monument', in S. Nuttall and C. Coetzee (eds) *Negotiating the Past – The Making of Memory in South Africa*. Cape Town: Oxford University Press, 161–80.

Deacon, Harriet. 2009. 'The Archival Platform, a New Networking, Advocacy and Research Initiative', presented at The First International Conference on African Digital Libraries and Archives (ICADLA-1), Addis Ababa, Ethiopia, 1–3 July 2009, http://wiredspace.wits.ac.za/bitstream/handle/10539/8933/18%20Deacon.pdf?sequence=1, accessed 17/08/11.

Delbo, Charlotte. 1990. *Days and Memory*. Rosette Lamont (trans.) Marlboro, Vermonth: Melboro Press.

Deleuze, Gilles. 1993. *The Deleuze Reader*. Constantin V. Boundas (ed.) New York: Columbia University Press.

Delisle, Jennifer. 2006. Finding the Future in the Past: Nostalgia and Community-Building in Mhlophe's *Have You Seen Zandile? Journal of Southern African Studies* 32: 2 (June), 387–401.

Delport, Peggy. 2008. 'No Matter Where We Are, We Are Here'. Beginnings: The Fresco Wall of the District Six Museum. *City – Site – Museum: Reviewing Memory Practices at the District Six Museum*. Cape Town: District Six Museum, 130–51.

Derrida, Jacques. 1994. *Specters of Marx: the State of the Debt, the Work of Mourning, and the New International*. Peggy Kamuf (trans.) New York and London: Routledge.

Derrida, Jacques. 1996. *Archive Fever*. Chicago: Chicago University Press.

Derrida, Jacques. 2002. 'Archive Fever in South Africa', in Hamilton, Carolyn *et al.* (eds). *Refiguring the Archive*. Cape Town: David Philip Publishers; Dordrecht: Kluwer Academic Publishers, 38–80, even pages only.

Dhlamini, Jacob. 2009. *Native Nostalgia*. Sunnyside: Jacana Press.

Dickow, Helga and Valerie Møller. 2002. South Africa's 'Rainbow People', National Pride and Optimism: A Trend Study. *Social Indicators Research* 59: 2 (Aug.), 175–202.

Diop, Cheikh Anta. 1987. *Precolonial Black Africa.* (trans.) Harold Saleman. New York: Lawrence Hill Books.

Dolan, Jill. 2005. *Utopia in Performance: Finding Hope at the Theater.* Ann Arbor: University of Michigan Press.

Doxtader, Erik and Philippe-Joseph Salazar (eds) 2007. *Truth & Reconciliation in South Africa – The Fundamental Documents.* Claremont: New Africa Books.

Dubin, Steven. 2006. *Transforming Museums: Mounting Queen Victoria in a Democratic South Africa.* New York: Palgrave Macmillan.

du Plessis, Theo and Chriss Wiegand. 1998. 'Interpreting at the hearings of the Truth and Reconciliation Commission: April 1996 to February 1997', in Alex Kruger, Kim Wallmach and Marion Boers (eds) *Language Facilitation and Development in Southern Africa.* Pretoria: South African Translators' Institute.

du Preez, Petrus. 2011. 'The Tall Tale of the Tall Horse: The Illusion (or manifestation) of African Cultural and Traditional Aesthetics in Hybrid Performances', in Igweonu, Kene (ed.) *Trends in Twenty-First century African Theatre and Performance.* Amsterdam/New York: Rodopi, 139–70.

du Toit, André. 1983. No Chosen People: the myth of the Calvinist origin of Afrikaner nationalism and racial ideology, *American Historical Review*, 88: 4, 20–52.

du Toit, Marijke. 2003. 'The Domesticity of Afrikaner Nationalism: Volksmoeders and the ACVV, 1904–1929'. *Journal of Southern African Studies*, 29: 1 (March), 155–176.

Dubois, F. 1897. *Tombouctou la mytérieuse.* Paris. Trans. *Timbuctoo the Mysterious*, trans. from the French by Diana White. London: Heinemann.

Dubouw, Jessica. 2010. 'Introduction to *REwind: A Cantata*', in Carol Martin (ed.). *Dramaturgy of the Real on the World Stage.* Basingstoke and New York: Palgrave Macmillan, 91–4.

Dubow, Saul. 1992. Afrikaner Nationalism, Apartheid and the Conceptualization of 'Race'. *The Journal of African History* 33: 2, 209–237.

Dubow, Saul. 1995. 'The Elaboration of Segregationist Ideology', in William Beinart and Saul Dubow (eds) *Segregation and Apartheid in Twentieth-Century South Africa.* London and New York: Routledge, 145–75.

Duggan, Jo-Ann. 2011. From Memory to Archive, posted on Archival Platform editorial for July on 26 July, www.archivalplatform.org/blog/entry/from_memory_to_archive/, accessed18/8/11.

Edelstein, Jillian. 1999. The Truth Commission. *Granta* 66, Summer, 107–45.

Edelstein, Jillian. 2001. *Truth & Lies.* New York: New Press.

Ehlers, Anton. 2003. Apartheid Mythology and Symbolism. Desegregated and Re-invented in the Service of the New South Africa: The Covenant and the Battle of Blood/Ncome River. Presented at 'Founding Myths of the New South Africa' conference, University of Reunion, Saint-Denis de La Réunion, 25–29 March 2003.

Ellis, Stephen. 1998. The Historical Significance of South Africa's Third Force. *Journal of Southern African Studies* 24: 2 (June), 261–99.

Eprile, Tony. 2004. *The Persistence of Memory.* New York: W.W. Norton & Co.

Epstein, Debbie. 1998. Marked Men: Whiteness and Masculinity. *Agenda* 37, The New Man?, 49–59.

Erasmus, Zimitri and Edgar Pieterse. 1999. 'Conceptualising Coloured Identities in the Western Cape Province', in M. Palmberg (ed.) *National Identity and Democracy in Africa.* Pretoria: Human Sciences Research Council.

Erasmus, Zimitri (ed.) 2001. Coloured by History, Shaped by Place: New Perspectives on Coloured Identity in Cape Town. Cape Town: Kwela and South African History Online.

Erlank, Natasha. 2003. Gender and Masculinity in South African Nationalist Discourse, 1912–1950. *Feminist Studies*, 29: 3, Women in Democratic South Africa (Autumn), 653–71.

Erlmann, Veit. 1990. Migration and Performance: Zulu Migrant Workers' *Isicathamiya* Performance in South Africa, 1890–1950. *Ethnomusicology* 34: 2 (Spring–Summer), 199–220.

Evans, Martha 2007. 'Amnesty and Amnesia: The Truth and Reconciliation Commission in Film', in Martin Botha (ed.) *Marginal Lives & Painful Pasts: South African Cinema after Apartheid*. Parklands: Genugtig!

Eyal, Gil. 2004. Identity and Trauma: Two Forms of the Will to Memory. *History & Memory* 16: 1 (Spring/Summer), 5–36.

Fanon, Frantz. 1963. *The Wretched of the Earth*. Preface by JP Sartre. New York: Grove Press.

Fanon, Frantz. 1986 (1968). *Black Skin, White Masks*. C.L. Markmann (trans.). London: Pluto Press.

Farber, Yael. 2008a. Interview with Amanda Stuart Fisher, in *Theatre as Witness*. London: Oberon, 19–28.

Finnegan, Ruth. 1970. *Oral Literature in Africa*. Nairobi: Oxford University Press.

Faulkner, William. 1953. *Requiem for a Nun*. London: Chatto & Windus.

Fisher, Mark. 2007. 'Truth in Translation', *Variety Review*, posted 8 Aug 2007, www. variety.com/review/VE1117934366?refCatId=33&ref=related, accessed 17/6/11.

Fleishman, Mark.1990. Workshop theatre's Oppositional Form. *South African Theatre Journal*, 4: 1, 88–118.

Fleishman, Mark. 2011. *Cargo*: Staging Slavery at the Cape. *Contemporary Theatre Review* 21: 1, 8–19.

Fleishman, Mark and Nadia Davids. 2007. Moving Theatre: An Exploration of the Place of Theatre in the Process of Memorialising District Six through an Examination of Magnet Theatre's production *Onnest'bo*. *South African Theatre Journal* 21, 149–65.

Flockemann, Gino Fransman, Linda Tini, and Ignatius Ticha. 2005. Furiously Enthused? Performing Identities, Encountering *iMumbo Jumbo*: A UWC Case Study. *South African Theatre Journal* 19, 191–205.

Foster, Don, Paul Haupt, and Maresa de Beer. 2005. *Narratives of Protagonists in the South African Conflict*. Rondebosch: Institutue for Justice and Reconciliation, CT: HSRC Press, Oxford: James Currey.

Foucault, M. 1972. *The Archaeology of Knowledge*. A.M. Sheridan-Smith (trans.). London: Routledge.

Foucault, M. 1987. *Language, Counter-Memory, Practice*. Bouchard, D.F. & Simon, S. (trans). Thaca: Cornell University Press.

Fox, R.E. 1986. Derek Walcott: History as Dis-ease. *Callaloo* 9: 2 (Spring), 331–40.

Francis, Kali. 2006. Theatre of Struggle and Transformation: A Critical Investigation into the Power of Oral Traditions as used by director Mark Fleischman. *South African Theatre Journal* 20, 102–27.

Fugard, Athol. 1983. *Notebooks 1960–1977*. Johannesburg: Ad Donker Publisher.

Fullard, Madeleine. 2004. *Dis-Placing race: The South Africans Truth and Reconciliation Commission (TRC) and Interpretatios of Violence*. Braamfontein: Centre for Violence and Reconciliation,

Gear, Sasha, 2005. Rules of Engagement: Structuring Sex and Damage in Men's Prisons and Beyond. *Culture, Health & Sexuality* May, 7: 3, 195–208.

Germann, Lars. 2008. Bertolt Brecht's 'Threepenny Opera' and 'Love, Crime and Johannesburg' by the Junction Avenue Theatre Company: A Comparison. Nordestedt: GRIN Verlag (e-book).

Ghosh, Bishnupriya. 2004. On Grafting the Vernacular: The Consequences of Postcolonial Spectrology. *boundary* 2, 31: 2, Summer, 197–218.

Gibson, James. 2004. *Overcoming Apartheid: Can Truth Reconcile a Divided Nation?* New York: Russell Sage Foundation.

Gilbert, Shirli. 2007. Singing against Apartheid: ANC Cultural Groups and the International Anti-Apartheid Struggle. *Journal of Southern African Studies* 33: 2 (June), 421–41.

Giliomee, Hermann. 1995. 'The Growth of Afrikaner Identity', in William Beinart and Saul Dubow (eds) *Segregation and Apartheid in Twentieth-Century South Africa.* London and New York: Routledge, 189–205.

Gilroy, Paul. 1987. *'There Ain't no Black in the Union Jack': The Cultural Politics of Race and Nation.* London: Hutchinson.

Gilroy, Paul. 2000. *Between Camps: Race, Identity and Nationalism at the End of the Colour Line.* London: Allen Lane.

Gilroy, Paul. 2004. *After Empire: Melancholia or Convivial Culture?* Abingdon: Routledge.

Goffman, Erving. 1959. *The Presentation of Self in Everyday Life.* New York: Doubleday.

Golan, Daphna. 1991. Inkatha and Its Use of the Zulu Past. *History in Africa* 18, 113–26.

Goldblatt, Beth and Sheila Meintjes. 1996 . Gender and the Truth and Reconciliation Commission. Unpublished submission to the Truth and Reconciliation Commission.

Goldblatt, Beth and Sheila Meintjes. 1997. Dealing with the Aftermath – Sexual Violence and the Truth and Reconciliation Commission. *Agenda* 36, 7–18.

Goldin, Ian. 1987. 'The Reconstitution of Coloured Identity in the Western Cape', in Shula Marks and Stanley Trapido (eds) *The Politics of Race, Class and Nationalism in Twentieth century South Africa.* London and New York: Longman, 156–81.

Govender, Krijay. 2001. Subverting Identity after 1994: The South African Indian Woman as Playwright. *Agenda*, 49, Culture: Transgressing Boundaries, 33–43.

Gqola, Pumla Dineo. 2010. *What is Slavery to me? Postcolonial/ Slave memory in post-apartheid South Africa.* Johannesburg: Wits University Press.

Graham, Shane (Shane Dwight). 2003. The Truth Commission and Postapartheid Literature in South Africa. *Research in African Literatures* 34: 1 (Spring), 11–30.

Graver, David. 1995. Theatre in the New South Africa. *Performing Arts Journal*, 17: 1 (Jan.), 103–9.

Greene, N. 1996. 'Empire as Myth and Memory' *in Cinema, Colonialism, Postcolonialism: Perspectives from the French and Francophone World.* Austin: University of Texas Press.

Groenewald, M. 2010. Songs about Zuma: Revelations of Divisions after Democracy. *Literator* 3: 1, April, 123–46, online. http://findarticles.com/p/articles/mi_7020/is_1_31/ai_n57491503/?tag=content;col1, accessed 16/11/11.

Grootboom, Mpumelo Paul (interview). 2008. 'Theatre Climate in South Africa has many Taboos', The Power of Culture, Nederlands (Sept.), http://krachtvancultuur.nl/en/current/2008/september/mpumelo-paul-grootboom, accessed 28/12/11.

Grootboom, Mpumelo Paul (interview). 2010. 'It's Fantasy to Believe the World Cup will help Reduce Poverty in South Africa', *The Observer*, Sunday 16 May. www.guardian.co.uk/culture/2010/may/16/mpumelelo-paul-grootboom-south-africa/print, accessed 28/12/11.

Grosz, Elizabeth. 1994. 'A Thousand Tiny Sexes: Feminism and Rhizomatics', in Constantine V. Boundas and Dorothea Olkowski (eds) *Gilles Deleuze and the Theater of Philosophy.* New York: Routledge, 187–210.

Grundlingh, A.M., 2001. A Cultural Conundrum? Old Monuments and New Regimes: The Voortrekker Monument as Symbol of Afrikaner Power in a Postapartheid South Africa. *Radical History Review*, 81 (Fall), 95–112.

Grundlingh, Albert and Hilary Sapire. 1989. From Feverish Festival to Repetitive Ritual? The Changing Fortunes of Great Trek Mythology in an Industrializing South Africa, 1938–1988. *South African Historical Journal* 21, 19–37.

Grunebaum, Heidi. 2002. Talking to Ourselves 'Amongst the Innocent Dead': On Reconciliation, Forgiveness and Mourning. *Publication of the Modern Language Association of America* 117: 2 (March), also DACOM Occasional Papers Series, No. 2 (2005).

Grunebaum, Heidi and Yazir Henri. 2003. 'Re-membering Bodies, Producing Histories: Holocaust Survivor Narrative and Truth and Reconciliation Testimony', in Jill Bennett and Rosanne Kennedy (eds), *World Memory: Personal Trajectories in Global Time*. Basingstoke: Palgrave Macmillan, 101–18.

Grunebaum-Ralph, Heidi. 2001. Re-Placing Pasts, Forgetting Presents: Narrative, Place & Memory in the Time of the Truth and Reconciliation Commission. *Research in African Literatures* 32: 3, 198–212; also DACOM Occasional Papers Series, No. 1 (2005).

Gunner, Liz. 2007. "'Those Dying Generations at their Song": Singing of Life, Death and AIDS in Contemporary Kwa-Zulu-Natal', in Susan Arndt, E. Breitinger and Marek Spitczok von Brisinski (eds) *Theatre, Performance and New Media in Africa*. Bayreuth: Bayreuth African Studies 82, 133–44.

Gunner, Liz. 2008. Jacob Zuma, the Social Body and the Unruly Power of Song. *African Affairs*,108/430, 27–48.

Hadland, Adrian. (ed.) 2008. *Violence and Xenophobia in South Africa: Developing Consensus, Moving to Action*. Produced by a partnership between the Human Sciences Research Council (HSRC) and the High Commission of the United Kingdom, October, based on a roundtable hosted at HSRC in June.

Hagen, Joshua. 2008. Parades, Public Space, and Propaganda: The Nazi Culture Parades in Munich. *Geografiska Annaler*: Series B, Human Geography 90: 4 (Dec.), 349–67.

Hall, C. 1996. 'Histories, Empires and the Post-colonial Moment', in I. Chambers and L. Curti (eds) *The Post-colonial Question: Common Skies, Divided Horizons*. London and New York: Routledge.

Hall, Edith 2010. *Greek Tragedy: Suffering under the Sun*. Oxford: Oxford University Press.

Hall, Martin, 1998. 'Earth and Stone: Archaeology as Memory', in S. Nuttall and C. Coetzee (eds) *Negotiating the Past – The making of Memory in South Africa*. Cape Town: Oxford University Press.

Halligey, Alex. 2005. Re-inventing Mythologies: Arguments towards Cultural Identity in *Medea* and *Rain in a Dead Man's Footprints*. *South African Theatre Journal* 19, 208–22.

Hamber, B. 1998. Living with the Legacy of Impunity: Lessons for South Africa about Truth, Justice and Crime in Brazil. *Latin American Report* 13(2): 4–16.

Hamilakis, Yannis and Jo Labanyi. 2008. Introduction: Time, Materiality, and the Work of Memory. *History & Memory* 20: 2, 5–17.

Hamilton, Carolyn. 1994. Against the Museum as Chameleon. *South African Historical Journal*, 31 (Nov.), 184–90.

Hamilton, Carolyn, Verne Harris, Jane Taylor, Michelle Pickover, Graeme Reid, Razia Saleh (eds) 2002. *Refiguring the Archive*. Dordrecht/Boston/London: Kluwer Academic Publishers.

Hamilton, Carolyn. 2011. 'Why Archive Matters: Archives, Public Deliberation and Citizenship', in Xolela Mangcu (ed.) *Becoming Worthy Ancestors: Archive, Public Deliberation and Identity in South Africa*. Johannesburg: Witwatersrand University Press, 119–44.

Hansen, Thomas Blom. 2005. Melancholia of Freedom: Humour and Nostalgia among Indians in South Africa. *Modern Drama* 48: 2 (Summer), 297–315.

Harris, Brent. 2002. 'The Archive, Public History and the Essential Truth: The TRC Reading the Past', in Carolyn Hamilton *et al.* (eds) *Refiguring the Archive*. Cape Town: David Philip; Dordrecht: Kluwer Academic Publishers, 161–77.

Harris, Verne. 2011. Madiba, Memory and the Work of Justice, 18th Alan Paton Lecture, organised by the Alan Paton Centre and Struggle Archives, University of Kwa-Zulu Natal, Pietermaritzburg Campus, 5 May.

Harrison, R.P. 2003. *Dominion of the Dead*. Chicago: Chicago University Press.

Hartman, G.H. (ed.) 1993. *Remembrance: The Shapes of Memory*. Cambridge: Blackwell Publishers.

Hass, Kristin Ann. 1998. *Carried to the Wall: American Memory and the Vietnam Veterans Memorial*. Berkeley, California and London: University of California Press.

Hauptfleisch, Temple. 2007. 'Festivals as Eventifying Systems', and 'In Search of the

Rainbow: The Little Karoo National Arts Festival and the Search for Cultural Identity in South Africa', in T. Hauptfleisch, S. Lev-Aladgem, J. Martin, W. Sauter, H. Schoenmakers (eds) *Festivalising! Theatrical events, Politics and Culture*. IFTR/FIRT. Amsterdam and New York: Rodopi, 39–49, 79–96.

Hayner, Priscilla. 1994. Fifteen Truth Commissions – 1974 to 1994: A Comparative Study. *Human Rights Quarterly* 16, 597–655.

Heddon, Deidre. 2008. *Autobiography and Performance*. Basingstoke: Palgrave Macmillan.

Hees, Edwin. 1996. The Voortrekkers on Film: From Preller to Pornography. *Critical Arts* 10: 1, 1–22.

Hees, Edwin. 2003. 'The Birth of a Nation – Contextualizing De Voortrekkers (1916)', in Isabel Balseiro and Ntongela Masilela (eds) *To Change Reels – Film and culture in South Africa*. Detroit: Wayne State University Press.

Heidegger, M. 1958. *Question of Being*. New York: Twayne Publishers.

Henri, Yazir 2003. 'Reconciling Reconciliation: A Personal and Public Journey of Testifying before the South African Truth and Reconciliation Commission', in P. Gready (ed.), *Political Transition: Politics & Cultures*. London: Pluto Press.

Henri, Yazir and Heidi Grunebaum. 2005. Re-Historicising Trauma: Reflections on Violence and Memory in Current-day Cape Town. (trans. by authors) Published in *Im Inneren der Globalisierung – Psychosoziale Arbeit in Gewaltkontexten*. Medico-International, Frankfurt, DACPM Occasional Papers Series, No. 6.

Heritage Agency, The. 2009. *Timbuktu Script & Scholarship* Media Report, January, 1–5. Accessed from Iziko, Cape Town, January 2010.

Herwitz, Daniel. 2003. *Race and Reconciliation*. Minneapolis: University of Minnesota Press.

Hlongwane, Ali Khangela. 2007. The Mapping of the June 16 1976 Soweto Student Uprisings Routes: Past Recollections and Present Reconstruction(s). *Journal of African Cultural Studies* 19: 1, Performing (In) Everyday Life (June), 7–36.

Hobsbawn, E. and Ranger, T. (eds) 1983. *Invention of Tradition*. Cambridge: Cambridge University Press.

Hofmeyr, Isabel. 1987. 'Building a Nation from Words: Afrikaans Language, Literature and Ethnic Identity, 1902–1924', in Shula Marks and Stanley Trapido (eds) *The Politics of Race, Class and Nationalism in Twentieth century South Africa*. London and New York: Longman, 95–123.

Hofmeyr, I. 1994. *We Live Our Lives as a Tale that is Told: Oral Historical Narrative in a South African Chiefdom*. London: James Currey.

Holdsworth, Nadine. 2010. *Theatre & Nation*. Basingstoke and New York: Palgrave Macmillan.

Homann, Greg. 2009a. Landscape and Body. *South African Theatre Journal* 23, 146–75.

Hughes, L. 1926. *The Weary Blues*. New York: W.W. Norton & Co.

Hugo, Maria. 1949. Die Vrou in ons Volkslewe – haar rol in die Groot Trek en in ons nasiebou (The woman in the life of our nation – her role in the Great Trek and in the building of our nation), in the *Inwyding van die Voortrekkermonument – Amptelike program en gedenkboek*. Johannesburg: Voortrekkerpers, Bpk, 72–85.

Hunwick, John O. and Alida Jay Boyce (eds). 2008. *The Hidden Treasures of Timbuktu*. London: Thames & Hudson.

Hutchison, Yvette. 2004. 'Memory & Desire in SA: The Museum as Space for Performing Cultural Identity?', in David Kerr (ed.) *African Theatre: Southern Africa*, London: James Currey, 51–67.

Hutchison, Yvette. 2009. Verbatim Theatre in South Africa: 'Living theatre in a Person's Performance', in Alison Forsyth and Chris Megson (eds) *Get Real: Documentary Theatre Past and Present*. Basingstoke and New York: Palgrave Macmillan, 209–23.

Hutchison, Yvette. 2010a. *African Theatre: Histories 1850 and 1950*. Woodbridge: James Currey/Boydell & Brewer Inc.

Hutchison, Yvette. 2010b. 'Post-1990s Verbatim Theatre in South Africa: Exploring an

African Concept of "Truth"', in Carol Martin (ed.) *Dramaturgy of the Real on the World Stage*. Basingstoke and New York: Palgrave Macmillan, 61–71.

Hutchison, Yvette. 2010c. The 'Dark Continent' Goes North: An Exploration of Intercultural Theatre Practice through Handspring and Sogolon Puppet Companies' Production of *Tall Horse*. *Theatre Journal 62: 1* (March), 57–73.

Hutton, P.H. 1993. *History as an Art of Memory*. Hanover and London: University Press of New England.

Ibn Khuldûn. 1987. *The Muqaddimah – An Introduction to History*. Franz Rosenthal (trans.), N.J. Dawood (abridged and ed.). London: Routledge. (1st edn, 1967).

Ingold, Tim. 2000. *The Perception of the Environment: Essays in Livelihood, Dwelling and Skill*. London and New York: Routledge.

Issawi, Charles (trans. and arranged) 1987. *An Arab Philosophy of History: Selections from the Prolegomena of Ibn Khuldûn of Tunis (1332–1406)*. Princeton: The Darwin Press.

Jackson, Shannon and Steven Robins. 1999. Miscast: The Place of Negotiating the Bushman Past and Present. *Critical Arts* 13: 1, 69–101.

Jaffer, Mansoor. 1997. Nation-wide Statement-Taking Drive Kicks Off, Truth Talks. *The Official Newsletter of the Truth and Reconciliation Commission* 2: 1.

Jappie, Saarah. 2011. History, Heritage, Identity: Arabic Manuscripts in Cape Muslim Families, http://archivalplatform.cmail5.com/t/y/e/qakht/hiudmikd/, accessed 18/04/11.

Jeffrey, Anthea. 1999. *The Truth about the Truth Commission*. Johannesburg: SA Institute of Race Relations.

Jeppie, Shamil. 1990. 'Popular Culture and Carnival in Cape Town', in Shamil Jeppie and Crain Soudien (eds) *The Struggle for District Six: Past and Present*. Cape Town: Buchu Books, 67–79.

Jeppie, Shamil and Souleymane Bachir Diagne (eds) 2008. *The Meanings of Timbuktu*. Cape Town: HSRC Press in association with CODESRIA, Dakar.

Jeppson, Patrice L. 1997. 'Leveling the Playing Field' in the Contested Territory of the South African Past: A 'Public' versus a 'People's' Form of Historical Archaeology Outreach. *Historical Archaeology* 31: 3 (In the Realm of Politics: Prospects for Public Participation in African-American and Plantation Archaeology), 65–82.

Jeyifo, B.1985. 'The Hidden Class War in *The Road*', in *The Truthful Lie: Essays in a Sociology of African Drama*. London: Port of Spain, 11–22.

Judin, Hilton and Ivan Vladislavić (eds) 1998. *Blank_Architecture, Apartheid and After*. Rotterdam: NAi Publishers.

Justice in Transition booklet, available at www.justice.gov.za/trc/legal/index.htm, accessed 10/8/11.

Justice in Transition. 1995. *Truth and Reconciliation Commission*. Rondebosch: Justice in Transition.

Kanyegirie, Andrew. 2008. 'The Timbuktu Manuscripts', in NEPAD Dialogue, Issue 242, in section 2: NEPAD Broadens Stakeholder Understanding of its African Development Agenda. Online weekly, English edn, 12 September, www.nepad.org.

Kapelianis, Angie and Darren Taylor (eds) 2000. *South Africa's Human Spirit: An Oral Memoir of the* Truth and Reconciliation Commission. 5 CDs. Johannesburg: SABC.

Kapteijns, L. 1977. African Historiography Written by Africans 1955–1973: the Nigerian case. Leiden: Afrika-Studiencentrum. Unpublished PhD.

Karp, Ivan, Corinne Kratz, Lynn Szwaja and Tomás Ybarra-Frausto (eds) 2006. *Museum Frictions – Public Cultures/Global Transformations*. Durham and London: Duke University Press.

Karsten, Luchien and Honorine Illa. 2001. *Ubuntu* as a Management Concept. *Quest: An African Journal of Philosophy* XV, 1–2, 91–112.

Kasfir, N. 1968. *Politics in Africa: An Introduction*. Kampala: Milton Obote Foundation, Adult Education Centre.

Kentridge, William. 1998. Director's Note in Taylor, Jane 1998. *Ubu and the Truth Commission*. Cape Town: University of Cape Town Press.

Kerr, David. 2004. 'Put me on the Stage', in David Kerr (ed.) *African Theatre: Southern Africa*. London: James Currey, 79–91.

Kerr, David (ed.) 2011. *African Theatre: Media and Performance*. Woodbridge: James Currey/New York: Boydell & Brewer Inc.

Khorana, Meena. 1988. Apartheid in South African Children's Fiction. *Children's Literature Association Quarterly* 13: 2 (Summer), 52–6.

Kohler, Adrian. 2009. 'Thinking through Puppets' in Jane Taylor (ed.) *Handspring Puppet Company*. Johannesburg: David Krut Publishing, 42–147.

Krog, Antjie. 1998. *Country of My Skull*. Johannesburg: Random House.

Krog, Antjie. 2006. 'Last time, This Time'. LitNet: 20 March, www.oulitnet.co.za/seminar room/krog_krog2.asp, accessed 16/6/11.

Krog, Antjie, Nosisi Mpolweni and Kopano Ratele. 2009. *There was this Goat: Investigating the Truth Commission Testimony of Notrose Nobombu Konile*. Scottsville: University of Kwa-Zulu Natal Press.

Krueger, Anton. 2010. *Experiments in Freedom – Explorations of Identity in New South African Drama*. Newcastle-upon-Tyne: Cambridge Scholars Publishing.

Kruger, Loren. 1997. The Drama of Country and City: Tribalization, Urbanization and Theatre under Apartheid. *Journal of Southern African Studies* 23: 4 (Dec.), 565–84.

Kruger, Loren. 1999. *The Drama of South Africa – Plays, Pageants and Publics since 1910*. London and New York: Routledge.

Kruger, Loren. 2001. Theatre, Crime, and the Edgy City in Post-Apartheid Johannesburg. *Theatre Journal* 53: 2, Theatre and the City (May), 223–52.

Kruger, Loren. 2004. *Post-imperial Brecht: Politics and Performance, East and South*. Cambridge and New York: Cambridge University Press.

Kryza, Frank T. 2006. *The Race for Timbuktu*. New York/London/Toronto/Sydney: Harper Collins.

Kumkum, Sangari. 1995. 'The Politics of the Possible,' in Bill Ashcroft *et al.* (eds) *The Post-Colonial Studies Reader*. London and New York: Routledge.

Kundera, Milan. 1996. *The Book of Laughter and Forgetting*. Aaron Asher (trans.). New York: HarperCollins.

LaCapra, Dominick. 1999. Trauma, Absence, Loss. *Critical Inquiry* 25: 4 (Summer), 696–727.

LaCapra, Dominick. 2001. *Writing History, Writing Trauma*. Baltimore and London: Johns Hopkins University Press.

Langer, Lawrence. 1991. *Holocaust Testimonies: The Ruins of Memory*. New Haven and London: Yale University Press.

Langer, Lawrence. 1995. *Admitting the Holocaust: Collected Essays*. Oxford: Oxford University Press.

Larlham, Daniel. 2007. Transforming Geographies and Reconfigured Spaces South Africa's National Arts Festival. *TDR: The Drama Review* 51: 3 (Fall), 182–8.

Larlham, Daniel. 2009. Brett Bailey and Third World Bunfight – Journeys into the South African Psyche. *Theater* 39: 1, 7–27.

Lawford, Mark. 2010. World Cup 2010: Live coverage of the opening ceremony from the Soccer City, Johannesburg, 11 June 2010. *Mail-online*, www.dailymail.co.uk/sport/worldcup2010/article-1285838/WORLD-CUP-2010-Opening-ceremony-live-co verage-Johannesburg.html, accessed 28/10/10.

Lebel, Roland. 1925. *L'Afrique Occidentale dans la Littérature Française depuis 1870*. Paris: Larouse.

Lefko-Everett, Kate, Rorisang Lekalake, Erica Penfold and Sana Rais. 2010. *SA Reconciliation Barometer Survey Report*. Wynberg: Institute for Justice and Reconciliation, at www.ijr.org.za/uploads/SA_Reconciliation_Barometer_10th_Rou nd_Report_web_FINAL.pdf, accessed 1/9/11.

Leiris, Michel. 1986. In the Musee de l'Homme. *Sulfur* 15, 109–11.
Leopard takes World Cup spotlight. *BBC Sport*, 22 September 2008, http://news.bbc. co.uk/sport1/hi/football/africa/7630454.stm, accessed 23/9/08.
Leprun, Sylviane. 1986. *Le Théâtre des colonies: Scénographie, acteurs et discours de l'imaginaire dans les expositions, 1855–1937*. Paris: L'Harmattan.
Levi Primo. 1988. *Drowned and the Saved*. Raymond Rosenthal (trans.) London: Abacus.
Lewin, Hugh. 2011. *Stones against the Mirror*. Cape Town: Random House.
Liebenberg, J.M. 1988. Mites Rondom Bloedriver en die Gelofte (Myths surrounding Blood River and the Vow). *South African Historical Journal* 20: 17–32.
Linenthal, Edward T. 1995. *Preserving Memory: The Struggle to Create America's Holocaust Museum*. New York: Viking Press.
Lotriet, Annelie. 2002. 'Can Short Interpreter training be Effective? The South African Truth and Reconciliation Commission Experience', in Eva Hung (ed.). *Teaching Interpretation and Interpreting 4*. Amsterdam and Philadelphia: John Benjamins Publishing Company, 83–98.
Loubser, J.A. 1987. *The Apartheid Bible: A Critical Review of Racial Theology in South Africa*. Cape Town: Maskew Miller Longman.
Louw, Dirk J. 2001. Ubuntu and the Challenge of Multiculturalism in Post-Apartheid South Africa. *Quest: An African Journal of Philosophy* XV, 1–2, 15–36.
Lovell, Colin Rhys. 1956. Afrikaner Nationalism and Apartheid. *The American Historical Review* 61: 2 (Jan.), 308–30.
Lowenthal, David. 1989. 'Nostalgia Tells it like it Wasn't', in M. Chase and C. Shaw (eds). *The Imagined Past: History and Nostalgia*. Manchester: Manchester University Press.
Lowenthal, David. 1997. *The Past is a Foreign Country*. Cambridge: Cambridge University Press.
Lucia, Christine. 2002. Abdullah Ibrahim and the Uses of Memory. *British Journal of Ethnomusicology* 11: 2, 125–43.
Lyotard, Jean-Francois. 1977. 'The Unconscious as Mise en scène', in Michel Benamou and Charles Caramello (eds) *Performance in Post-Modern Culture*. Madison: Coda.
Mackey, Robert. 2010. 'Shakira Remixes African Hit for World Cup', blog *New York Times*, posted 24/5/10, http://thelede.blogs.nytimes.com/2010/05/24/shakira-remixes-african-hit-for-world-cup/, accessed 8/12/11.
Mackintosh-Smith, Tim (ed.) 2002. *The Travels of Ibn Battutah*. Basingstoke and Oxford: Picador.
Madonda, Bongani. 2004. Trekker Chic. *Sunday Times*, 2/5/04.
Mail and Guardian, 2011. 'Call for SA to debate "Kill the Boer"', 14/4/11, http://mg.co.za/article/2011-04-15-call-for-sa-to-debate-kill-the-boer, accessed 16/12/11.
Maingard, Jacqueline. 1997. Imag(in)ing the South African Nation: Representations of Identity in the Rugby World Cup 1995. *Theatre Journal* 49, 15–28.
Mamdani, Mahmood. 2001. Beyond Settler and Native as Political Identities: Overcoming the Political Legacy of Colonialism. *Comparative Studies in Society and History* 43: 4 (Oct.), 651–64.
Mamdani, Mahmood. 2002. Amnesty or Impunity? A Preliminary Critique of the Report of the Truth and Reconciliation Commission of South Africa (TRC). *Diacritics* 32: 3, 33–59.
Mandela, Nelson. 16/12/1995. Message on National Reconciliation Day, www.anc.org.za/show.php?id=3646, accessed 14/8/11.
Mangcu, Xolela (ed.) 2011. *Becoming Worthy Ancestors: Archive, Public Deliberation and Identity in South Africa*. Johannesburg: Witwatersrand University Press.
Marchetti-Mercer, M.C. 2003. Family Murder in Post-apartheid South Africa: Reflections for Mental Health Professionals. *Health/ Gesondheid*, 8: 2 (June), 83–91.
Marschall, Sabine. 2001. The Search for Essence: 'Africanness' in 20th century South African architecture. *Southern African Humanities* 13, 139–54.
Marschall, Sabine. 2004. Serving Male Agendas: Two National Women's Monuments in South Africa. *Women's Studies: An inter-disciplinary journal* 33: 8, 1009–33.

Marschall, Sabine. 2006a. Visualizing Memories: The Hector Pieterson Memorial in Soweto. *Visual Anthropology* 19: 2, 145–69.

Marschall, Sabine. 2006b. Commemorating 'Struggle Heroes': Constructing a Genealogy for the New South Africa. *International Journal of Heritage Studies* 12: 2, 176–193.

Martin, Denis-Constant. 1999. *Coon Carnival: New Year in Cape Town, Past and Present.* Cape Town: David Philip Publishers.

Marx, Gerhard. 2009. 'A Matter of Life and Death: The Function of Malfunction in the Work of Handspring Puppet Company', in Jane Taylor (ed.) *Handspring Puppet Company.* Johannesburg: David Krut Publishing, 225–49.

Matshikaza, Johan. 2003. Foreword to *The Plays of Miracle and Wonder.* Cape Town: Double Story, 6–7.

Mayo, Jr. James M. 1978. Propaganda with Design: Environmental Dramaturgy in the Political Rally. *JAE* 32: 2, Politics and Design Symbolism (Nov.), 24–27, 32.

Mbembe, Achille. 2001. *On the Postcolony.* Berkeley, CA: University of California Press.

Mbembe, Achille. 2004. Aesthetics of Superfluity. *Public Culture* 6: 3 (Fall), 373–405.

Mbeki, Thabo. 1998. The African Renaissance, South Africa and the World. Speech at the United Nations University, 9 April 1998. www.unu.edu/unupress/mbeki.html, 15 pages, accessed 15/3/08.

Mbeki, Thabo. 2001. 'I am an African', speech published in *Quest – An African Journal of Philosophy* XV, 1–2, 9–15, see www.quest-journal.net/Quest_2001_pdf/introduction.pdf, accessed 1/10/08.

Mbeki, Thabo. 2005. Address at the SA-Mali project fundraising dinner, Cape Town International Convention centre, Cape Town, 8 April 2005. www.anc.org.za/ancdocs/history/mbeki/2005/tm0408.html, accessed 1/10/08. Also available on www.dfa.gov.za/docs/speeches/2005/mbek0413.htm.

Mbeki, Thabo. 2006. The South Africa-Mali Timbuktu project – Utilizing Skills and Talents to Advance the African Renaissance. Address at a fundraising dinner in Tshwane, South Africa, October 1, 2005. *The Journal of Pan African Studies* 1: 3 (March), 62–8.

Mbotwe, Mandla. 2010. Dissecting the aesthetics of identity in *Isivuso Sama Phupha. South African Theatre Journal* 24, 241–58.

McClintock, A. 1993. Family feuds: gender, nationalism and the family. *Feminist Review* 44 (Summer), 61–80.

McEachern, Charmaine. 2002. *Narratives of Nation Media, Memory and Representation in the Making of the new South Africa.* New York: Nova Science.

Mcleod, J. 2000. *Beginning Postcolonialism.* Manchester: Manchester University Press.

Mda, Zakes. 1996. 'Introduction: An Overview of Theatre in South Africa', in Z. Mda (ed.) *Four Plays.* Florida Hills: Vivlia, vi–xxvi.

Mda, Zakes. 2002. 'SA theatre in an era of reconciliation', in Frances Harding (ed.). *The Performance Arts in Africa.* London: Routledge, 279–89.

Mecoamere, Victor. 2008. Literacy Defeats Ignorance, *Sowetan* 17 December, 17.

Mellet, Patric Tariq. 2011. Kratoa or Kratoa 'Eva' van Meerhof?, http://cape-slavery-heritage.iblog.co.za, 23/1/11, accessed 28/4/11.

Meltzer, David J. 1981. 'Ideology and Material Culture', in Gould, R.A. and Schiffer, M.B. (eds) *Modern Material Culture: The Archeology of Us.* New York: Academic Press.

Meltzer, Lalou, Katie Mooney, Fiona Clayton, Shanaaz Galant and Shamila Rahim. 2010. *Ghoema & Glitter.* Cape Town: Iziko.

Mengel, Ewald, Michela Borzaga and Karin Orantes (eds) 2010. *Trauma, Memory, and Narrative in South Africa – Interviews. Matatu* 38. Amsterdam and New York: Rodopi.

Merrington, Peter. 1997. Masques, Monuments, and Masons: The 1910 pageant of the Union of South Africa. *Theatre Journal* 49, 1–14.

Merrington, Peter. 1999. 'State of the Union': The 'new pageantry' and the performance of identity in North America and South Africa, 1908–1910. *Journal of Literary Studies* 15: 1–2, 238–63.

Millar, Mervyn. 2006. *Journey of the Tall Horse: A story of African Theatre.* London: Oberon Books.

Milton, Sybil and Nowinski, Ira. 1992. *In Fitting Memory: The Art and Politics of Holocaust Memorials.* Detroit: Wayne State University Press.

Miner, Horace. 1965. *The Primitive City of Timbuctoo.* Garden City, New York: Anchor Books.

Minkley, Gary and Leslie Witz. 1994. Sir Harry Smith and his Imbongi: Local and National Identities in the Eastern Cape, 1952. *History Workshop Conference,* University of the Witwatersrand, 12–16 July 1994. http://wiredspace.wits.ac.za/bitstream/handle/10539/8015/HWS-285.pdf?sequence=1, accessed 15/11/11.

Moffett, Helen. 2010. 'Gender is a Matter of Life and Death', in Mengel, Ewald *et al.* (eds) *Trauma, Memory, and Narrative in South Africa – Interviews. Matatu* 38. Amsterdam and New York: Rodopi, 227–47.

Momberg, Eleanor. 2002. Mandela Tribute to 'Freedom Fighter'. *The Citizen* 7 March, 1–2.

Monaghan, Rachel. 1999. 'Popular Justice' in South Africa. *Fortnight* No. 378 (May), 15–16.

Moodie, T. Dunbar. 1975. *The Rise of Afrikanerdom: Power, Apartheid, and the Afrikaner Civil Religion.* Berkeley and London: University of California Press.

Moodley, Nashen. 1999. Home Truths. *Mail and Guardian,* 16 September 1999, 4.

Morell, Robert (ed.) 2001. *Changing Men in Southern Africa (Global Masculinities).* Pietermaritzburg: University of Natal Press; London and New York: Zed Books.

Morell, Robert. 2006. 'Fathers, Fatherhood and Masculinity in South Africa', in Linda Richter and Robert Morrell (eds) *Baba – Men and Fatherhood in South Africa.* Cape Town: HSRC Press, 13–16.

Morris, Gay. 2008. Institutional arrangements of theatre in the Cape: the case of township theatre. *South African Theatre Journal* 22, 102–18.

Morton, Patricia. 2000. *Hybrid Modernities: Architecture and Representation at the 1931 Colonial Exposition. Paris.* Cambridge, Massachusetts: Massachusetts Institution of Technology.

Motsei, Mmatshilo. 2007. *The Kanga and the Kangaroo Court – Reflection on the Rape Trial of Jacob Zuma.* Auckland Park: Jacana Media.

Motshoba, Mtutuzeli. 2002. 'Nothing but the Truth: The ordeal of Duma Khumalo', in Deborah Posel and Graeme Simpson (eds) *Commissioning the Past: Understanding South Africa's Truth and Reconciliation Commission.* Johannesburg: Witwatersrand University Press, 131–44.

Moyo, Awelani. 2011. Problematising 'Indigeneity' in/for South Africa's 'Rainbow Nation': the role of Festivals. Paper given at *Building Reconciliation and Social Cohesion through Indigenous Festival Performance* Symposium, at the University of London Institute in Paris, 17–18 November.

Mtshali, Mbongeni. 2009. Sounding the Body's Meridian: Signifying Community and 'the body national' in Post-apartheid South African theatre. University of Kwa-Zulu Natal, Pietermaritzburg: Unpublished MA dissertation.

Munslow, Alan. 2007. *Narrative and History.* Basingstoke and New York: Palgrave Macmillan.

Nabudere Dani W. 2002. Ubuntu Philosophy, Memory and Reconciliation. *Quest: An African Journal of Philosophy* XVI, 1–2, 1–20.

Nabudere, Dani W. 2008. Ubuntu Philosophy, Memory and Reconciliation, NA. Web/Electronically generated www.grandslacs.net/doc/3621.pdf, accessed 25/8/10.

Naidoo, Muthal. 1993. *The Search for a Cultural Identity: A Personal Odyssey.* Indic Theatre Monograph Series, 1.

Naidoo, Muthal. 2010. 'Kill the Boer', a response to Mcebisi Ndletyana's article, posted 7/4/10, www.muthalnaidoo.co.za/articles-and-papers-othermenu-86/223–kill-the-boer, accessed 23/12/11.

Nathan, A.J. 1999. Boer Prisoners of War on the Island of St Helena. *Military History Journal* 11: 3/4 (Oct.), http://samilitaryhistory.org/vol113an.html, accessed 10/11/11.

Naudé, Charles. 2000. Veroeningsdaag – Almal saam verantwoordelik. *Beeld* 14/12/00, 14.
Ndebele, N. 1994. *South African Literature and Culture: Rediscovery of the Ordinary*. Manchester: Manchester University Press.
Ndebele, Njabulo. 1998. 'Memory, Metaphor, and the Triumph of Narrative', in S. Nuttall and C Coetzee (eds) *Negotiating the Past – The making of Memory in South Africa*. Cape Town: Oxford University Press, 19–28.
Ndletyana, Mcebisi. 2010. 'Kill the Boer'. *The Sunday Independent* 4 April 2010, 13.
Ndlovu, Sifiso Mxolisi. 2000. Johannes Nkosi and the Communist Party of South Africa: Images of 'Blood River'and King Dingane in the Late 1920s-1930. *History and Theory*, 39: 4, Theme Issue: 'Not Telling': Secrecy, Lies, and History (Dec.), 111–32.
Neale, Caroline. 1985. *Writing 'Independent' History: African Historiography 1960–1980*. Westport and London: Greenwood Press.
Neethling-Pohl, A. 1974. *Dankbaar die Uwe*. Cape Town: Human and Rousseau.
NEPAD. 2008. Nepad Lays out Vision for Africa. 14/11/08, see www.southafrica.info/ business/economy/development/nepad.htm, accessed 14/11/08.
Nietzsche, F. 1956. *The Birth of Tragedy* (trans.) Francis Golffing. New York: Doubleday.
Nora, Pierre. 1989. Between Memory and History: Les Lieux de Memoire. *Representations* 26, Spring, 7–24.
Norval, Aletta. 1996. *Deconstructing Apartheid Discourse*. London and New York: Verso.
Nuttall Sarah and Carli Coetzee (eds) 1998. *Negotiating the Past – The Making of Memory in South Africa*. Cape Town: Oxford University Press.
Nuttall, Sarah and Cheryl-Ann Michael. 2000. 'Introduction', in S. Nuttall and C.A. Michael (eds) *Sense of Culture: South African Cultural Studies*. Cape Town: Oxford University Press.
Odom, Glenn A. 2011. South African Truth and Tragedy: Yael Farber's *Molora* and Reconciliation Aesthetics. *Comparative Literature* 63: 1, 47–63.
Okumu, Washington A.J. 2002. *The African Renaissance*. Trenton/Asmara: Africa World Press, Inc.
Omotoso, Kole. 2004. *A History of Theatre in Africa*. Martin Banham (ed.) Cambridge: Cambridge University Press.
Ong, Walter. 1982. *Orality and Literacy: The Technologizing of the Word*. London and New York: Routledge.
Ouzgane, Lahoucine and Robert Morrell. 2005. *African Masculinities: Men in Africa from the Late Nineteenth Century to the Present*. New York and Basingstoke: Palgrave Macmillan; Scottsville, South Africa: University of KwaZulu-Natal Press.
Parker, Louis-Napoleon 1928. *Several of My Lives*. London: Chapman and Hall.
Patel, Khadija. 2012. Timbuktu: SA's Uncertainty as Rebels Move in. *Daily Maverick* 8 May 2012. www1.dailymaverick.co.za/article/2012-05-08-timbuktu-sas-uncertainty-as-rebels-move-in, accessed 11/5/12.
Patrimony. 2004. Catalogue of Sogolon Puppet Exhibition in Stellenbosch, South Africa. AngloGold Ashanti.
Pearson, Bryan. 1996. '"Sarafina" AIDS Sequel Sparks Jo'burg protests'. *Variety* 25/3/96, 362: 8.
Perkins, Kathy 1998. 'Introduction', in K. Perkins (ed.) *Black South African Women: An Anthology of Plays*. London: Routledge, 1–5.
Peterson, Bhekizizwe 1995. 'A Rain a Fall but the Dirt It Tough': Scholarship on African Theatre in South Africa. *Journal of Southern African Studies* 21: 4, Special Issue on South African Literature: Paradigms Forming and Reinformed (Dec.), 573–84.
Peterson, Bhekizizwe and Suleman, Ramadan. 2009. *Zulu Love Letter – a Screenplay*. Johannesburg: Wits University Press.
Pigou, P. 2009. 'Accessing the Records of the Truth and Reconciliation Commission,' in K. Allan (ed.). 2009. *Paper Wars: Access to Information in South Africa*. Johannesburg: Wits University Press, 17–55.

Pohlandt-McCormick, Helena. 2000. 'I Saw a Nightmare...': Violence and the Construction of Memory (Soweto, June 16, 1976). *History and Theory* 39: 4, Theme Issue: 'Not Telling': Secrecy, Lies, and History (Dec.), 23–44.

Posel, Deborah. 1995. 'The Meaning of Apartheid before 1947: Conflicting Interests and Forces within the Afrikaner Nationalist Alliance', in William Beinart and Saul Dubow (eds) *Segregation and Apartheid in Twentieth-Century South Africa*. London and New York: Routledge, 206–30.

Posel, Deborah. 2002. 'The TRC Report: What kind of History? What kind of Truth?', in Deborah Posel and Graeme Simpson (eds) *Commissioning the Past: Understanding South Africa's Truth and Reconciliation Commission*. Johannesburg: Witwatersrand University Press, 147–72.

Posel, Deborah and Graeme Simpson. 2002. *Commissioning the Past: Understanding South Africa's Truth and Reconciliation Commission*. Johannesburg: Witwatersrand University Press.

Preller, G.S. 1917 (1988). *Piet Retief*. Melville: Scripta Africana. (Facsimile of the 1937 edn).

Preller, G.S. 1937 (1988) *Andres Pretorius*. Melville: Scripta Africana. (Facsimile of the 1937 edn).

Promotion of National Unity and Reconciliation Act. 1995. Republic of South Africa, *Government Gazette* 361(16579), preamble.

Proust, M. 1983. *Remembrance of Things Past* (1913–27). C.K. Scott-Moncrieff and T. Kilmartin (trans.), 3 volumes, London: Penguin.

Prussin, Labelle. 1986. *Hatumere: Islamic Design in West Africa*. Berkeley: University of California Press.

Rabinow, Paul. 1989. *French Modern: Norms and Forms of Social Environment*. Cambridge, Massachusetts and London: MIT Press.

Radstone, Susannah and Katharine Hodgkin (eds) *Memory Cultures: Memory, Subjectivity and Recognition*. New Brunswick and London: Transaction Publishers.

Ramose, Mogobe B. 1999. *African Philosophy through Ubuntu*. Harare: Mond Books.

Ramose, Mogobe B. 2002. 'The Ethics of *ubuntu*', and 'The philosophy of *ubuntu* and *ubuntu* as philosophy', in P.H. Coetzee and A.P.J. Roux (eds) *Philosophy from Africa*. Oxford: Oxford University Press, 324–30, 230–8.

Ramphele, Mamphela. 1995. 'The Challenge Facing South Africa' in A. Boraine and J. Levy (eds) *The Healing of a Nation?* Cape Town: Justice in Transition.

Ramphele, Mamphela. 2000. 'Teach me how to be a Man: An Exploration of the Definition o Masculinity', in Veena Das, Arthus Kleinman, Mamphela Ramphele and Pamela Reynolds (eds) *Violence and Subjectivity*. Berkeley: University of California Press, 192–219.

Randall, Keith. 1991. *France, 1814–70: Monarchy, Republic and Empire*. London: Hodder Arnold.

Rassool, Ciraj and Witz, Lesley. 1993. The 1952 Jan van Riebeeck Tercentenary Festival: Constructing and Contesting Public National History in South Africa. *Journal of African History* 34: 447–68.

Rassool, Ciraj. 2007. 'Key Debates on Memorialisation, Human Rights and Heritage Practice', in Bonita Bennett, Christchené Julius and Crain Soudien (eds) *Reflections on the Conference Hands on District Six - Landscapes of Post-colonial Memorialisation*. Cape Town: District Six Museum, 34–7.

Rassool, Ciraj. 2008. 'Contesting "Museumness": Towards an Understanding of the Values and Legacies of the District Six Museum', in Bonita Bennett, Christchené Julius and Crain Soudien (eds) *City - Site - Museum: Reviewing Memory Practices at the District Six Museum*. Cape Town: District Six Museum, 68–75.

Rebellato, Dan. 2008. 'From the State of the Nation to Globalization: Shifting Political Agendas in Contemporary British playwriting', in Nadine Holdsworth and Mary Luckhurst (eds) *A Concise Companion to British and Irish Drama*. Oxford: Blackwell, 245–62.

Reddy, Thiven. 2001. 'The Politics of Naming: The Constitution of Coloured Subjects in South Africa', in Z. Erasmus (ed.), *Coloured by History, Shaped by Place: New perspectives on Coloured Identity in Cape Town*. Cape Town: Kwela and South African History Online.

Richner, Jürg Emil. 2005. The Historiographical Development of the Concept 'mfecane' and the Writing of Early Southern African History, from the 1820s to 1920s. MA Thesis, University of Rhodes, http://eprints.ru.ac.za/155/1/Richner-M.A.-Thesis.pdf, accessed 15/11/11.

Ricoeur, Paul. 1984. *Time and Narrative*. Kathleen McLaughlin and David Pellauer (trans.), vol. 1. Chicago: University of Chicago Press, 1–51.

Ricoeur, Paul. 2004. *Memory, History, Forgetting*. Kathleen Blamey and David Pellauer (trans.). Chicago: University of Chicago Press. Electronic text and image data, Ann Arbor, Michigan: University of Michigan (2010).

Right Perspective, The. 2010. 'South Africa Bans "Shoot The Boer" Song', posted by NewsGuy, 26/03/10. www.therightperspective.org/2010/03/26/south-africa-bans-shoot-the-boer-song/, accessed16/12/11.

Roach, Joseph. 1996. *Cities of the Dead: Circum-Atlantic Performance*. New York: Columbia University Press.

Robinson, David. 2009. Review of Jeppie, Shamil and Souleymane Bachir Diagne's *The Meanings of Timbuktu* (2008). H-NET Reviews in the Humanities and Social Sciences, http://h-net.msu.edu/cgi-bin/logbrowse.pl, accessed 25 January 2010.

Rokem, Freddie. 2000. *Performing History – Theatrical Representations of the Past in Contemporary Theatre*. Iowa City: University of Iowa Press.

Roos, Gideon. 1950. The Great Trek. *The Australian Quarterly* 22: 4 (Dec.), 35–40.

Ross, Fiona C. 2003. *Bearing Witness: Women and the Truth and Reconciliation Commission in South Africa*. London and Sterling, Virginia: Pluto Press.

Rudakoff, Judith 2004. Somewhere, Over the Rainbow: White-Female-Canadian Dramaturge in Cape Town. *TDR* 48: 1 (Spring), 126–63.

Rumney, Philip, N.S. and Charnelle van der Bijl. 2010. Rape, Attitudes, and Law Enforcement in South Africa. *New Criminal Law Review* 13: 4 (Fall), 826–40.

Saad, Elias N. 1983. *Social History of Timbuktu: The Role of Muslim Scholars and Notables 1400–1900*. Cambridge: Cambridge University Press.

Saage-Maaß, Miriam and Wiebke Golombek. 2010. Transnationality in Court: In Re South African Apartheid Litigation, 02–MDL-1499, U.S. District Court, Southern District of New York (Manhattan), 8 April 2009. *European Journal of Transnational Studies* 2: 2 (Aut.), 1–10.

Sachs, Albie. 1991. Preparing Ourselves for Freedom: Culture and the ANC Guidelines. *TDR* 35: 1, 187–93.

Sachs, Albie. 2009. *The Strange Alchemy of Life and Law*. Oxford and New York: Oxford University Press.

Sacks, Oliver. 1995. *An Anthropologist on Mars*. New York: Vintage Books.

SAHA on Access to Information Bill, www.saha.org.za.

SAHA Sept. 2011. Dr. Wouter Basson's Conduct was 'in breach of medical protocols', 26/9/11. www.saha.org.za/news/2011/September/dr_wouter_basson_s_conduct_was_in_breach_of_medical_protocols.htm

SAHA. May 2011. The Truth and Reconciliation Commission Archive: 15 years on, www.archivalplatform.org/news/entry/the_truth_and_/, accessed 17/5/11

SAHO (South African History Organisation), Great Trek 1835–1846, www.sahistory.org.za/south-africa-1806–1899/great-trek-1835–1846, accessed 10/11/11.

SAHO. Origins of Battle of Blood River. www.sahistory.org.za/origins-battle-blood-river-1838, accessed 10/11/11.

Said, E.W. 1991. *Orientalism*. London: Penguin.

Said, E.W. 1994. *Culture and Imperialism*. New York: Alfred A. Knopf Inc.

Sanders, Mark. 2007. *Ambiguities of Witnessing – Law and Literature in the time of the Truth Commission*. Johannesburg: Witwatersrand University Press.

SAPA. 1996a. Churches Slam Indifference of Whites. 30/12/96. www.justice.gov.za/trc/media/1996/9612/s961230a.htm

SAPA. 1996b. Police who Shot Gugulethu Seven should be Prosecuted: Mothers. 23/4/96. www.justice.gov.za/trc/media/1996/9604/s960423c.htm.

Scarry, Elaine. 1985. *The Body in Pain: The Making and Unmaking of the World*. New York: Oxford University Press.

Schaffer, Kay and Sidonie Smith. 2004. *Human Rights and Narrated Lives*. Basingstoke: Palgrave Macmillan.

Schechner, Richard. 1993. *The Future of Ritual: Writings on Culture and Performance*. London: Routledge.

Schechner, Richard. 1998. *Performance Theory*. New York and London: Routledge.

Schechner, Richard. 2003. *Performance Studies: An Introduction*. London and New York: Routledge.

Schoeman, Karel. 2007. *Early Slavery at the Cape of Good Hope 1652-1717*. Pretoria: Protea Book House.

Schönfeldt-Aultman, Scott M. 2006. Monument(al) Meaning-Making: The Ncome Monument and Its Representation of Zulu Identity. *Journal of African Cultural Studies* 18: 2 (Dec.), 215–34.

Schramm, Katharina. 2011. Landscapes of Violence: Memory and Sacred Space. *History & Memory* 23: 1 (Spring/Summer), 5–23.

Senne, Damario. 2008. Riding the International Wave. *Built* (Nov.), 10–16.

Serote, Mongane Wally. 2005. 'Week of Reconciliation: Wars that have Shaped our Democracy', Day of Reconciliation speech, Mpumulanga, 16/12/05, at www.freedompark.co.za/cms/index, accessed 24/11/11.

Serote, Mongane Wally. 2006. 'The Significances and Relevance of the Freedom Park in the South African Context', speech as CEO of Freedom Park for The Central University of Technology, Free State, 15 May 2006.

Serote, Mongane Wally. 2010. *Revelations*. Sunnyside: Jacana Media.

Shell, R.C. 1994. 'Children of Bondage: A Social History of the Slave Society at the Cape of Good Hope', in C. Saunders and H. Phillips (eds) *Studies in the History of Cape Town* 5. Cape Town: University of Cape Town.

Shillington, Kevin. 2011. *Luka Jantjie – The Resistance Hero of the South African Frontier*. London: Aldridge Press, Johannesburg: Wits University Press, New York: Palgrave Macmillan.

Sicher, Efraim. 2000. The Future of the Past: Countermemory and Postmemory in Contemporary American Post-Holocaust Narratives. *History & Memory* 12: 2, Fall/Winter. 56–91.

Sinclair, Thornton. 1938. The Nazi Party Rally at Nuremberg, *The Public Opinion Quarterly* 2: 4 (Oct.), 570–83.

Smith, David. 2009. Quarter of Men in South Africa Admit Rape. guardian.co.uk, 17 June www.guardian.co.uk/world/2009/jun/17/south-africa-rape-survey, accessed 29/6/09.

Smith, Richard Cándida. 2002. 'Performing the Archive', in Richard Cándida Smith (ed.) *Art and the Performance of Memory – Sounds and Gestures of Recollection*. London and New York: Routledge, 1–12.

Solberg, Rolf. 2003. *South African Theatre in the Melting Pot*. Grahamstown: Institute for the Study of English in South Africa, Rhodes University.

Sonkosi, Zola. 2003. 'Amnesty from an African Point of View', in Charles Villa-Vicencio and Erik Doxtader (eds) *The Provocations of Amnesty: Memory, Justice and Impunity*. Claremont, SA: David Philip.

Sorkin, A.J. 1989. 'Politics and the Muse: Voices and Visions at the Crossroads', in A. Sorkin (ed.) *Politics and the Muse – Studies in Recent American Literatures*. Bowling Green: Bowling Green University Popular Press.

Spector, J. Brooks. 2011. Now Appearing Nightly on Stage: Winnie Agonistes. *The Daily Maverick*, Sunday 8 May 2011.www.thedailymaverick.co.za/article/2011-05-08-now-appearing-nightly-on-stage-winnie-agonistes, accessed 10/7/11.

Speer, A. 1970. *Inside the Third Reich*. New York: Macmillan.
Steenveld, L. and L. Strelitz. 1998. The 1995 Rugby World Cup and the Politics of Nation-building in South Africa. *Media, Culture & Society* 20: 4, 609–29.
Stets, J.E. and Burke, P.J. 2000. Identity Theory and Social Identity Theory. *Social Psychology Quarterly*, 63, 224–37.
Stewart, Susan. 1993. *On Longing: Narratives of the Miniature, the Gigantic, the Souvenir, the Collection*. Durham, NC and London: Duke University Press.
Taylor, Diana. 2007a. Trauma and Performance: Lessons from Latin America. *Paragraph* 30: 1, 9–29.
Taylor, Diana. 2007b. *The Archive and the Repertoire: Performing Cultural Memory in the Americas*. Durham and London: Duke University Press.
Taylor, Jane. 2008. Reform, Perform: Sincerity and the Ethnic Subject of History. *South African Theatre Journal* 22, 9–24.
Taylor, Jane (ed.) 2009a. *Handspring Puppet Company*. Johannesburg: David Krut Publishing.
Taylor, Jane. 2009b. 'Introduction', in Jane Taylor (ed.) *Handspring Puppet Company*, 19–39.
Teer-Tomaselli, R. 1995. Moving Towards Democracy: The South African Broadcasting Corporation and the 1994 election. *Media, Culture and Society* 17, 577–601.
Temu, A. and Swai, B. 1981. *Historians and Africanist History: A critique – Post-colonial Historiography Examined*. London: Zed Publishers.
Tennyson, Alfred. 1829. *Timbuctoo*. Cambridge: John Smith. Full version accessed from http://pathguy.com/timbuc.htm on 20/08/10, fragment from www.sc.edu/library/spcoll/sccoll/africa/tenn.html, accessed 27/8/10.
Thacker, Andrew and Moya Lloyd (eds). 1997. *The Impact of Michel Foucault on the Social Sciences and Humanities*. Basingstoke: Macmillan.
Thompson, James. 2005. *Digging up Stories: Applied Theatre, Performance and War*. Manchester: Manchester University Press.
Thompson, J.H. 2006. *An Unpopular War: From Afkak to Bosbefok: Voices of South African National Servicemen*. Cape Town: Zebra Press.
Thompson, Leonard. 1985. *The Political Mythology of Apartheid*. New Haven and London: Yale University Press.
Thurman, Chris. 2010. Classics Revisited. *Financial Mail* 19 Aug 2010. www.fm.co.za/Article.aspx?id=118494#, accessed 4/7/11.
Tombouctou Manuscripts Project and Iziko Social History Collections Department. 2008. *Timbuktu Scripts and Scholarship*. Cape Town: Iziko Museums of Cape Town for the Department of Arts and Culture.
TRC (Truth and Reconciliation Commission of South Africa). 1998. *Final Report*. London: Macmillan.
TRC. Online *Final Report*, volumes 1– 5, 1998, volumes 6–7, 2003, see www.justice.gov.za/trc/report/index.htm, accessed July and August 2011.
TRC Pamphlets. 1995. The Committee on Amnesty, The Committee on Human Rights Violations, and Truth. *The Road to Reconciliation*. Rondebosch: Justice in Transition.
Triulzi, A. 1996. 'African Cities, Historical Memory and Street Buzz', in I. Chambers and L. Curti (eds) *The Post-colonial question: Common Skies, Divided Horizons*. London and New York: Routledge.
Trouillot, Michel-Rolph. 1995. *Silencing the Past*. Boston: Beacon Press.
Turner, Victor. 1982. *From Ritual to Theatre*. New York City: Performing Arts Journal Publication.
Unsworth, Andrew. 1996. Tokyo's Groot Trek. *Sunday Times* 15 December 1996.
van der Merwe, Chris and Pumla Gobodo-Madikizela. 2008. *Narrating our Healing: Perspectives on Working through Trauma*. Newcastle: Cambridge Scholars Publishing.
van der Watt, L. 1996. Art, Gender and Afrikaner Nationalism: a History of the Voortrekker Monument tapestries. Unpublished MA thesis, University of Cape Town.

van Graan, Mike. 2006. From Protest Theatre to the Theatre of Conformity? *South African Theatre Journal* 20, 276–88.

van Heerden, Johann. 2008. Theatre in a New Democracy – Some Major Trends in South African Theatre from 1994 to 2003. Unpublished PhD, University of Stellenbosch.

van Jaarsveld, F.A. 1964. *The Afrikaner's interpretation of South African History*. Cape Town: Simondium Publishers.

van Jaarsveld, F.A. 1979. *Die Evolusie van Apartheid en ander Geskiedkundige Opstelle*. Cape-Town: Tafelburg Publishers.

van Tonder, Deon. 1994. From Mausoleum to Museum: Revisiting Public History at the Inauguration of Museum Africa, Newtown. *South African Historical Journal* 31 (Nov.), 165–83.

van Wyk, Johan. 1996. Poor White Satyrs and Nationalist Blueprints. *Alternation*, 3: 2, 157–73. http://graham.stewart.tw/johanvanwykweb/index/2mpoor.htm, accessed 15/11/11.

van Zyl Slabbert, Frederick. 2003. 'Truth Without Reconciliation, Reconciliation Without Truth', in Charles Villa-Vicencio and Erik Doxtader (eds). *The Provocations of Amnesty*. Claremont, SA: David Philip.

van Zyl Slabbert, Frederick. 2011. 'Some Do Contest the Assertion that I am an African', in Xolela Mangcu (ed.) *Becoming Worthy Ancestors: Archive, Public Deliberation and Identity in South Africa*. Johannesburg: Witwatersrand University Press, 47–58.

van Zyl Smit, Betine. 2008. 'Multicultural Reception: Greek Drama in South Africa in the late Twentieth and early Twenty-first Centuries', in L. Hardwick and C. Stray (eds) *A Companion to Classical Receptions*. Oxford: Blackwell Publishing, 373–85.

van Zyl Smit, Betine. 2010. Orestes and the Truth and Reconciliation Commission. *Classical Receptions Journal* 2: 1, 114–35.

Vatcher, William Henry Jr. 1965. *White Laager – The rise of Afrikaner Nationalism*. London: Pall Mall Press.

Vermeulen, Irma. 1999. *Man en Monument: Die Lewe en Werk van Gerard Moerdijk*. Pretoria: van Schaik.

Villa-Vicencio, Charles and Wilhelm Verwoerd. 2000. *Looking Back, Reaching Forward: Reflections on the Truth and Reconciliation Commission of South Africa*. Cape Town and London: University of Cape-Town Press/Zed Books.

Villa-Vicencio, Charles and Erik Doxtader (eds) 2003. *The Provocations of Amnesty*. Claremont, SA: David Philip.

Villa-Vicencio, Charles. 2009. *Walk with us and Listen: Political Reconciliation in Africa*. Cape Town: University of Cape Town Press.

von Henneberg, Krystyna Clara. 2004. Monuments, Public Space, and the Memory of Empire in Modern Italy. *History and Memory* 16: 1 (Spring/Summer), 37–85.

wa Thiong'o, Ngugi. 1994. *Decolonising the Mind: The Politics of Language in African Literature*. London: James Currey, Nairobi: EAEP, Portsmouth: Heinemann.

Wake, Caroline. 2009. The Accident and the Account: Towards a Taxonomy of Spectatorial Witness in Theatre and Performance Studies. *Performance Paradigm*, 5.1 (May), www.performanceparadigm.net/wp-content/uploads/2009/07/wake.pdf, accessed 25/10/11.

Walcott, D. 1965. 'Codicil' in *The Castaway*. London: Jonathan Cape.

Walcott, D. 1974. 'The Muse of History', in Orde Coombs (ed.) *Is Massa Day Dead?* Garden City: New York, 1–27.

Walder, Dennis. 1998. 'Spinning out the Present: Narrative, Gender and the Politics of South African Theatre', in D. Attridge and R. Jolly (eds) *Writing South Africa*. New York: Cambridge University Press, 204–20.

Walder, Dennis. 2011. *Postcolonial Nostalgias: Writing, Representation and Memory. Routledge Research in Postcolonial Literatures, 31*. Abingdon and New York: Routledge.

Webb, Steven. 2008. *Ops Medic: A National Serviceman's Border War*. Alberton: Galago Publishing Company.

Weeder, Michael. 2008. 'Topographies of the Forgotten: Prestwich and Cape Town's Nineteenth Century Cemeteries', in Bonita Bennett, Christchené Julius and Crain

Soudien (eds) *City – Site – Museum: Reviewing Memory Practices at the District Six Museum.* Cape Town: District Six Museum, 32–49.

White, Hayden. 1973. *Metahistory: The Historical Imagination in Nineteenth-Century Europe.* Baltimore: Johns Hopkins University Press.

Wicomb, Zoë. 1996. 'Postcoloniality and Postmodernity: The Case of the Coloured in South Africa', in Herman Wittenberg and Loes Nas (eds) *AUETSA Proceedings of the Conference of Association of University English Teachers of South Africa.* Bellville: University of Western-Cape.

Wicomb, Zoë. 1998. 'Shame and Identity: The Case of the Coloured in South Africa', in Derek Attridge and Rosemary Jolly (eds) *Writing South Africa: Literature, Apartheid and Democracy, 1970–1995.* Cambridge: Cambridge University Press, 91–107.

Wilcocks, R.W. 1932. *The Poor White.* Stellenbosch: Report of the Carnegie Commission.

Williamson, Eagan. 2005. Monument boos oor sepiester op senotaaf. *Beeld* 18/3/05, front page.

Wilson, Richard A. 2001. *The Politics of Truth and Reconciliation in South Africa: Legitimizing the Post-Apartheid State.* Cambridge: Cambridge University Press.

Winter, Jay. 1995. *Sites of Memory; Sites of Mourning.* Cambridge: Cambridge University Press.

Witz, Leslie. 2003. *Apartheid's Festivals: Contesting South Africa's National Past.* Bloomington: Indiana University Press and Cape Town: David Philip.

Wolford, Lisa. 1999. Guillermo Gómez-Peña: An Introduction. *Theatre Topics* 9.1, 89–91.

World Cup Jabulani Adidas ball. *Shine* 2010. 4 December 2009. www.shine2010.co.za/Community/blogs/goodnews/archive/2009/12/04/official-2010–world-cup-match-ball-jabulani-launched.aspx, accessed 6/12/09.

Wright, John and Aron Mazel. 1991. Controlling the Past in the Museums of Natal and KwaZulu. *Critical Arts* 5: 3, 59–77.

Yaeger, Patricia (ed.) 1996. *The Geographies of Identity.* Ann Arbor: University of Michigan Press.

Young, James E. 1993. *The Texture of Memory: Holocaust Memorials and Meaning.* New Haven and London: Yale University Press.

Young, James. 2000. *At Memory's Edge: After-images of the Holocaust in Contemporary Art and Architecture.* New Haven: Yale University Press.

Programmes/booklets museums

Afrikaanse Taal- en Kutuurvereeniging (ATKV). 1938. *Gedenkboek van die Ossewaens op die Pad van Suid-Afrika,* eeufees: 1938–1939.

Board of Control of the Voortrekker Monument. 1954. *The Voortrekker Monument, Pretoria.* Pretoria: Board of Control of the Voortrekker Monument.

Central Committee for the Jan van Riebeeck Festival. 1952. *Official Programme of the van Riebeeck Festival* (1952). Cape Town: Nasionale Pers Bpk.

Freedom Park Trust. 2004. Slavery, Commemoration of National Day of Reconciliation, 16 December 2004, Cape Town, available in Freedom Park library online archives, Speeches, Slavery.

Freedom Park Trust. 2007. The Freedom Park Trust Dialogue with the Nation: The Way Forward. Press release, 8 February, see website.

Groot Trek Herdenkensfees 1838–1988 – Commemorative Book and Programme/Historical record of the Opening of the Voortrekker Monument. 16/12/1949. Pretoria: Insercor Industrial Services.

Historical Sketch. 1910. *Historical Sketch and Description of the Pageant Held at Cape Town on the Occasion of the Opening of the First Parliament of the Union of South Africa.* Cape Town: Pageant Committee.

Searle, Richard. ca. 1998 *Die Cecile de Ridder Volkspele Nagedagtenis.* Handwritten with photos.

Sentrale Volksmonumentekommitee. ca 1938. *Gedenkboek: Voortrekker-Eufees 1838–1938*. Johannesburg: I.S. Gray & Co.

Sentrale Voortrekker Eufees 1838-1938 Program. Pretoria, 14–16 December 1938 (Programme of Central Voortrekker Festival). Johannesburg: Afrikaanse Pers Bpk.

Souvenir and Programme of the Pageant of South Africa. 1910. Cape Town: The Pageant Committee.

van den Berg, Mossie. 1999. Geloftesterk jou stand, abridged and translated by Hannes van der Merwe, *The Blood River Vow by the Voortrekkers of 1838 and what it really means to us in Modern Times*. Montana Park: Hannes van der Merwe.

Voortrekkermonument-inwydingskomitee (Inauguration Committee). 1949. *Inwyding can die Voortrekkermonument – Amptelike program en gedenkboek* (Inauguration of the Voortrekker Monument – Official Programme and Memorial Book), 13–16 December 1949. Johannesburg: Voortrekkerpers Bpk.

Plays

Akerman, Anthony. 1993. *Somewhere on the Border*, in Stephen Gray (ed.), *South Africa Plays*. London: Heinemann-Centaur, 2–140.

Bailey, Brett. 2003. *The Plays of Miracle and Wonder – Ipi Zombi?, iMumbo Jumbo, The Prophet*. Cape Town: Double Story.

Brink, Andre 1997. *Die Jogger* (The Jogger). Cape Town/Pretoria/Johannesburg: Human & Rousseau.

Burns, Kephra. 2006. *Tall Horse* script (2005 version), in Mervyn Millar, *Journey of the Tall Horse: A story of African Theatre*. London: Oberon Books.

Chakela, Walter. 1997. *Isithukuthu*. Unpublished.

Coetzee, Greig. 2009. *White Men with Weapons*, in *Johnny Boskak is feeling Funny*. Scottsville: University of KwaZulu-Natal Press.

Davids, Nadia. 2006. *At her Feet*. Cape Town: Oshun Books.

de Wet, Reza. 1991. *Vrystaat-trilogie*. Pretoria: HAUM.

de Wet, Reza. 1993. *Trits*. Pretoria: HAUM.

de Wet, Reza. 2000. *Plays One: Missing, Crossing, Miracle*. London: Oberon Books.

de Wet, Reza, 2005. *Plays Two: African Gothic, Good heavens, Breathing*. London: Oberon.

Farber, Yael and Thembi Mtshali. [1999] 2008. *A Woman in Waiting*, in Yael Farber, *Theatre as Witness*. London: Oberon Books.

Farber, Yael. 2008b. *Molora*. London: Oberon Books.

Farber, Yael. 2008c. *Amajuba: Like Doves We Rise, in Theatre as Witness*. London: Oberon Books.

Fourie, Charles (ed.) 2006. *New South African Plays*. London: Aurora Press.

Fugard, Athol. 2000. *Sizwe Bansi is Dead* and *The Island* in *Township Plays*. Oxford: Oxford University Press.

Gerryts, U.M. 1937. *Na Vyftig Jaar en ander toneelstukkies vir Voortrekkers*. (After Fifty years and other plays for Voortrekkers). Kaapstad, Bloemfontein, Pretoria: Nasionale Pers.

Gopie, Rajesh. 2010. *Out of Bounds*. Junkett Publishers, ebook.lighteningsource.com.

Graver, David (ed.) 1999. *Drama for a New South Africa*. Bloomington and Indianapolis: Indiana University Press.

Grootboom, Mpulelelo Paul and Presley Chweneyagae. 2006. *Relativity: 'Township Stories'*. Sunnyside: Dung Beetle Dramas, STE Publishers.

Grootboom, Mpulelelo Paul. 2009. *Foreplay*. London: Oberon Books.

Hamilton, Nan. 1997. *No. 4*. Unpublished site-specific performance.

Herzberg, Paul. 1997. *The Dead Wait*. Unpublished play script

Herzberg, Paul. 2002. *The Dead Wait*. London: Oberon Books.

Homann, Greg (ed.) 2009b. *At this Stage – Plays from Post-apartheid South Africa*. Johannesburg: Wits University press.

Junction Avenue Theatre Company. 2001. *Sophiatown*, in Martin Orkin (ed.) *At the Junction*. Johannesburg: Witwatersrand University Press, 144–209.

Kani, John. 2002. *Nothing but the Truth*. Johannesburg: Witwatersrand University Press.

Krige, Uys. 1940. *Magdalena Retief*. (3rd edn). Kaapstad: Unie-Volkspers Bpk.

Krog, Antje. 1999. *Waarom is do Wat Voor Toyi-Toyi Altyd so Vet?* (Why are those who Toyi-Toyi in front always so fat?) Unpublished, 1st performed at Aardklop Kunstefees.

Kuhlamani Support Group. 1999. *The Story I'm about to Tell*, unpublished.

Mahomed, Ismail 1999. *Purdah*, in David Graver (ed.) *Drama for a New South Africa*. Bloomington and Indianapolis: Indiana University Press, 154–65.

Mann, Chris Zithulele. 2004. *Thuthula: Heart of the Labyrinth*. Braamfontein: Ravan Press.

Mhlophe, Gçina. 2002. *Have you Seen Zandile?* Pietermaritzburg: University of Natal Press.

Miller, Phillip. 2006. *REwind: A Cantata for Voice, Tape and Testimony*. (1st performed). Libretto in Carol Martin (ed.) 2010. *Dramaturgy of the Real on the World Stage*. Basingstoke and New York: Palgrave Macmillan, 95–108.

Mtwa, Percy. 1986. *Bopha!*, in Duma Ndlovu (ed.) *Woza Afrika!* New York: George Braziller.

Naidoo, Muthal. 2008. *WIP Theatre Plays*. Durban: MN Publications.

Perkins, Kathy (ed.) 1998. *Black South African Women*. London and New York: Routledge.

Simon, Barney, et al. 1986. *Born in the RSA*, in Duma Ndlovu (ed.) *Woza Afrika!* New York: George Braziller.

Simon, Barney, Mtwa, Mbongeni Ngema's 2009. *Woza Albert!* London: Methuen Drama.

Slabozelpszy, Paul. 1985. *Saturday Night at the Palace*. Jeppestown: Ad Donker Publishers.

Taylor, Jane. 1998. *Ubu and the Truth Commission*. Cape Town: University of Cape Town Press.

Truth in Translation. (2006–09), collaboratively created by Michael Lessac, Paavo TomTammi, Hugh Masekela and Colonnades Theatre Lab.

Uys, Pieter Dirk. 1996. *Truth Omissions*, unpublished.

van Graan, Mike. 1996. *Dinner Talk*, unpublished.

Van Graan, Mike. 2006. *Green Man Flashing*, in Charles Fourie (ed.), *New South African Plays*. London: Aurora Metro Press, 172–221.

van Wyk Louw, N.P. 1942. *Die Dieper Reg*. Kaapstad, Bloemfontein, Port Elizabeth: Nasionale Pers.

Films and documentaries

Amandla! A Revolution in Four Part Harmony. 2002. Hirsch, Lee (director and writer). ATO Pictures/ Kwela Productions.

The Ancient Astronomy of Timbuktu. 2009. Guy Spiller (director) Dogged Films.

The Cradock Murders: Matthew Goniwe and the Demise of Apartheid ([2003] 2010) David Forbes (producer/director/DOP), Michel Noll (producer – France). Distributed ICTV, France. Evolved from 52-min TV version of 2003.

Die Voortrekkers/Winning a Continent. 1916. H. Shaw (director), G.S. Preller screenplay, South African Film Productions.

Du Preez, Max. *Special Report*. Broadcast by SABC 21 April 1996–29 March 1998. SABC. Also digitalised by the Yale Law School Lillian Goldman Library and available via streaming video via www.law.yale.edu/trc/index.htm.

Forgiveness. 2004. Ian Gabriel (director) DV8.

Handspring Puppet Company. 2005. *Tall Horse* promotional DVD, Cape-Town.

Have you seen Drum Recently? 1989. Jürgen Schadenberg. Produced by the Schadenberg Movie Company.

In My Country. 2005. John Boorman (director) Sony Pictures. Based on Antje Krog's *Country of my Skull*.

Long day's Journey into Day: South Africa's Search for Truth and Reconciliation. 2000. Frances Reid and Deborah Hoffman (directors), feature length documentary following four cases from TRC.

Mapantsula. 1988. Oliver Schmit (director). Produced by Haverbeam and One Look Productions.
Red Dust. 2006. Hooper, Tom (director) HBO.
Shoreline. 2009. SABC. Jacob Loubser (series producer).
The Lost Libraries of Timbuktu. BBC 4, broadcast 12/2/09.
Zulu Love Letter. 2004. Suleman, Ramadan (writer and director) and Bhekizizwe Peterson (writer and producer). France: JBA Productions.

Websites

African Renaissance Institute (ARI): www.africarenaissance.org/ [this has been replaced by SACAR, see below]
Archival Platform: www.archivalplatform.org
Freedom Park: www.freedompark.co.za
Magnet Theatre: www.magnettheatre.co.za/
South African Chapter of the African Renaissance (SACAR): www.sacar.org.za/home.html
SA–Mali project: www.sa-maliproject.co.za/Timbuktu/Index.html
SAHA: www.saha.org.za/
Third World Bunfight: www.thirdworldbunfight.co.za/
Timbuctoo the Mysterious: www.the153club.org/timbuctoo.html
TRC material online: www.justice.gov.za/trc/report/index.htm

INDEX

Note: 'n.' after a page number indicates a note on that page.